THE
LYLE
OFFICIAL
ARTS
REVIEW 1989

D1374449

While every care has been taken in the compiling of information contained in this volume the publishers cannot accept any liability for loss, financial or otherwise, incurred by reliance placed on the information herein.

All prices quoted in this book are obtained from a variety of auctions in various countries during the twelve months prior to publication and are converted to dollars at the rate of exchange prevalent at the time of sale.

The publishers wish to express their sincere thanks to the following for their involvement and assistance in the production of this volume:

KAREN DOUGLASS (Art Editor)
JANICE MONCRIEFF (Assistant Editor)
ANNETTE CURTIS
SALLY DALGLIESH
TANYA FAIRBAIRN
FRANK BURRELL
ROBERT NISBET
LOUISE SIMPSON
JONN DUNLOP
EILEEN BURRELL
SARAH RITCHIE
MACDONALD GREEN
LISA JONES
ALAN KIDD

ISBN 0-86248-111-2

Printed by A. Wheaton & Co. Ltd., Exeter, Devon.
Bound by Dorstel Press, Harlow, Essex.

THE LYLE OFFICIAL

ARTS
REVIEW 1989

COMPILED & EDITED BY
TONY CURTIS

Auction Acknowledgements

Anderson & Garland, Anderson House, Market Street, Newcastle-upon-Tyne NE1 6XA
Australian Fine Art, 62/65 Market Street, Sydney 2000
Barbers Fine Art Auctioneers, Smarts Heath Road, Mayford, Woking, Surrey
Bearnes, Rainbow, Avenue Road, Torquay TQ2 5TG, Devon
Bermondsey Antique Market, Tower Bridge Road, London
Bloomsbury Book Auctions, 3 & 4 Hardwick Street, London EC1R HRY
Bonhams, Montpelier Galleries, Montpelier Street, Knightsbridge, London SW7 1HH
Capes Dunn and Co., The Auction Galleries, 38 Charles Street, Manchester, Lancashire M1 7DB
Chancellors Hollingsworth, 31 High Street, Ascot, Berkshire SL5 7HG
Christie's, Cornelis Schuystraat 57, 1071 JG, Amsterdam
Christie's (International) S.A., 8 Place De La Talonwerie, 1204 Geneva
Christie's (Hong Kong) Ltd., 3607 Edinburgh Tower, 15 Queens Road, Hong Kong
Christie's, 8 King Street, St James's, London SW1Y 6QT
Christie's (Monaco) S.A.M., Park Palace, 98000 Monte Carlo
Christie's, 502 Park Avenue, New York, NY 10022
Christie's, 219 East 67th Street, New York, NY 10021
Christie's Scotland, 164-166 Bath Street, Glasgow, Scotland G2 4TG
Christie's South Kensington Ltd., 85 Old Brompton Road, London SW7 3LD
Chrystals Auctions, Unit 32, Spring Valley Industrial Estate, Braddan, Isle of Man
Bruce D. Collins, Fine Arts Gallery, Box 113, Denmark, Maine
County Group, 102 High Street, Tenterden TN30 6AU, Kent
Dreweatt Neate, Donnington Priory, Donnington, Newbury, Berkshire RG13 2JE
Du Mouchelles Art Galleries Co., 409 E. Jefferson Avenue, Detroit, Michigan 48226
Elliott & Green, Emsworth Road, Lymington, Hampshire SO41 9BL
Fellows and Sons, Bedford House, 88 Hagley Road, Edgbaston, Birmingham, West Midlands
John D. Fleming & Co., 8 Fore Street, Dulverton, Somerset TA22 9EX
Geering & Colyer, 22/26 High Street, Tunbridge Wells, Kent TN1 1XA
Graves, Son & Pilcher, 71 Church Road, Hove, East Sussex BN3 2GL
W. R. J. Greenslade & Co., 13 Hammet Street, Taunton, Somerset TA1 1RN
Giles Haywood, The Auction House, St John's Road, Stourbridge DY8 1EW, West Midlands
Hobbs & Chambers, 'At the Sign of the Bell', Market Place, Cirencester, Gloucestershire
Hobbs & Chambers, 15 Royal Crescent, Cheltenham, Glos.
Edgar Horn, Auction Galleries, 46/50 South Street, Eastbourne, BN21 4XB
G. A. Key, Aylsham Salerooms, Palmers Lane, Aylsham, Norfolk NR11 6EH
King & Chasemore, West Street, Midhurst, West Sussex GU29 9NG
Lalonde Fine Art, 71 Oakfield Road, Clifton, Bristol, Avon BS8 2BE
W. H. Lane & Son, Fine Art Auctioneer & Valuers, 64 Morrab Road, Penzance Cornwall
Langlois Ltd., Westaway Rooms, Don Street, St Helier, Jersey, Channel Islands
Lawrence Fine Art, South Street, Crewkerne TA18 8AB, Somerset
Lawrence's, Fine Art Auctioneers, Norfolk House, 80 High Street, Bletchingley, Surrey
Lots Road Chelsea Auction Galleries, 71 Lots Road, Chelsea, London SW10 0RN
Mallans, Fine Art Auctioneers, 24 St Michaels Street, Oxford, Oxfordshire
Morphets, 4-6 Albert Street, Harrogate, North Yorkshire HG1 1JL
D. M. Nesbit & Co., 7 Clarendon Road, Southsea, Hampshire PO5 2ED
James Norwich Auctions Ltd., Head Office, 33 Timberhill, Norwich, Norfolk NR1 3LA
Osmond, Tricks, Regent Street, Auction Rooms, Clifton, Bristol, Avon BS8 4HG
Phillips, 65 George Street, Edinburgh EH2 2JL
Phillips, 207 Bath Street, Glasgow G2 4DH
Phillips, Blenstock House, 7 Blenheim Street, New Bond Street, London W1Y 0AS
Phillips New York, 406 East 79th Street, New York, NY 10021
Phillips, The Old House, Station Road, Knowle, Solihull, West Midlands B93 0HT
Prudential Fine Art Auctioneers, Millmead Auction Rooms, Guildford, Surrey
Prudential Fine Art Auctioneers, 5 Woodcote Close, Kingston Upon Thames, Surrey KT2 5LZ
Prudential Fine Art Auctioneers, Trinity House, 114 Northenden Road, Sale, Manchester
Russell, Baldwin & Bright, The Fine Art Saleroom, Ryelands Road, Leominster HR6 8JG
Sotheby's, 34-35 New Bond Street, London W1A 2AA
Henry Spencer & Sons, 20 The Square, Retford, Notts. DN22 6DJ
St John Vaughan with John Hogbin, 8 Queen Street, Deal, Kent CT14 6ET
Louis Taylor & Sons, Percy Street, Hanley, Stoke-on-Trent, Staffordshire ST1 1NF
Warners, Wm. H. Brown, The Warner Auction Rooms, 16/18 Halford Street, Leicester LE1 1JB
Peter Wilson Fine Art Auctioneers, Victoria Gallery, Market Street, Nantwich, Cheshire
Worsfolds Auction Galleries, 40 Station Road West, Canterbury, Kent

Introduction

Published annually and containing details of thousands of oil paintings, watercolours and prints, The Lyle Official Arts Review is the most comprehensively illustrated reference work on the subject available at this time.

Each entry is listed alphabetically under the Artist's name for easy reference and includes a description of the picture, its size, medium, auctioneer and the price fetched at auction during the twelve months prior to publication.

As regards authenticity of the works listed, this is often a delicate matter and throughout this book the conventional system has been observed:

The full Christian name(s) and surname of the artist denote that, in the opinion of the auctioneer listed, the work is by that artist.

The initials of the Christian name(s) and the surname denote that, in the opinion of the auctioneer listed, the work is of the period of the artist and may be wholly or partly his work.

The surname only of the artist denotes that, in the opinion of the auctioneer listed, the work is of the school or by one of the followers of the artist or painted in his style.

The word 'after' associated with the surname of the artist denotes that, in the opinion of the auctioneer listed, the picture is a copy of the work of the artist. The word 'signed' associated with the name of the artist denotes that, in the opinion of the auctioneer listed, the work bears a signature which is the signature of the artist.

The words 'bears signature' or 'traces of signature' denote that, in the opinion of the auctioneer listed, the work bears a signature or traces of a signature which may be that of the artist.

The word 'dated' denotes that the work is dated and, in the opinion of the auctioneeer listed, was executed at that date.

The words 'bears date' or 'inscribed' (with date) denotes that, in the opinion of the auctioneer listed, the work is so dated and may have been executed at about that date.

All pictures are oil on canvas unless otherwise specified. In the dimensions (sight size) given, the height precedes the breadth.

Although the greatest possible care has been taken to ensure that any statement as to authorship, attribution, origin, date, age, provenance and condition is reliable, all such statements can only be statement of opinion and are not to be taken as statements or representations of fact.

The Lyle Official Arts Review offers a unique opportunity for identification and valuation of paintings by an extremely broad cross section of artists of all periods and schools.

Unless otherwise stated descriptions are placed immediately underneath the relevant illustrations.

We firmly believe that dealers, collectors and investors alike will treasure this and subsequent annual editions of the Lyle Official Arts Review (published in September each year) as changing trends in the fluctuating world of art values are revealed.

Tony Curtis

FRONT COVER

'The Picnic' by **Sir Noel Coward** *(Christie's)*
'Portrait de Jeune Fille' by **Moise Kisling** *(Sotheby's)*
'A Good Joke' by **Louis Charles Moeller** *(Christie's)*
'A Hound And A Goldfinch' by **Jean-Baptiste Oudry** *(Sotheby's)*
'A Basket Of Cherries' by **John F. Francis** *(Christie's)*

SPINE

'Portrait de Mario' by **Amedeo Modigliani** *(Christie's)*

BACK COVER

'Potipher, A Bay Hunter, In A Stable' by **William Barraud** *(Sotheby's)*
'Foxwood' by **Carel Weight, R.A.** *(Sotheby's)*
'Femme Nue Assise Sur Un Lit' by **Claude Emile Schuffenecker** *(Christie's)*

ARTS REVIEW

*Sir Noel Coward – 'Jamaica Bay' – signed – gouache and oil on canvas – 24 x 30in.
(Christie's)*   **$80,500 £46,000**

What a difference a name makes! Pictures by famous people who paint as a hobby were at one time regarded as the jokey side of the saleroom — but then Noel Coward came along and changed all that.

A sale devoted to his works was held by Christie's in the spring of this year and prices were exceptionally keen. Coward, who died in 1973, began painting as a child but stuck to watercolours till the 1930's when he was converted to oils by Winston Churchill, another pastime painter. Coward was reluctant to expose his pictures to the public, fearing that they would be valued only because of "celebrity snobbism" but his ability as a painter was fully recognised at Christie's sale when hammer prices soared well above estimates, and sometimes even doubled them. Many of his best pictures were painted in Jamaica and an example is his colourful study of Jamaica Bay which sold for £46,000, a price which many professional and much collected artists would be hard put to match. Since Christie's sale other Coward canvases have been popping up at auction, including one at Phillips which was given by Coward to Dame Sybil Thorndike — a case of getting

*Sir Noel Coward – 'Two Nuns' – signed – gouache and oil on canvas – 24 x 30in.
(Christie's)* $73,500 £42,000

*Sir Noel Coward – 'The Gardener At
Firefly, Jamaica – signed – oil on
canvas – 18 x 14in.
(Christie's)* $13,125 £7,500

*Sir Winston Churchill, Hon. R.A. –
'Villa On Cap Martin' – signed with
initials – oil on canvas – 24 x 20in.
(Christie's)* **$39,160 £22,000**

two famous names at once. It was a gouache and watercolour landscape which went for around £6,000.

Coward's mentor Churchill has also suffered in the past from "celebrity snobbism" but his painting was patchy and prices paid for his work varies considerably from five figures to around £5,000. The name however ensures that Churchills will always be sought after by someone and American buyers are particularly interested in his work.

His arch enemy Hitler, is thought by some, to have been a more accomplished painter than Churchill and when paintings by him come up for auction, they go for very high prices but they are rare and none have appeared on the market for some years.

A famous name always does wonders for the price of even a scrap of a drawing . . . witness the sketches of John Lennon, especially the ones he did of Yoko Ono, which are fought over by collectors. A small light hearted sketch by Dylan Thomas was sold by Phillips in London in the spring of '88 for around £300.

Another thing that helps an artist's price is a new book about them or a dramatic death. Georgia O'Keefe is a highly regarded American painter but her prices rose to even greater heights after a biography of her by Laurie Lisle was published in 1988. Watercolour cartoons by Andy Warhol were selling for around £3,000 until he died unexpectedly on the operating table in New York last year and his vast and varied collection of possessions were auctioned for staggering sums. Since then small sketches like his "Cupid with Pussy Cats" which sold for £5,500 have escalated dramatically in price.

*Andy Warhol – 'Cupid With Pussy Cats' –
signed – pen, ink and watercolour on
paper – 14 x 20in.(Sotheby's)* **$9,680 £5,500**

Sometimes scraps of esoteric information about a picture or a drawing can make it more desirable. Jean Cocteau's self portraits, listed by Sotheby's as having been made 'under the influence of opium', fetched around £5,000 each. The auctioneers must have thought that if the pictures had been made while he was in a normal state of mind, they would perhaps have been less attractive to buyers.

The "name game" is becoming so popular that in the summer of 1988 Christie's persuaded a collection of famous people to draw or paint their idea of the perfect garden and the pictures were put on display at Glasgow's Garden Festival before being auctioned in the autumn. Most of the contributors were not famous for being artists and they included model Twiggy; comedian Billy Connolly; actor Larry Hagman or, as everyone knows him, J.R. Ewing from "Dallas"; actor Sir Alex Guinness and Catherine Cookson, the novelist.

Contemplating the escalation of interest in part-time painters who happen to be famous for other reasons, a well known art expert sighed, "Wouldn't it be wonderful if we found out that Marilyn Monroe was a Sunday painter!"

Vincent Van Gogh — 'Portrait Of Adeline Ravoux' – dated 1890 – oil on canvas – 29 x 21½in. (Christie's)
$14,175,000 £7,500,000

Vincent Van Gogh – 'Irises' – signed – oil on canvas – 28 x 36¾in.
(Sotheby's)   **$53,900,000   £30,111,731**

The year in review has been a very interesting one because it has shown the resillience of the art market in spite of the cataclysm of the Stock Market Crash which shook the financial world on October 19th, 1987. The quick profit taking which had distinguished all areas of a booming art market during the early part of the year, initially took a shake as buyers held off in the middle ranges of all categories. For a while they were happier to wait to see exactly what was going to happen and middle range Impressionists were the most obviously affected but that uncertainty did not last long.

It was the force of Japanese buying that put nerve back into the market and what better boost was needed than the £30.2m ($53.9m) paid by a Japanese insurance company in New York for Van Gogh's "Irises"? This price took the world by

surprise for even the most sanguine of Sotheby's experts had set their sights on getting only around $20m for the picture which was consigned for sale by Mr John Whitney Payson whose mother had bought the picture in 1947 for under $100,000. The art world was universally delighted and reassured when the price for "Irises" surpassed the previous record of £24.75m that Christie's had obtained in London in the spring of 1987 for Van Gogh's "Sunflowers". Because confidence is all important in a speculative market it was a relief to know that Van Gogh had come to the rescue, providing all the encouragement needed that art was alive and thriving in spite of shivering among Wall Street investors. As a consequence, some financial advisers have actually been urging wealthy clients to see art as an alternative investment and prices paid for good quality pictures from the top

Edgar Degas — 'Danseuse Russe' — signed — pastel — 23¾ x 15in. (Sotheby's)
$442,750 £253,000

echelons have gone on rising steadily since then.

So much so that by May, 1988, Impressionist and Modern pictures had established themselves as the world's Number One refuge investment, taking over the position from Japanese real estate. Their rise has been steady, marked by milestones along the way like the 5.22 million francs paid at a Parisian Art auction for a Toulouse Lautrec of Jane Avril; Monet's water lily study, "Nympheas" which went for an auction house record of $3.3m or £1.85m at Christie's New York and Renoir's study of a girl with a basket of flowers, sold for another record price of $5.28m (£2.96) to a Japanese fine art and real estate dealer. Then came the $202,400 (£126,500) paid for Edgar Degas' "Mlle Becat aux Ambassadeurs" showing a singer performing in her characteristic style. This picture was estimated to sell for around £40,000 so its price was a notable signpost on the way up. Degas' star has gone on

*Edgar Degas – 'Les Blanchisseuses' –
signed – oil on canvas – 32 x 30in.
(Christie's)* **$13,613,600 £7,480,000**

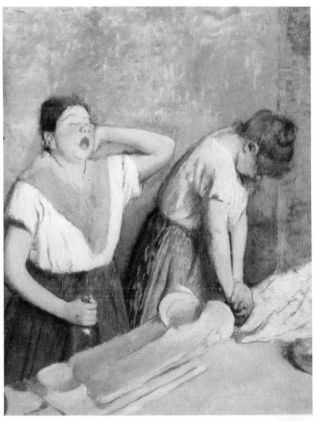

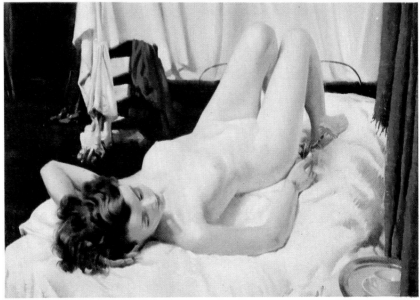

*Arthur Royce Bradbury – 'Marigold' – signed and dated 1935 – oil on canvas –
30 x 36in.
(Christie's)* **$18,496 £10,450**

rising and at the end of the year, Christie's held a special evening sale of his "Les Blanchisseuses" which is thought to have been painted around 1882. This graphic scene of women working in a laundry shop sold for a staggering £7,480,000.

In May, 1988, the Renoir record price was again broken when his painting of his mistress Aline feeding their baby was sold to a German client for $8.8m (£4.6m) at Sotheby's in New York in spite of being described by a dealer, in rather sour grape fashion, as being "rather dreary".

A distinctive feature of the new Impressionist interest is the rise in price of lesser regarded artists like Fantin-Latour and Pissarro to the front rank. This may be because of the huge prices being paid for mega-stars like Renoir, Degas and Manet but nonetheless a Fantin-Latour which would have been lucky to fetch £9,000 in the 1950's is now making at least £800,000.

At the same sale a Cezanne landscape of Pontoise made an auction house record of $9.24m (£4.86m) and was sold to Japan. A Picasso record was set when his Cubist still life of souvenirs collected on a trip to Le Havre in 1912 was sold at Sotheby's for £4.18m to a Swiss dealer. Yet another record was set for a Matisse when his study of a

*Tsuguharu Foujita –
'Madonne A La Grotte' –
signed twice – oil on
canvas – 18¼ x 15¼in.
(Sotheby's)*
$365,750 £209,000

Ben Shahn – 'Unemployment' – signed – tempera on paper laid down on masonite –
13¾ x 16¾in.
(Christie's)   **$49,500 £30,536**

vase of flowers against figured wallpaper was sold to an American client for $5.72m (£3m) against an estimate of around $1.75m. It had been sent for sale by the New York Museum of Modern Art because it was surplus to requirements and in this they were following a trend set by several American museums who, encouraged by the enthusiasm of Japanese bidders, have been selling surplus pictures to raise funds.

Nothing brings pictures out of storage or off sitting room walls more readily than publicity and a surge of saleroom interest. A case in point is St Ives artist Dorothea Sharpe, who died in 1955. She is one of the most recent artists to be hit by a wave of popularity. Ten years ago, a good example of her work could be picked up for around £500; last year the price had risen to about £4,000; this year estimates have been

hovering around the £20,000 and £30,000 mark for good examples and every saleroom is anxious to feature her in their sales of Modern artists. She is best known for her clear, fresh seascapes with figures of mothers and children in the foreground.

Stanley Spencer's prices also took a great jump upward during the past year. His previous top price, dating from June 1986, was £82,500 but that was made to look small when, in the summer of 1987, his "Punts Meeting", part of his "Christ Preaching at Cookham Regatta" series, sold in London for £429,000.

Other Modern artists making good money include Sir Alfred Munnings and there are plenty of his pictures around for he was extremely prolific. Pictures of horses always sell well anyway because they are regarded as safe for decorating purposes.

Dorothea Sharp – 'The Shrimpers' – signed – oil on canvas – 15 x 22in.
(Sotheby's)   **$28,875 £16,500**

Dorothea Sharp – 'Mother And Children By The Sea' – signed with initials – oil on
canvas – 20 x 24in.
(Phillips)   **$16,400 £10,000**

Sir Alfred Munnings, P.R.A. – 'Near Mendham Mill, On The Waveney' – signed and dated '99, and inscribed on the reverse – pencil and watercolour – 8 x 10¾in. (Christie's)   **$14,696 £8,800**

Sir Alfred Munnings, P.R.A. – 'A Meet Of The Norwich Staghounds' – signed and dated 1906 – watercolour and gouache – 17¾ x 23¾in. (Christie's)   **$74,404 £41,800**

Sir William Russell Flint,
R.A. – 'Two Models And
A Mirror' – signed and
signed again, inscribed
and dated on the reverse –
tempera – 24¾ x 20¼in.
(Christie's)

$56,783 £31,900

The same applies to the work of Russell Flint whose pictures continue to increase in price in spite of the number of them there are to be found. Less easily found is Harold Harvey, Montague Dawson, Laura Knight and Dame Ethel Walker, all of whom are consistently rising in value. Glyn Philpot is another name to watch. He was painting in the 1930's and his pictures have now soared into the £30,000 range.

Even lesser Edwardian artists like Helen Allingham, whose work used to be regarded as merely 'pretty', has now been elevated to a higher status since her picture "At The End Of The Garden" showing a little girl in a flower filled landscape sold for a record £22,500 at Phillips. It had been estimated in Allingham's usual range of between £4,000 and £5,000. Her pictures always sell better if there is a figure in the pretty gardens which she made her speciality.

Still in the Modern field, the Scottish Colourists go on from strength to strength with enthusiastic local buying as well as bidders coming from abroad, especially USA, Canada and Australia. The Colourists are now sharing their popularity with 'The Glasgow Boys' of the same period and enthusiasm for both categories shows no sign of disappearing. Christie's in Edinburgh set records when they sold John Duncan Fergusson's "A Farm Among the Hills" for £49,500 and George Leslie Hunter's "Houseboats, Loch Lomond" for £35,200.

*Dame Laura Knight, R.A. – 'Studio
Reflections' – signed – oil on
canvas – 40 x 50in.
(Christie's)*　　**$9,185　£5,500**

*Helen Allingham, R.W.S. – 'Picking Buttercups In An Orchard' – signed – watercolour
heightened with scratching out – 10 x 14in.
(Sotheby's)*　　　　　　　　　　**$15,785　£9,020**

Lawrence Stephen Lowry, R.A. –
'A Street' – signed and dated 1962,
signed again and inscibed and dated
on the reverse – oil on panel – 11 x
8¾in.
(Christie's) $23,881 £14,300

Montague Dawson – 'The Clipper Ships At Night' – signed – oil on canvas – 40 x 50in.
(Sotheby's) $74,844 £39,600

Edward Atkinson Hornel, R.O.I. – 'Primrose Day' – signed and dated 1926 – oil on canvas – 25 x 30in.
(Christie's) **$28,650 £15,000**

When Francis Campbell Boileau's painting of "Marigolds" was sold at Sotheby's it tripled its estimate to make £28,600 and Samuel John Peploe's prices keep on rising and rising. In March a still life by him sold at Sotheby's Hopetoun House sale for £68,200. The popularity of Edward Atkinson Hornel, one of "The Glasgow Boys", also continues though he is not to everyone's taste. A painting by him reached the £50,000 level during the year under review.

Other Modern British painters whose prices have taken a great leap forward include L. S. Lowry, whose "Up North" painted in 1957, sold for a record £66,000, and Paul Nash whose "Changing Scene" made £57,200 although his previous highest price had been in the region of £10,000.

Top price Modern painters have not been lagging behind either because artists like Modigliani and Kandinsky have both been enjoying great popularity especially among Japanese buyers. A Modigliani study

Edward Atkinson Hornel, R.O.I. – 'Geisha Girl' – signed and dated 1901, oil on canvas laid down on panel – 18 x 13¾in.
(Christie's) **$29,605 £15,500**

*Amedeo Modigliani –
'Portrait De Mario' – oil
on canvas – 45¾ x 28¾in.
(Christie's)*
$9,002,400 £4,840,000

of a woman recently made £3.4m while a Kandinsky landscape sold for £1.36m, a record for the artist. In New York a Jackson Pollock sold for $1.1m and a De Koonig for $2m.

Once the art market realised that the world had not come to an end when the Stock market fell, prices in other sections began to show signs of increasing confidence as well. After having been for some time in a state of suspension, the pre-Raphaelites fought back when Dante Gabriel Rossetti's

"Proserpine" became the most expensive Victorian picture ever sold when an anonymous collector paid £1.43m to secure it. This picture was a study of Rossetti's beloved Jane Morris, the wife of his friend William Morris. Rossetti painted eight versions of this picture and the one that made the record price was begun in 1873 but was damaged and repainted. It later belonged to artist L. S. Lowry who had a great admiration for the Pre-Raphaelites.

Lawrence Stephen Lowry, R.A. – 'Figure On A Seat' – signed and dated 1960 – oil on canvas – 20 x 24in. (Christie's).　　**$12,859　£7,700**

Wassily Kandinsky – 'Bindung' – signed and dated '32 – oil on canvas – 27½ x 23½in. (Christie's)
$593,340　£319,000

*James Millar, Attributed to − 'Portrait Of An Officer With His Family' − oil on canvas −
39½ x 50½in.*
(Sotheby's) $7,568 £4,400

*William Duffield − 'Still Life Of Pots And Fruit' − signed and dated twice 15th Jan. 1852 −
oil on canvas − 14 x 19½in.*
(Sotheby's) $8,085 £4,620

Abraham Cooper, R.A. – 'A Saddled Grey Arab Stallion In A Landscape' – signed with monogram and indistinctly dated 1820 (?) – oil on canvas – 23½ x 29½in. (Sotheby's) **$24,596 £14,300**

Louis Charles Moeller – 'Your Move' – signed – oil on canvas – 18 x 24in. (Christie's) **$38,500 £21,509**

Federigo Andreotti – 'The Love Letter' – signed – on panel – 41 x 29in.
(Christie's) **$52,910 £28,600**

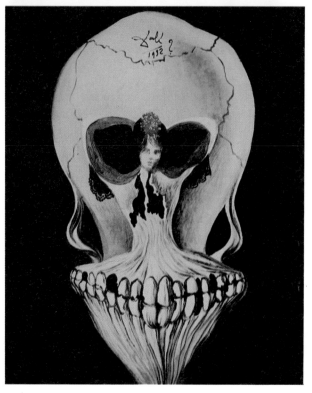

Salvador Dali 'Ballerine' – signed and dated 1932 – oil on canvas – 9¾ x 7¾in.
(Christie's) **$66,880 £41,800**

David Roberts, R.A. – 'The Pool Of Bethesda, Jerusalem' – signed, inscribed and dated 1839 – watercolour and bodycolour over pencil – 32 x 47.5cm. (Phillips)   **$63,720 £36,000**

Another world record price was made in November for David Roberts, the 19th century Edinburgh born artist who specialised in scenes of the Middle East but whose prices were thought to be in decline during the past two or three years. All doubts were cast aside however when his watercolour of "The Pool of Bethesda, Jerusalem", from 1839, sold for £36,000 at Phillips in London.

Old Masters and paintings by Renaissance artists have not been appearing in great numbers at auction for some time but when the 16th century Bolognese artist Annibale Carracci's painting "The Holy Family Accompanied by St Lucy" turned up for sale, it was nearly overlooked. The granddaughter of the man who bought it for £5 in 1930 took it to an auction house for valuation in the summer of 1987 and was told it was worth around £400. Later

however it was entered for sale at Phillips who initially did not recognise it as a Carracci either but found out the truth in time. The picture was sold in the end to a New York dealer for £847,000.

Prints are another area that is showing a great increase in activity, partly because of Japanese interest in that field as well. Sotheby's scored a fine coup when they sold British Rail Pension Fund's collection of Japanese prints for high prices. They included 41 prints of Hokusai's celebrated series "The Thirty Six Views of Fuji". One of these prints, "The Great Wave of Kanagawa" is said to have influenced the French Impressionists and inspired Debussy's composition "La Mer".

There is today an extraordinary demand for good prints in all categories from Old Masters to Modern American and prices are always rising. For example, two years ago

*Edwin F. Bayha – 'Boy
With Toy Soldiers' –
signed – oil on canvas –
39 x 32in.
(Christie's)*
$37,400 £22,914

*George Barbier – 'Two Ladies In A Salon' – signed and dated 1924 – pen and ink
and bodycolour – 7½ x 12½in. (Christie's)* **$11,803 £6,380**

*Norman Rockwell –
'Give Me A Boy' – 29 x
22½in.
(Christie's)*
   $38,500 £21,509

a set of Matisse's "Jazz" could be bought for $100,000 but recently Sotheby's sold a set in New York for $410,000 to a Continental collector. Modern British prints too are appreciating in price and an example is a set of six by Christopher Nevinson, sold for £22,000 although only seven years ago they were priced at £5,500. There is always a broad range of bidders for American contemporary prints which can be picked up for prices ranging from $1,000 to $100,000. There was a great surge of print making in the USA in the 1950's and '60's and top range prices are demanded by the work of

people working then, including Jasper Johns, Frank Stella and Richard Diebenkorn. They chose their paper to enhance the overall appearance of the print and immaculate condition is extremely important if the print is to sell for a top price. It is also preferable if each impression is hand signed and hand numbered although some artists, including Andy Warhol, often had editions stamp signed and this does not affect the value of their prints.

LIZ TAYLOR

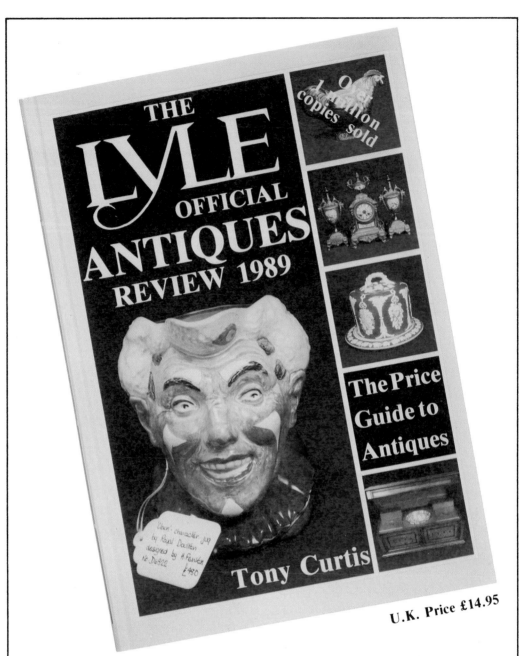

A brand new publication each year *The Lyle Official Antiques Review* is the most comprehensive, up-to-date price guide to antiques available.

Its 800 pages are packed with precisely the kind of profitable information the professional Dealer needs – including descriptions, photographs and values of thousands and thousands of individual items carefully selected to give a representative picture of the current market in antiques and collectibles .

ARTS
REVIEW 1989

OSWALD ACHENBACH – Ischia – signed and dated '84 – 26 x 35in.
(Christie's) $49,896 £30,800

JULIUS ADAM – Cats At Play – signed – 10½ x 15¾in.
(Christie's) $30,294 £18,700

OSWALD ACHENBACH – The Bay Of Naples – signed – 26 x 37in.
(Christie's) $39,204 £24,200

OSWALD ACHENBACH – In The Garden Of The Villa Borghese – signed – 32 x 45¼in.
(Christie's) **$14,520** **£8,800**

PATRICK WILLIAM ADAM – Interior Of Argyll House, Chelsea – the artist's label on the reverse – oil on panel – 10½ x 6¾in.
(Christie's) $1,653 £990

ADAMS

JOHN QUINCY ADAMS – Portrait Of Countess
Michael Karolyi Reclining, Full Length, On A
Divan – signed and dated 1918 – unframed – 71 x
68¾in.
(Christie's) **$23,166** **£14,300**

JULES ADLER – Scene de Village en Bretagne –
signed, dated and inscribed 1922 – oil on canvas –
27¼ x 23¼in.
(Christie's) **$5,405** **£2,970**

LUCIEN ADRION – Le Pont Bir Hakeim, Paris
– signed – oil on canvas – 25½ x 32in.
(Christie's) **$3,603** **£1,980**

AELFAFFER – Figures Before Ruins In An
Extensive Campagna Landscape – signed,
inscribed and dated 1845 – oil on panel – 121 x
196cm.
(Phillips) **$2,160** **£1,200**

IVAN CONSTANTINOVITCH AIVASOWSKY –
A Coastal Landscape With Shipping Off
Trebizond; and Shipping On The Marmara Sea At
Sunset – both signed and dated 1888 – 9½ x
14½in.
(Christie's) **$33,858** **£20,900 Pair**

JOHAN AKKERINGA – A Day At The Seaside –
signed – 25 x 34½in.
(Christie's) $62,370   £38,500

ADAM EMORY ALBRIGHT – Young Fishermen
In A Rowboat – signed and dated 1909 – oil on
canvas – 24 x 30¼in.
(Christie's) $18,700   £11,536

JOSEF ALBERS – Study For Homage To The
Square 'Earthbound' – signed, inscribed and dated
1959 on the reverse – oil on canvasboard – 24 x
24in.
(Christie's) $18,018   £9,900

K. ALCHIMOWICZ – The Honoured Hero –
signed and dated 1901 – 51½ x 79in.
(Christie's) $4,989   £3,080

ERNEST ALBERT – Snow Mantle – signed and
dated 1937 – oil on canvas – 25 x 30¼in.
(Christie's) $13,200   £7,374

CECIL CHARLES WINDSOR ALDIN – Pekinese;
Foxes; and Sleeping Tiger Cubs – each signed –
pen and ink on ivorine – the largest, 18 x 23cm.
(Sotheby's) $673   £385 Four

ALECHINSKY

PIERRE ALECHINSKY – Untitled – signed and dated '61 – oil on canvas – 100 x 107.5 cm.
(Sotheby's) **$71,808 £37,400**

PIERRE ALECHINSKY – Peinture du Chevet – inscribed and dated 1966 on the reverse – oil on canvas – 37 x 25¾in.
(Christie's) **$32,076 £19,800**

PIERRE ALECHINSKY – Zero De Conduite – signed, and signed and dated 1961 – oil on canvas – 97 x 129.5 cm.
(Sotheby's) **$84,480 £44,000**

PIERRE ALECHINSKY – Overland – signed, inscribed and dated 1981 – watercolour on printed paper map mounted on canvas – unframed – 27 x 22¼in.
(Christie's) **$10,410 £5,720**

PIERRE ALECHINSKY – Lieu du delit – signed and dated '61 – brush and black ink on paper mounted on board – 10 x 15in.
(Christie's) **$4,455 £2,750**

HENRY ALKEN, Jnr. – The Cock-Pit; and The Prize Ring – one signed – oil on panel – 17.5 x 25.5cm.
(Sotheby's)   **$11,730   £6,820 Pair**

HELEN ALLINGHAM – Picking Buttercups In An Orchard – signed – watercolour heightened with scratching out – 25.5 x 35.5cm.
(Sotheby's)   **$15,785   £9,020**

JACOB ALT – Peasants On A Path In The Nasswald – signed – 13½ x 18in.
(Christie's)   **$5,445   £3,300**

SIR WILLIAM ALLAN – Portrait Of Mohammed Ali Bey – inscribed on label attached to reverse – oil on panel – 36 x 27.5cm.
(Sotheby's)   **$2,849   £1,540**

CHARLES CURTIS ALLEN – 'Summer, Mt. Monadnock' – signed, and inscribed on reverse – oil on canvas – 24 x 36in.
(Robt. W. Skinner Inc.)   **$2,700   £1,636**

E. ALTRUI – Italiante Landscapes – signed – oil – 12 x 9in.
(Messrs. G. A. Key)   **$600   £330 Pair**

AMADEO

AMADEO, 5th Count Preziosi – A Turkish Lady In A Carriage – signed and dated 1850 –
watercolour over pencil with touches of white – 26.5 x 37.5 cm. *(Sotheby's)*
$5,698 £3,080

AMADEO, 5th Count Preziosi – A Lady Playing
The Lute – signed – watercolour over pencil – 37
x 27 cm.
(Sotheby's) **$5,087 £2,750**

AMERICAN SCHOOL – Reading In The Parlour
– oil on canvas – unframed – 21¼ x 14¾ in.
(Christie's) **$2,640 £1,628**

AMERICAN SCHOOL, early 19th century –
Four Trout In Landscape – oil on canvas –
11½ x 18in.
(Bruce D. Collins)　　$1,045　　£590

AMERICAN SCHOOL, late 19th century –
Summer Landscape Scene – oil on board – 14½ x
24in.
(Robt. W. Skinner Inc.)　　$550　　£333

AMERICAN SCHOOL, 19th century – Mountain
Lore – oil on canvas – 17 x 21in.
(Bruce D. Collins)　　$880　　£497

AMERICAN SCHOOL, 19th century – Farm In
Summer – oil on canvas – 16¾ x 23in.
(Christie's)　　$1,980　　£1,106

AMERICAN SCHOOL, 19th century – Young
Woman Reading – oil on canvas – 21 x 26in.
(Bruce D. Collins)　　$412　　£232

AMERICAN SCHOOL, late 19th century – Tug
And Squarerigger – oil on board – 5½ x 6½in.
(Bruce D. Collins)　　$77　　£43

AMERICAN SCHOOL

AMERICAN SCHOOL, late 19th century –
Schooners At Dusk – signed – watercolour –
9½ x 14in.
(Bruce D. Collins)   **$825**   **£466**

AMERICAN SCHOOL, late 19th century – Kettle
And Fish – oil on canvas – 16 x 22in.
(Bruce D. Collins)   **$132**   **£74**

AMERICAN SCHOOL, 20th century – The Polo
Match – signed and monogrammed – gouache on
paper, figures laid on backing board – 28 x 21½in.
(Robt. W. Skinner Inc.)   **$275**   **£166**

AMERICAN SCHOOL, 20th century – Mother
And Child – oil on canvas – 24 x 18in.
(Robt. W. Skinner Inc.)   **$800**   **£446**

AMERICAN SCHOOL, 20th century – Predators
– signed – oil on canvas – 33 x 23½in.
(Robt. W. Skinner Inc.)   **$850**   **£515**

FRIEDRICH VON AMERLING – Portrait Of
Count Zichy, Half Length – signed – 26 x 20½in.
(Christie's) **$1,936** **£1,100**

SOPHIE ANDERSON – Peek-a-Boo! – signed with
initials – on canvas – 11½ x 9¾in.
(Phillips) **$4,576** **£2,600**

PAUL-JEAN ANDERBOUHR – Les Peupliers –
signed and inscribed on the reverse – oil on canvas
– 29 x 23¾in.
(Christie's) **$1,336** **£825**

TOM ANDERTON – 'The Coombe, Newlyn,
Penzance', A Wooded Lane – signed and dated
1934 on the reverse – oil on canvas – 65½ x
61cm.
(W. H. Lane & Son) **$660** **£400**

ANDREOTTI

ALEXANDRE ANITCHKOF – An Autumn Gale
– signed – oil on panel – 32 x 40cm.
(Phillips) $684   £380

FEDERIGO ANDREOTTI – The Proposal –
signed – 28¾ x 23¼in.
(Christie's) $42,592   £24,200

GEORGE HENRY ANDREWS – Cotton Bazaar,
Smyrna – signed – watercolour over pencil
heightened with white – 15 x 19cm.
(Sotheby's) $1,933   £1,045

GEORGE HENRY ANDREWS – Unloading Fruit,
Istanbul – signed and dated 1862 – watercolour
over traces of pencil heightened with bodycolour
and touches of gum arabic – 49 x 93.5cm.
(Sotheby's) $36,630   £19,800

THOMAS POLLOCK ANSHUTZ – The Pose –
signed – watercolour on paper laid down on board
– 28½ x 19¼in.
(Christie's) $15,400   £9,435

KAREL APPEL – Portrait – signed and dated '81
– oil, black chalk, coloured chalk, coloured crayon,
gouache and watercolour on paper – 33½ x 27½in.
(Christie's)   **$5,605**   **£3,080**

KAREL APPEL – Five Designs For Windows –
gouache on five sheets of paper – 59 x 41in.
(Christie's)   **$22,022**   **£12,100**

KAREL APPEL – Tete eclatee – signed and dated
'58 – oil on canvas – 31¾ x 25¾in.
(Christie's)   **$28,028**   **£15,400**

KAREL APPEL – Little Boy – signed and dated
'51 – oil on canvas – 110 x 75cm.
(Sotheby's)   **$380,160**   **£198,000**

APPEL

KAREL APPEL – Le Grand Chef Cobra – signed
and dated '50 – oil on canvas – 39¼ x 35¼in.
(Christie's)   **$320,760   £198,000**

KAREL APPEL – Untitled – signed and dated '72
– oil on canvas – unframed – 38 x 51in.
(Christie's)   **$20,020   £11,000**

KAREL APPEL – Untitled – signed and dated
'59 – gouache, black and coloured crayon on
paper mounted on board – 21¾ x 29½in.
(Christie's)   **$9,266   £5,720**

KAREL APPEL – Premiers Jeux – signed –
gouache, paper collage and black crayon on paper
mounted on composition board – 43¼ x 29½in.
(Christie's)   **$35,640   £22,000**

KAREL APPEL – Untitled – signed and dated
'54 – gouache and coloured crayon on paper –
19¼ x 25¼in.
(Christie's)   **$8,910   £5,500**

GEORGE OWEN WYNNE APPERLEY – The Watching Satyr – inscribed and dated 1914 – gouache, brush, black ink and pencil – 13½ x 15½in.
(Christie's)   **$1,443**   **£825**

ALEXANDER ARCHER – Samuel Clark's Prize Stallion The Emperor Held By A Groom In A Landscape – inscribed on the reverse – oil on board – 51 x 61.5cm.
(Sotheby's)   **$6,054**   **£3,520**

JOSEPH APPLEYARD – The Fourth Test Match At Heddingley March July 1953 – signed – oil – 24 x 35¼in.
(Anderson & Garland)   **$1,743**   **£1,050**

WARREN WILLIAMS ARCA – Morning, Landing The Catch–Modre Bay, Anglesey – signed – watercolour – 21½ x 41½in.
(Prudential Fine Art Auctioneers)   **$3,465**   **£2,100**

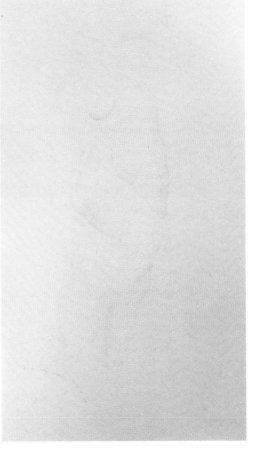

ALEXANDER ARCHIPENKO – Nu – signed and dated '48 – pencil on paper – 19¾ x 15¾in.
(Christie's)   **$5,280**   **£3,300**

ARIOLA

FORTUNATO ARIOLA – Western Calm – signed and dated 1871 – oil on canvas – 12 x 24in.
(Christie's)   **$8,800**   **£4,916**

ARMAN (ARMAND FERNANDEZ) – Untitled – Cafetiere en Metal – signed and dated 1960 – sliced metal coffee pot on panel – 14½ x 47in.
(Christie's)   **$22,022**   **£12,100**

ARMAN – Violon Casse – mixed media collage – 151 x 113cm.
(Sotheby's)   **$31,680**   **£16,500**

ARMAN (ARMAND FERNANDEZ) – Black Indian Invasion – signed – accumulation of black ink bottles and blobs of ink in polyester and plexiglas – 58½ x 72 x 2in.
(Christie's)   **$50,050**   **£27,500**

ARMAN (ARMAND FERNANDEZ) –
Accumulation de compteurs – signed, and also signed, inscribed and dated 1963 on reverse – metal counter wheels in polyester mounted on board – 27½ x 11¾in.
(Christie's)   **$26,026**   **£14,300**

GEORGE ARMFIELD – Terriers At A Badger Set
– signed – on canvas – 27¾ x 36in.
(Phillips)   **$8,800**   **£5,500**

GEORGE ARMFIELD – The Woodland Stalker –
signed – on canvas – 18¼ x 24½in.
(Phillips)   **$1,600**   **£1,000**

ALFRED ARMITAGE – The Boisterous Musicians
– signed – on canvas – 22 x 16in.
(Phillips)   **$3,200**   **£2,000**

MAXWELL ARMFIELD – Taurus – inscribed –
watercolour and pencil – 18 x 18in.
(Christie's)   **$2,117**   **£1,210**

GEORGE DENHOLM ARMOUR – Heavy Going
– signed – black chalk and wash heightened with
white – 45 x 31cm.
(Phillips)   **$1,770**   **£1,000**

ARMOUR

GEORGE DENHOLM ARMOUR – Salmon
Fishing – signed – watercolour, bodycolour and
pencil – 13 x 17in.
(Christie's)   **$2,421**   **£1,540**

JOHN ARMSTRONG – Study Of Reclining Nude
– signed with initials – coloured crayon and
pencil – 16½ x 14in.
(Christie's)   **$577**   **£330**

DR. MARY NEILL NICOL ARMOUR – Roses
And Pinks – signed and dated '70 – oil on canvas
– 61 x 51cm.
(Phillips)   **$5,012**   **£2,800**

JOHN ARMSTRONG – Still Life With A Pear,
A Green Pepper And A Pomegranate – signed and
dated '58 – oil on panel – 17 x 30in.
(Christie's)   **$4,041**   **£2,420**

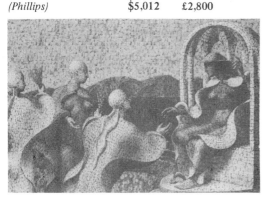

JOHN ARMSTRONG – Odyssey – signed with
initials and dated '46 – gouache – 31.5 x 47.5cm.
(Phillips)   **$2,970**   **£1,800**

JOHN ARMSTRONG – Pain Eluded (Maquette
For Ceiling) – signed and dated '53 – oil on
panel – 12¼ x 18¼in.
(Christie's)   **$4,408**   **£2,640**

JOHN ARMSTRONG – The Family – signed with
initials – oil on canvas – 36 x 22in.
(Christie's) $3,674   £2,200

JOHN ARMSTRONG – Roman Centurion And
Two Nudes – signed with initials – oil on canvas –
21 x 14½in.
(Christie's) $2,695   £1,540

WILLIAM ARMSTRONG – Niagara Falls –
signed and dated 1866 – watercolour heightened
with bodycolour – 13¼ x 20in.
(Sotheby's) $1,831   £990

CONSTANT ARTZ – Family Of Ducks – signed –
oil on panel – 18 x 24cm.
(Phillips) $1,260   £700

DAVID ADOLF CONSTANT ARTZ – A Boy In A
Pink Cap – signed – 18½ x 12¼in.
(Christie's) $3,484   £1,980

ASPERTINI

JOHN ATKINSON – A Ploughman And Team –
signed – watercolour – 10¾ x 14½in.
(Anderson & Garland)   **$1,992   £1,200**

AMICO ASPERTINI – Portrait Of A Cleric
Holding A Scroll – oil on panel – 62.5 x 48.5cm.
(Sotheby's)   **$589,930   £341,000**

JOHN ATKINSON – A Haycart In A Field –
signed – watercolour – 10¾ x 14½in.
(Anderson & Garland)   **$1,294   £780**

ENRIQUE ATALAYA – Trocadero – signed,
inscribed and dated '11 – 4½ x 2in.; and four
sketches, including views of St. Cloud, Chaville,
and the Bois de Boulogne.
(Christie's)   **$1,258   £715 Five**

JEAN ATLAN – Composition – signed – oil on
hessian – 81 x 100cm.
(Sotheby's)   **$88,704   £46,200**

JEAN ATLAN – Sans Titre – signed – oil on canvas – 100 x 65 cm.
(Sotheby's) $65,824   £37,400

GEORGE COPELAND AULT – A Newark Home – signed and dated '20 – oil on panel – 14 x 9¾ in.
(Christie's) $3,300   £1,843

GEORGE COPELAND AULT – My Studio – signed and dated '28 – watercolour on paper – 13½ x 11 in.
(Christie's) $2,420   £1,352

ARTHUR EVERETT AUSTIN, Jnr. – Synchronism – signed and dated 1926 – oil on gold ground on panel – 10 x 7½ in.
(Christie's) $3,850   £2,375

AUSTRALIAN SCHOOL

AUSTRALIAN SCHOOL, 1888 — A Folio Of Watercolours — inscribed on label — watercolour over pencil — 14.5 x 22cm. and smaller.
(Sotheby's)   **$1,831**   **£990 Eight**

AUSTRIAN SCHOOL, circa 1820 — Military Officers And Gathered Civilians In An Ornamental Garden — oil on metal — 31.5 x 43cm.
(Phillips)   **$810**   **£450**

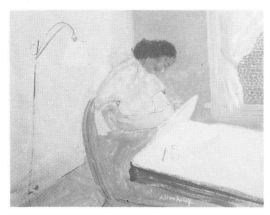

MILTON AVERY — Woman Sketching — signed — gouache, pen and black ink and pencil on paper — 17¾ x 24in.
(Christie's)   **$12,100**   **£6,760**

MILTON AVERY — Nude With Nets — signed — marker and sepia ink on paper — 16¾ x 13¾in.
(Christie's)   **$1,100**   **£678**

MILTON AVERY — March And Sally — signed — pastel on black paper laid down on board — 18 x 12in.
(Christie's)   **$8,250**   **£5,089**

MILTON AVERY – Child In Water – signed – oil on canvasboard – 25¾ x 27½in.
(Christie's)   **$12,100**   **£6,760**

MILTON AVERY – Figurines – signed – oil on canvas laid down on board – 23¾ x 18in.
(Christie's)   **$5,500**   **£3,072**

MILTON AVERY – Still Life, Mandolin In Case – signed and dated 1948, and signed and dated again and inscribed on the reverse – oil on canvas – 27¾ x 36in. *(Christie's)*
$49,500 £27,655

MILTON AVERY – Swirling Trees – signed –
watercolour and gouache on paper – 17¾ x 23¾in.
(Christie's) **$6,050 £3,380**

JOHN B. BACHELDER – 'C. Bachelder My Wife
At Lowell Mass. July 1853' – oil on canvas – 16
x 20in.
(Bruce D. Collins) **$825 £466**

FRANCIS BACON – Study For A Portrait –
inscribed and dated 1966 on the reverse – oil on
canvas – 33 x 27¼in.
(Christie's) **$677,160 £418,000**

HENRY BACON – Hauling A Ship – signed and dated 1887 – oil on canvas – 20¼ x
30½in. *(Christie's)* **$5,500 £3,072**

LIEUTENANT PHILIP JAMES BAINBRIGGE –
The Ice Cone, Montmorency Falls – watercolour
over pencil with scratching out and touches of
bodycolour – 17¾ x 23¼in.
(Sotheby's) $6,105   £3,300

LIEUTENANT PHILIP JAMES BAINBRIGGE –
The Ice Cone, Montmorency – inscribed and
dated 1837 – watercolour over pencil – 6¾ x
10in.
(Sotheby's) $1,526   £825

GEORGE ARNALD BAKER – The Armchair
Angler – signed – oil on canvas – 38 x 53.5cm.
(Sotheby's) $9,081   £5,280

HENDRIK VAN DE SANDE BAKHUYZEN – A
Wooded River Landscape With A Peasant Woman
and A Shepherd With His Flock Of Goats Resting
By A Bridge – signed and dated 1827 – on panel
– 19¾ x 24½in.
(Christie's) $9,982   £6,050

**JULIUS JACOBUS VAN DE SANDE
BAKHUYZEN** – Figures Attending A Barge
Before A Farm – signed and dated 1872 – oil on
canvas – 68 x 104cm.
(Phillips) $14,400   £8,000

GASTON BALANDE – Paysage – signed and
dated '52 – oil on canvas – 53 x 70cm.
(Phillips) $5,376   £3,200

BALDWIN

SAMUEL BALDWIN – The Gamekeeper's Bag, Found – signed and dated 1863 – on canvas – 20 x 16in.
(Phillips) **$2,400** **£1,500**

VINCENT R. BALFOUR-BROWNE – In Difficulties: An Exhausted Stag Approaching A Herd In The Snow – signed with initials and dated 1906 – pencil and watercolour heightened with white – 11¾ x 15¾in.
(Christie's) **$1,443** **£825**

GIACOMO BALLA – Trasformazione forme spiriti – signed – watercolour and pencil on paper – 4¼ x 7in.
(Christie's) **$7,040** **£4,400**

ANTONIO BALESTRA, Attributed to – The Departure Of Hector From Andromache – on canvas – 96½ x 60¼in.
(Phillips) **$13,104** **£7,200**

JULES FREDERIC BALLAVOINE – The Masked Ball – signed – 39 x 25½in.
(Christie's) **$4,989** **£3,080**

BALTHUS (COUNT BALTHAZAR KLOSSOWSKI DE ROLA) – Le Bouquet de Fleurs – signed and dated 1941 on the reverse – oil on board – 28¾ x 36¼in.
(Christie's) $105,600   £66,000

ALF BANNER – Unloading The Haycart – signed and dated 1891 – on canvas – 9¼ x 15in.; also a companion.
(Phillips) $1,936   £1,100 Pair

EDWARD MITCHELL BANNISTER – New England Coast – signed and dated '91 – oil on canvas – 14 x 24¼in.
(Christie's) $5,500   £3,392

FILIPPO BARATTI – The Life Guards Passing Hyde Park Corner, London – signed and dated 1885 – 25½ x 37in.
(Christie's) $142,560   £88,000

GEORGES BARBIER – Le Flamenco – watercolour, brush and black ink on paper – 9½ x 12in.
(Christie's) $2,673   £1,650

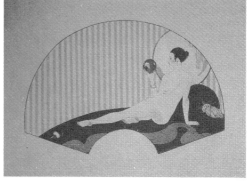

GEORGES BARBIER – Odalisque a la Boulle de Crystal – signed and dated 1920 – watercolour and black ink on paper – 12½ x 19½in.
(Christie's) $4,455   £2,750

BARBIER

GEORGES BARBIER – Le Tango – watercolour, pen and black ink on paper – 12 x 19½in.
(Christie's) $9,801   £6,050

GEORGES BARBIER – Eve – gold paint and watercolour on paper – 15 x 22in.
(Christie's) $4,455   £2,750

GEORGES BARBIER – Colin Maillard – signed and dated 1915 – watercolour, brush and black ink on paper – 15 x 22¼in.
(Christie's) $4,989   £3,080

GEORGES BARBIER – Femme nue sur un Divan – signed – watercolour, brush and black ink on paper – 12¼ x 19½in.
(Christie's) $3,564   £2,200

GIOVANNI FRANCESCO BARBIERI, Called Il Guercino – Judith With The Head Of Holofernes – pen and brown ink – 230 x 197mm.
(Sotheby's) $68,112   £39,600

MIQUEL BARCELO – Untitled – oil and collage on card – 59¼ x 39¼in.
(Christie's) $24,024   £13,200

EDUARD BARGHEER – Figuren, Ischia – signed and dated '49 – watercolour – 8½ x 10¾in.
(Christie's) $800   £440

EDUARD BARGHEER – Am Strand, Ischia – signed and dated '48 – watercolour on paper – 8½ x 10¾in.
(Christie's) $1,401   £770

MYRON BARLOW – Mementos – signed – oil on canvas – 39¾ x 39¾in.
(Christie's) $8,800   £4,916

WILLIAM D. BARKER – Still Life With Summer Flowers – signed and dated 1862 – watercolour – 23 x 16in.
(Prudential Fine Art Auctioneers) $1,485   £900

JAMES MacDONALD BARNSLEY – A Venetian Canal – signed and dated 1887 – oil on paper laid down on card – 12½ x 8½in.
(Sotheby's) $1,058   £572

ARO

JOSE TAPIRO Y BARO – Wayfarer – signed –
watercolour on paper – 13¾ x 9in.
(Robt. W. Skinner Inc.)   **$2,600**   **£1,452**

ANTONIO BARONE – The Lady In Black –
signed – oil on canvas – 71¾ x 35¾in.
(Christie's)   **$22,000**   **£13,479**

PAUL BARTHEL – The Choir – signed – 41¼ x 55¼in. *(Christie's)*   **$12,474 £7,700**

WILLIAM H. BARTLETT – An April Morning On The Colne – signed and dated '96 – oil on panel – 9 x 13in.
(Christie's) **$1,155** **£660**

EDWARD LE BAS – Breakfast In Majorca – signed – oil on canvas – 61 x 67in.
(Christie's) **$22,044** **£13,200**

WALLACE BASSFORD – Fishing Fleet – signed – oil on canvas – 29¾ x 24in.
(Christie's) **$1,980** **£1,221**

GEORGE BASELITZ – Grosser Bernhard – signed and dated '68, and also signed, inscribed and dated on the reverse – oil on canvas – 63¾ x 51¼in.
(Christie's) **$120,120** **£66,000**

JOAQUIN SOROLLA Y BASTIDA – Portrait Of Charles Harrison Tweed – signed and indistinctly inscribed, and dated 1909 on the reverse – oil on canvas – 41 x 30½in.
(Robt. W. Skinner Inc.) **$9,000** **£5,027**

BASTIEN-LEPAGE

JULES BASTIEN-LEPAGE – Portrait Of The Artist – signed and dated 1882 – on panel – 10½ x 8¾in.
(Christie's)   **$49,896   £30,800**

FREDERICK S. BATCHELLER – Still Life With Yellow Roses – signed – oil on board – 12 x 9in.
(Robt. W. Skinner Inc.)   **$1,900   £1,151**

HENRY MAYO BATEMAN – The Football Match: 'The Man Who Stopped To Smoke A Bar One' – signed – pencil, pen and black ink, watercolour and bodycolour – 13 x 13in.
(Christie's)   **$1,212   £693**

HENRY MAYO BATEMAN – The Billiard Game: 'The Man Who Stopped To Smoke A Bar One' – signed – pencil, pen and black ink, watercolour and bodycolour – 13 x 13in.
(Christie's)   **$1,347   £770**

ARTHUR BATT – A Territorial Dispute – signed and dated 1883 – on canvas – 24¼ x 36¼in.
(Phillips)   **$8,800   £5,500**

CARL BAUM – Still Life With Fruit – signed
with conjoined initials – oil on canvas – 30 x
25¼in.
(Christie's)   **$7,700**   **£4,717**

EDWIN F. BAYHA – Boy With Toy Soldiers –
signed – oil on canvas – 39 x 32in.
(Christie's)   **$37,400**   **£22,914**

WALTER BAYES – The Drinking Place – signed
with monogram – oil on board – 25 x 18.5cm.
(Phillips)   **$3,300**   **£2,000**

**GIOVANNI ANTONIO BAZZI, Circle of, Called
Il Sodoma** – The Man Of Sorrows – on panel –
14½ x 12in.
(Phillips)   **$12,740**   **£7,000**

BEAL

GIFFORD BEAL – Horse Tent At The Circus – signed – oil on masonite – 16¼ x 32in.
(Christie's) **$16,500 £9,218**

REYNOLDS BEAL – Upstate New York – signed
– graphite and charcoal – 10½ x 12½in.
(Bruce D. Collins) **$330 £186**

REYNOLDS BEAL – Sells Floto – signed –
crayon and graphite on paper – 12 x 12½in.
(Robt. W. Skinner Inc.) **$1,200 £670**

REYNOLDS BEAL – Country Carnival – signed –
pastel, crayon and graphite on paper – 12 x 12½in.
(Robt. W. Skinner Inc.) **$950 £530**

JAMES HENRY BEARD – Where's Dinner? –
signed and dated 1882 – oil on board – 11¾ x
14¼in.
(Christie's) **$12,100 £6,760**

ARNOLD BEAUVAIS – The Law Courts From A
Window In Carey Street – signed, and signed
again, inscribed and dated 1938 on the reverse –
oil on canvasboard – 19¾ x 15¾in.
(Christie's) **$770** **£440**

MAX BECKMANN – Orchester – signed and
dated '32 – oil on canvas – 35 x 54½in.
(Christie's) **$220,220 £121,000**

MAX BECKMANN – Peter, lesend – signed and
dated '22 – pencil on paper – 12 x 8¾in.
(Christie's) **$6,688** **£4,180**

MAX BECKMANN – Stourdza–Kapelle bei Baden-
Baden – signed with initials and dated '36 –
pencil on squared paper – 7¾ x 4¾in.
(Christie's) **$1,408** **£880**

C

BECKWITH

ZEDEKIAH BELKNAP, Attributed to –
Woman With Red Shawl – oil on canvas –
31 x 26in.
(Bruce D. Collins)   **$1,650**   **£932**

JAMES CARROLL BECKWITH – Portrait Of
William Coffin – signed, dated 1885 and
inscribed, and signed again, dated and inscribed –
oil on canvas – 20¼ x 15¼in.
(Christie's)   **$12,100**   **£6,760**

BELGIAN SCHOOL – Portrait Of The Duc De
Braban, Standing Three-Quarter Length In
Military Uniform – 47½ x 39in.
(Christie's)   **$1,200**   **£682**

ROBERT ANNING BELL – The Amazon Patrol –
signed, inscribed and dated '27 – pencil and
watercolour – 35 x 25cm.
(Phillips)   **$445**   **£270**

VANESSA BELL – Berkshire Farm – signed – oil on canvas – 21½ x 28¾in.
(Christie's) $6,429   £3,850

VANESSA BELL – Portrait Of Lytton Strachey Reading – oil on panel – 36 x 24in.
(Christie's) $146,960   £88,000

GEORGE WESLEY BELLOWS – Tending The Lobster Traps, Early Morning – signed – oil on panel – 16¼ x 19¼in.
(Christie's) $60,500   £37,068

VANESSA BELL – Snow At Charleston; A View From The Studio – oil on canvas – 20 x 16in.
(Christie's) $7,348   £4,400

FRANK MOSS BENNETT – A Peaceful Pipe – signed and dated 1915 – oil on canvas – 33 x 28cm.
(Sotheby's) $9,838   £5,720

BENOIS

ALEXANDRE BENOIS – Costume Design–Le Negre – signed, dated '36 and inscribed – pencil and bodycolour and annotated with instructions to the dressmaker – 32 x 23cm.; also two other costume designs, all three mounted as one. *(Phillips)* $6,048 £3,600

FRANK WESTON BENSON – Portrait Of A Young Woman With Necklace – signed and inscribed – oil on canvas – 21 x 17¼in. *(Christie's)* $22,000 £12,291

FRANK WESTON BENSON – Canoeing – signed and dated '26 – watercolour and pencil on paper laid down on board – 22¾ x 15¼in. *(Christie's),* $13,200 £8,087

FRANK WESTON BENSON – North Haven, Maine – signed and dated '25 – watercolour on paper – 14¾ x 20in. *(Christie's)* $14,300 £7,989

THOMAS HART BENTON — Spring — signed and
dated '44 — tempera on masonite — 33¼ x 21in.
(Christie's)   **$49,500   £27,655**

THOMAS HART BENTON — Study For America
Today Murals — signed — oil on canvasboard — 15¼
x 19½in.
(Christie's)   **$49,500   £27,655**

THOMAS HART BENTON — Rich Penny — signed
— tempera on masonite — 28¼ x 23¾in.
(Christie's)   **$82,500   £50,547**

JEAN BERAUD — La Modiste — signed —
watercolour, pen and black ink on paper — 10½ x
6¾in.
(Christie's)   **$4,400   £2,750**

BERGAMINI

PIERRE EMILE BERNEDE – The Finishing Touch – signed and dated 1859 – on panel – 15½ x 13in.
(Christie's)   **$8,131**   **£4,620**

FRANCESCO BERGAMINI – Vestry Vandals – signed – 19½ x 12in.
(Christie's)   **$7,260**   **£4,400**

L. BERNARD – An Arab Market Scene – signed – on panel – 21 x 17in.
(Christie's)   **$5,445**   **£3,300**

OSCAR EDMUND BERNINGHAUS – Looking Elk – signed, dated '17 and inscribed – oil on board – 13 x 9in.
(Christie's)   **$4,400**   **£2,458**

OSCAR EDMUND BERNINGHAUS – Indian
With Two Horses – signed and inscribed – oil on
canvasboard – 9 x 13in.
(Christie's) $15,400 £9,435

PIERRE M. BEYLE – Fishermen At Work,
Newfoundland – signed and dated 1887 – oil on
canvas – 41 x 56½in.
(Sotheby's) $4,070 £2,200

JOHANN BERTHELSEN – Winter In Central
Park – signed – oil on canvas laid down on
canvasboard – 20¼ x 16in.
(Christie's) $1,980 £1,221

JOHANN BERTHELSEN – Snow Storm In The
City – signed – oil on canvas – 20 x 23¾in.
(Christie's) $3,300 £2,035

SID BICKFORD – Brook Trout Rising – oil on
canvas – 28 x 17in.
(Bruce D. Collins) $4,510 £2,548

BIEGEL

PETER BIEGEL — Mallards Rising — signed —
watercolour and bodycolour — 11¾ x 16½in.
(Christie's) **$2,117 £1,210**

ALBERT BIERSTADT — Top Of The Falls —
signed with conjoined initials and dated 1850 —
oil on canvas — 18¼ x 21¾in.
(Christie's) **$27,500 £15,364**

ALBERT BIERSTADT — In The Yosemite
Valley — signed with initials conjoined — oil on
paper laid down on board — 18¾ x 27¾in.
(Christie's) **$33,000 £20,219**

ALBERT BIERSTADT — Call Of The Wild —
signed with initials conjoined — oil on paper laid
down on canvas — 13½ x 19¼in.
(Christie's) **$24,200 £13,520**

ALBERT BIERSTADT — Tropical Coast — signed with initials conjoined — oil on paper
laid down on masonite — 13¼ x 10¾in. *(Christie's)* **$22,000 £12,291**

GIOVANNI BILIVERTI – Judith – on canvas –
46½ x 36¼in.
(Phillips)   **$80,080**   **£44,000**
A. J. BILLINGSHURST – Thames View –
watercolour – 9.5 x 13.5in.
*(Prudential Fine Art
    Auctioneers)*   **$296**   **£160**

JACOB BILTIUS – A Trompe L'Oeil: A Brace Of
Snipe, A Capercaillie, A Musket, A Gun Powder
Pouch And Other Hunting Equipment, Hanging
From A Nail In The Wall – signed and indistinctly
dated – on canvas – 45¾ x 36in.
(Phillips)   **$87,360**   **£48,000**

HARALDUR BILSON – A Nun With Her Charges
– signed – oil on canvas – 92 x 92cm.
(Phillips)   **$792**   **£480**

JACOB BILTIUS – A Trompe L'Oeil: On A Wall
Hanging By A Hook Is A Dead Hare, A Brace Of
Quail, A Musket, A Powder Pouch, A Whistle And
Other Implements Of The Chase – signed and
dated 1672 – on canvas – 45¾ x 36in.
(Phillips)   **$76,440**   **£42,000**

BIMBO

BARTOLOMMEO DEL BIMBO, Called il Bimbi –
A Still Life Of A Basket Of Strawberries In A
Landscape – oil on canvas – 37 x 49.5cm.
(Sotheby's)   **$79,926**   **£46,200**

SAMUEL JOHN LAMORNA BIRCH – Farm In
Summer – signed – oil on canvas – 51 x 61cm.
(Phillips)   **$7,160**   **£4,000**

SAMUEL JOHN LAMORNA BIRCH – The Pool
Under The Mill – signed and dated 1947 – oil on
canvas – 20 x 25in.
(Christie's)   **$8,223**   **£4,620**

SAMUEL JOHN LAMORNA BIRCH – Bright
Summer – signed and dated 1947 – oil on panel –
11 x 13½in.
(Christie's)   **$2,937**   **£1,650**

SAMUEL JOHN LAMORNA BIRCH – Fishing On
The Itchen – signed and dated 1947 – oil on
canvas – 12 x 16in.
(Christie's)   **$8,223**   **£4,620**

SAMUEL JOHN LAMORNA BIRCH – The Last
Long Streaks Of Snow – signed and dated 1902,
and signed and inscribed on a label on the
stretcher – oil on canvas – 76 x 132cm.
(Phillips)   **$25,060**   **£14,000**

CESARE BISEO – Outside Cairo – signed and dated 1883 – 20½ x 28in.
(Christie's)   **$12,474**   **£7,700**

SAMUEL JOHN LAMORNA BIRCH – A Spate In The Gorge, Wales – signed – oil on canvas – 76.5 x 63.5cm.
(Phillips)   **$4,428**   **£2,700**

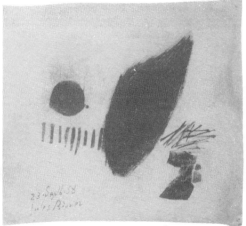

JULES BISSIER – Untitled – signed and dated '58 – egg tempera on canvas – 6¾ x 7¾in.
(Christie's)   **$12,012**   **£6,600**

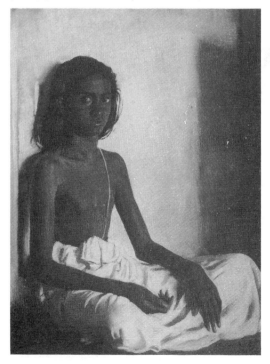

SIR OSWALD BIRLEY – An Indian Boy – signed and dated 1927 – oil on canvas – unframed – 40½ x 30½in.
(Christie's)   **$23,881**   **£14,300**

JULES BISSIER – Univerkeinflick – signed and dated '61, and inscribed and dated on the reverse – egg tempera and black ink on linen – 6½ x 8¾in.
(Christie's)   **$17,017**   **£9,350**

BISSIER

JULES BISSIER – Tamara – signed, inscribed and dated '61 – watercolour on paper – 7 x 8in.
(Christie's)   **$15,147**   **£9,350**

WILLIAM KAY BLACKLOCK – The Mill-Pool At Houghton, Hunts. – signed and inscribed on the reverse – oil on board – unframed – 14 x 12in.
(Christie's)   **$5,143**   **£3,080**

OLIVE PARKER BLACK – Early Fall – signed – oil on canvas – 20 x 24¼in.
(Christie's)   **$3,520**   **£2,171**

OLIVE PARKER BLACK – Spring Solitude – signed – oil on canvas – 24¼ x 36in.
(Christie's)   **$4,950**   **£3,053**

WILLIAM KAY BLACKLOCK – Portrait Of A Woman, Half Length – signed and dated 1905 – oil on canvas – 27 x 20in.
(Christie's)   **$11,940**   **£7,150**

E. BLANC-GARIN – Arranging Flowers – signed and dated 1887 – 44½ x 29in.
(Christie's)   **$12,474**   **£7,700**

EDWIN HOWLAND BLASHFIELD – The Moon And The Stars – oil on canvas – 72 x 48in.
(Christie's)   **$13,200**   **£8,087**

ARBIT BLATAS – La Table – signed – oil on panel – 23½ x 36¼in.
(Christie's)   **$4,950**   **£3,053**

THOMAS BLINKS – Waiting For The Guns – signed and dated '94 – 34 x 55in.
(Christie's)   **$80,190**   **£49,500**

F. B. DeBLOIS – Catch Of The Day – signed and dated 1865 – oil on canvas – 25 x 30¼in.
(Christie's)   **$5,500**   **£3,072**

BLOOMFIELD

HARRY BLOOMFIELD – Nus en Foret – signed, and inscribed on a label on the reverse – oil on canvas – 22 x 28in.
(Christie's) **$1,925** **£1,100**

FRANK BOGGS – Scene de Rue devant l'Eglise de Saint-Medard, Paris – signed and inscribed – oil on canvas – 28¾ x 36¼in.
(Christie's) **$14,080** **£8,800**

ROBERT FREDERICK BLUM – The Blind Shampooer – signed – brush and black and brown ink and chinese white on board – 15¼ x 13¼in.
(Christie's) **$4,180** **£2,335**

FRANK MYERS BOGGS – Notre Dame – signed and dated 1904 – oil on canvas – 15¼ x 18½in.
(Christie's) **$3,300** **£2,035**

AUGUST VILHELM BOESEN – Romsdalen, Norway – signed – 44 x 63in.
(Christie's) **$1,089** **£660**

FRANK MYERS BOGGS – Docks At Sunset – signed – oil on canvas – 10¾ x 14in.
(Christie's) **$1,650** **£1,010**

FRANK MYERS BOGGS – In Port – signed –
oil on canvas – 15 x 21¾in.
(Christie's) $8,800   £5,391

ALEXEI-PETROWITSCH BOGOLJABOFF –
Helsingor Castle By Moonlight – signed and
indistinctly inscribed – 17 x 25¼in.
(Christie's)   **$1,815**   **£1,100**

FRANK MYERS BOGGS – Charenton – signed
and dated '82, and dated again and inscribed – oil
on canvas – 15 x 21¾in.
(Christie's) $7,150   £3,994

GUY PENE DU BOIS – At The Station – signed
and dated 1921 – watercolour, brush and black
ink on board – 14¾ x 12½in.
(Christie's) $6,050   £3,706

FRANK MYERS BOGGS – Les Quais De La
Seine – signed – oil on canvas – 23¾ x 28¾in.
(Christie's) $28,600   £17,523

CONSTANTINOS BOLANACHI – Shipwrecked
Sailors On A Raft With Shipping Beyond – signed
– 25 x 51¼in.
(Christie's)   **$178,200**   **£110,000**

BOLDINI

WILLIAM JOSEPH J. C. BOND – An Angler On A
Bridge In An Extensive Wooded Landscape –
signed and dated '95 – on panel – 6½ x 8½in.
(Phillips) $528   £300

GIOVANNI BOLDINI – Portrait Of A Gentleman,
Head And Shoulders – signed and dated 1891 –
`9 x 8in.
(Christie's) $3,872   £2,200

PIERRE BONNARD – L'Eglise sur la Hauteur –
oil on canvas – 15¼ x 20¼in.
(Christie's) $120,120   £66,000

DAVID BOMBERG – San-Miguel, Toledo,
Afternoon – signed, dated '29 and inscribed on
the reverse – oil on canvas – 28 x 28in.
(Christie's) $119,405   £71,500

PIERRE BONNARD – Le Boxeur (Autoportrait)
– signed – oil on canvas – 21¼ x 29in.
(Christie's) $720,720 £396,000

PIERRE BONNARD – La Seine a Vernon –
signed – oil on canvas – 13¼ x 14¾in.
(Christie's) $120,120   £66,000

PIERRE BONNARD – Jardin vu de la Terrasse
(Jardin meridional au Cannet) – signed – oil on
canvas – 22¼ x 24¼in.
(Christie's)   **$400,400 £220,000**

PIERRE BONNARD – Personnages dans la Rue –
oil on canvas – 15¾ x 11¼in.
(Christie's) $167,200   £104,500

PIERRE BONNARD – Portrait de jeune Fille –
pencil on paper – 25¼ x 18¼in.
(Christie's) $7,007   £3,850

LEON JOSEPH FLORENTIN BONNAT – Antique
Archway – signed – oil on canvas – 31 x 23cm.
(Phillips) $1,596   £950

BORG

CARL OSCAR BORG – Sierra Mountains, California – signed – watercolour and pencil on paper – 14 x 18½in.
(Christie's) $1,760 £1,085

BERNARD LOUIS BORIONE – L'Amateur – signed and dated 1920 – on panel – 13¾ x 10½in.
(Christie's) $2,722 £1,650

JESSIE ARMS BOTKE – Bouquet In A Blue Vase – signed – oil on canvas mounted on board – 26¼ x 24in.
(Christie's) $4,620 £2,850

FRANCOIS BOUCHER – Young Girl Reclining – red and white chalks over black chalk underdrawing (partially stumped) – 316 x 462mm.
(Sotheby's) $491,920 £286,000

EUGENE BOUDIN – Camaret, Bateaux de Peche – signed and dated '73 – oil on canvas – 27 x 38in.
(Christie's) $283,360 £176,000

EUGENE BOUDIN – Antibes, Le Fort Carre – signed, inscribed and dated '93 – oil on canvas – 18¼ x 26in.
(Christie's) $96,800 £60,500

EUGENE BOUDIN – Un Coin du Bassin de
Deauville – signed – oil on panel – 13¾ x 10¼in.
(Christie's)   **$80,080**   **£44,000**

EUGENE BOUDIN – Le Port a Maree basse –
signed – pastel and charcoal on paper – 7½ x
10¼in.
(Christie's)   **$14,960**   **£9,350**

EUGENE BOUDIN – Le Bateau – watercolour
and pencil on paper – 4 x 5¼in.
(Christie's)   **$5,005**   **£2,750**

EUGENE BOUDIN – Laveuses au Bord de la
Touques – signed – oil on panel – 5¼ x 8¼in.
(Christie's)   **$114,400**   **£71,500**

GEORGE HENRY BOUGHTON – Puritan –
signed – oil on panel – 12 x 10¼in.
(Christie's)   **$1,320**   **£814**

GEORGE HENRY BOUGHTON – Winter
Evening – signed – oil on panel – 9¾ x 14in.
(Christie's)   **$8,800**   **£5,391**

BOULLOGNE

LOUIS DE BOULLOGNE, The Younger – Study Of A Satyr – red chalk with touches of black chalk, heightened with white chalk, on blue paper – 402 x 274mm.
(Sotheby's)   **$21,758**   **£12,650**

FRANCIS CECIL BOULT – 'A Forlorn Hope' – signed and dated 1885 – on canvas – 11½ x 17½in.
(Phillips)   **$1,232**   **£700**

ANTOINE BOUVARD – Venetian Canal Scene – signed – oil on canvas – 41 x 56cm.
(Phillips)   **$2,688**   **£1,600**

JACQUES BOUYSSOU – Le Port – signed – oil on panel – 65 x 81cm.
(Phillips)   **$1,344**   **£800**

ALEXANDER BOWER – Winter Light – signed – watercolour on paper – 18¾ x 27in.
(Robt. W. Skinner Inc.)   **$425**   **£257**

FRANK LOUVILLE BOWIE – 'The White House' – signed – oil on artist's board – 11½ x 16in.
(Robt. W. Skinner Inc.)   **$1,500**   **£909**

JANE MARIA BOWKETT – 'Companions' – signed and dated 1882 – on canvas – 23½ x 17½in.
(Phillips)   **$1,936**   **£1,100**

ALEXANDER STUART BOYD, Attributed to – Portrait Of A Woman In A Fur Stole – oil on canvas – 40.5 x 30.5cm.
(Phillips)   **$346**   **£210**

HERCULES BRABAZON BRABAZON – An Eastern Bath – watercolour with pencil heightened with bodycolour on brown paper – 24 x 33.5cm.
(Sotheby's)   **$1,526**   **£825**

SIDNEY LAWRENCE BRACKETT – Wayside Inn – signed – oil on canvas – 18 x 24in.
(Bruce D. Collins)   **$2,090**   **£1,180**

ROBERT BRACKMAN – Study For Autumn Light – signed, and signed again and inscribed on the reverse – oil on canvas – 20¼ x 12¼in.
(Christie's)   **$3,850**   **£2,375**

BRADFORD

WILLIAM BRADFORD – Seascape, Cliffs At
Sunset – oil on canvas laid down on board – 9 x
14in.
(Christie's) $13,200   £8,143

WILLIAM BRADFORD – Arctic Caravan –
signed – oil on canvas – 17¾ x 30¾in.
(Christie's) $33,000   £20,219

WILLIAM BRADFORD – Shipwrecked Off
Labrador – signed and dated 1867 – oil on canvas
– 20 x 30¼in.
(Christie's) $28,600   £15,978

WILLIAM BRADFORD – Trapped In Packed Ice
– signed and dated '77 – oil on canvas – 17½ x
29¾in.
(Christie's) $28,600   £15,978

WILLIAM BRADFORD – The Valley – signed –
oil on canvas – 13¾ x 21in.
(Christie's) $2,750   £1,684

HELEN BRADLEY – On A Warm Spring
Afternoon . . . – signed and inscribed on a label
on the reverse – oil on canvas-board – 10 x 12½in.
(Christie's) $8,266   £4,950

HELEN BRADLEY – Going Home Along Spring
Lane . . . – signed and inscribed on a label on the
reverse – oil on canvas-board – 9¼ x 12½in.
(Christie's) $9,185   £5,500

CARLO BRANCACCIO – A Canal Scene – signed
– 20 x 24¼in.
(Christie's)   **$5,263**   **£3,190**

SIR FRANK BRANGWYN – Timber Loading –
signed and dated 1890 – oil on canvas en
grisaille – 76 x 58cm.
(Phillips)   **$2,624**   **£1,600**

SIR FRANK BRANGWYN, Circle of – A Moorish
Market – oil on canvas – 29½ x 39½in.
(Christie's)   **$1,828**   **£1,045**

GIOVANNI BRANCACCIO – Ritratto di un
Ragazzo Maschere – signed, inscribed and dated
'63 – oil on board – 72 x 44cm.
(Phillips)   **$1,008**   **£600**

CHARLES BROOKE BRANWHITE – 'A Hard
Frost' – signed and dated 1856 – on board – 14 x
22in.
(Phillips)   **$4,576**   **£2,600**

BRAQUE

GEORGES BRAQUE – Baigneuse (aux trois Fruits) – signed and dated '26 – oil on canvas – 39¼ x 31¾in.
(Christie's)   **$900,900**   **£495,000**

GEORGES BRAQUE – Nature morte – signed – oil on canvas – 18¼ x 23¾in.
(Christie's)   **$177,100**   **£110,000**

GEORGES BRAQUE – Tournesols – signed – oil on cradled panel – 23¼ x 23¾in.
(Christie's)   **$247,940**   **£154,000**

GEORGES BRAQUE – Nature morte a l'As de Trefle – signed on the reverse – oil on canvas – 12¼ x 12¼in.
(Christie's)   **$193,600**   **£121,000**

GEORGES BRAQUE – Nature Morte aux Figues – signed with initials – pastel on paper – 7¼ x 10in.
(Christie's)   **$56,320**   **£35,200**

JOHN BRATBY – Piazza San Marco – signed
twice – oil on masonite – 23½ x 35½in.
(Christie's)   **$1,925**   **£1,100**

JOHN BRATBY – Portrait Of Eileen Joyce Seated
Full Length In A Flowered Concert Dress – signed,
inscribed and dated '59 – charcoal – 37½ x 27¼in.
(Christie's)   **$1,386**   **£792**

VICTOR BRAUNER – Le Reueil III – signed and
dated 1956 – oil on canvas – 28¾ x 36¼in.
(Christie's)   **$22,880**   **£14,300**

JOHN BRATBY – Sunflowers – signed – oil on
canvas – unframed – 48 x 36in.
(Christie's)   **$4,408**   **£2,640**

VICTOR BRAUNER – Composition a deux Tetes
– signed and dated 1955 – oil on paper laid down
on canvas – 19¼ x 25¼in.
(Christie's)   **$17,463**   **£10,780**

BREAKSPEARE

MARTYN BREWSTER – After Dark – signed, inscribed and dated 1986 on the reverse, and signed again on the reverse – oil on canvas – 71 x 60in.
(Christie's)   **$1,010**   **£605**

WILLIAM A. BREAKSPEARE – Lost In Thought – signed – on panel – 9 x 6¼in.
(Phillips)   **$1,056**   **£600**

ALFRED DE BREANSKI – The Haymakers' Rest – signed and dated 1876 – on canvas – 19½ x 29½in.
(Phillips)   **$4,576**   **£2,600**

HEINRICH BRELING – The Highwayman – signed – on panel – 5 x 6in.
(Christie's)   **$1,548**   **£880**

MAURICE BRIANCHON – Vase bleu aux Oeillets rouges et aux Mimosas – signed and dated 1941 – oil on canvas – 36¼ x 25¾in.
(Christie's)   **$52,800**   **£33,000**

MAURICE BRIANCHON – Idyll am Meer – signed – on board – 34 x 44cm. *(Phillips)*
$5,880 £3,500

ALFRED THOMPSON BRICHER – Light Winds
– signed with initials in monogram – oil on canvas
– 12¼ x 22¼in.
(Christie's) $14,300   £8,761

MAURICE BRIANCHON – L'Arlequin – signed –
oil on board – 16½ x 12¾in.
(Christie's) $24,948   £15,400

ALFRED THOMPSON BRICHER – Low Tide,
Southhead, Grand Manan Island – signed with
initials in monogram – oil on canvas – 26 x 48in.
(Christie's) $44,000   £26,958

BRICHER

ALFRED THOMPSON BRICHER – Bakers
Island – signed with initials, signed again and
inscribed – oil on canvas – 15¼ x 33in.
(Christie's) $14,300   £8,761

ALFRED THOMPSON BRICHER – Summer
Reverie – watercolour on paper – 11¾ x 21in.
(Christie's) $22,000   £13,479

ALFRED THOMPSON BRICHER – Seascape –
signed with initials in monogram – oil on canvas
– 13 x 29in.
(Christie's) $30,800   £18,871

ELEANOR FORTESCUE BRICKDALE – The
Shrine – signed and inscribed on old label on
backboard – watercolour – 50 x 35cm.
(Phillips) $8,142   £4,600

ALFRED THOMPSON BRICHER – Rocky Shore
– signed and dated 1873 – oil on canvas – 24¼ x
20¼in.
(Christie's) $16,500   £9,218

FREDERICK ARTHUR BRIDGMAN – An Arab
Family By A Stream – signed and dated 1925 –
24¾ x 16½in.
(Christie's) $2,129   £1,210

LOUIS LE BROCQUY – Crane surmodele et Peint
– signed, and signed again, inscribed and dated
1965 – oil on canvas – 25½ x 21½in.
(Christie's) $5,090   £2,860

MARJORIE BROOKS – A Hand Of Cards –
signed – oil on canvas – 39½ x 30in.
(Christie's) $3,490   £2,090

HARRY BROOKER – The Model Airplane – signed and dated 1918 – oil on canvas – 71 x
91.5cm. *(Sotheby's)* $6,622   £3,850

BROWN

ALEXANDER KELLOCK BROWN – The Woodland Path – signed with initials, and also signed and inscribed on the reverse – on canvas – 10¼ x 6½in.
(Phillips)   **$1,040**   **£650**

HENRY HARRIS BROWN – A Drummer In The XXth Hussars – signed and dated 1892 – on canvas – 21½ x 13½in.
(Phillips)   **$2,024**   **£1,150**

HARRISON BIRD BROWN – Landscape Scene/ Sunset – signed – oil on canvas – 13 x 11in.
(Robt. W. Skinner Inc.)   **$750**   **£454**

HUGH BOYCOTT BROWN – Idle Boats, Pinmill, Suffolk – signed – oil on board – 10¼ x 15½in.
(Christie's)   **$616**   **£352**

SIR JOHN ARNESBY BROWN — Extensive
Landscape — signed — oil on canvas — 16 x 20in.
(Christie's)   **$4,235   £2,420**

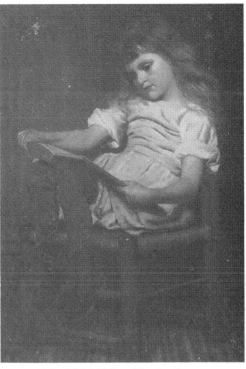

JOHN GEORGE BROWN — First Reader —
signed and dated 1881 — oil on canvas — 22¼ x
16¼in.
(Christie's)   **$15,400   £9,435**

JOHN GEORGE BROWN — Among The Trees —
signed — oil on canvas — 23½ x 15in.
(Christie's)   **$30,800   £18,871**

JOHN GEORGE BROWN — Best Friends — signed
and inscribed — oil on canvas — 24¼ x 20in.
(Christie's)   **$15,400   £9,500**

BROWN

JOHN LEWIS BROWN – An Elegant Riding Party On The Outskirts Of A Village – signed – on panel – 8½ x 6¼in.
(Christie's) **$907** **£550**

JENNIE AUGUSTA BROWNSCOMBE – Ready For The Oven – signed – oil on canvas – 29 x 21in.
(Christie's) **$3,300** **£1,843**

BYRON BROWNE – Jug With Flowers – signed and dated April 29, 1957 – tempera on paper – 26 x 20¼in.
(Christie's) **$1,100** **£673**

LAJOS BRUCK – A Rest In The Fields – signed – 17½ x 13¼in.
(Christie's) **$3,630** **£2,200**

PIETER BRUEGHEL III — The Tax Collector's Office — oil on panel — 74.5 x 106.5 cm.
(Sotheby's) $57,090 £33,000

PIETER BRUEGHEL, the Younger — The Drunkard Pushed Into The Pigsty; and The Woodcutters —
oil on panel — 17.7 cm. diam. *(Sotheby's)* $152,240 £88,000 Pair

BRUNING

GEORGE DE FOREST BRUSH – Onatoga In The Forest – signed – oil en grisaille on canvas – 28 x 21¾in.
(Christie's) $550   £336

PETER BRUNING – Untitled – signed and dated 1963, and dated on the reverse – oil on canvas – 23¾ x 19¾in.
(Christie's) $16,016   £8,800

PETER BRUNING – Haus am Wilden – signed, dated '62 and inscribed – oil and coloured crayon on canvas – 51¼ x 56¾in.
(Christie's) $35,640   £22,000

GEORGE DE FOREST BRUSH – Classical Hommage – signed – pastel on brown paper – 12½ x 9¾in.
(Christie's) $7,150   £3,994

FRANCOISE ANTOINE DE BRUYCKER –
Children Playing With A Boat – signed – on panel
– 17¼ x 20¾in.
(Christie's) **$6,776** **£3,850**

JOHANN GEORG BUCHNER – Portrait Of A
Woman With Her Three Children – signed and
dated 1836 – 21 x 26¾in.
(Christie's) **$7,744** **£4,400**

BUCKNER – A Full Length Portrait Of A Girl And
Boy In A Landscape – oil – 30 x 23¼in.
(Anderson & Garland) **$2,573** **£1,550**

THEODORE PETROS BRYSAKIS – A Turkish
Warrior – signed – on panel – 10½ x 7½in.
(Christie's) **$6,969** **£3,960**

ALICE STANDISH BUELL – The Last Load –
signed in pencil – drypoint – 7½ x 10½in.
(Bruce D. Collins) **$154** **£87**

BUFFET

BERNARD BUFFET – Bouquet de Fleurs sur une Table – signed and dated '52 – oil on canvas – 18 x 25in. *(Christie's)*   **$24,948 £15,400**

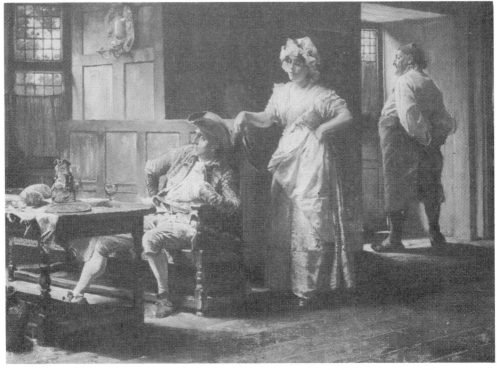

EDGAR BUNDY – A Doubtful Customer – signed and dated 1896 – on canvas – 30 x 40in. *(Phillips)*   **$6,400 £4,000**

ELBRIDGE AYER BURBANK – Lo-Mash-EE, Hopi – signed and dated 1904 – oil on canvas – 13 x 9in.
(Bruce D. Collins)   **$1,540**   **£870**

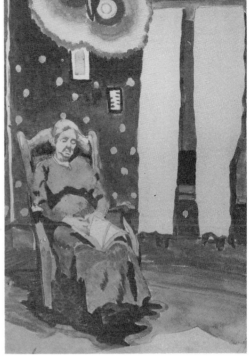

CHARLES EPHRAIM BURCHFIELD – In The Parlour – signed and dated 1916, and dated Sep. 22, 1916 and inscribed on the reverse – watercolour and pencil on paper – 20 x 14in.
(Christie's)   **$8,800**   **£5,391**

CHARLES EPHRAIM BURCHFIELD – House On The S.E. Corner Of Fourth And Vine Streets, Salem, Ohio – signed with initials and dated 1917, and dated and inscribed on the reverse – tempera, watercolour and gouache on paper laid down on board – 18 x 22in.
(Christie's)   **$27,500**   **£15,364**

CHARLES EPHRAIM BURCHFIELD – Rainstorm On Rooftops – signed and dated 1916, and dated 6-17-1916 on the reverse – watercolour and pencil on paper – unframed – 14 x 19¾in.
(Christie's)   **$4,950**   **£3,032**

BURCHFIELD

CHARLES EPHRAIM BURCHFIELD – Barn At Evening – signed with monogrammed initials and dated 1919 – watercolour and pen and purple ink and pencil on paper – 8¾ x 11½in.
(Christie's) **$7,150** **£3,994**

CHARLES EPHRAIM BURCHFIELD – Moon Halo – signed and dated 1916, and dated August 13, 1916 and inscribed on the reverse – watercolour and pencil on paper – 20 x 14in.
(Christie's) **$22,000** **£13,479**

CHARLES EPHRAIM BURCHFIELD – Old Houses – signed and dated 1918 – watercolour, pencil and chinese white on paper – 9¾ x 13¾in.
(Christie's) **$7,150** **£3,994**

CHARLES EPHRAIM BURCHFIELD – Backyards In New York – inscribed on the reverse – watercolour on paper – unframed – 19¾ x 14in.
(Christie's) **$7,150** **£4,380**

HORACE ROBBINS BURDICK – Landscape – signed – oil on board – 8 x 10in.
(Bruce D. Collins) **$286** **£161**

SYDNEY RICHMOND BURLEIGH — Gardener
Wheeling Barrow — initialled — watercolour —
5 x 3in.
(Bruce D. Collins) $467   £263

DAVID BURLIUK — The Letter — signed — oil on
canvas — 31 x 31½in.
(Christie's) $3,520   £2,171

DAVID BURLIUK — Peasant; and Edgewater
Yacht Basin — signed — the first watercolour,
pencil and pen and black ink — the second
watercolour, gouache, crayon and pencil — on
paper — 11½ x 15½in. and 12 x 15¾in.
(Christie's) $1,760   £1,085 Two

SIR EDWARD COLEY BURNE-JONES, Bt. — A
Study Of Heads — pencil — 26 x 16.5cm.; verso —
A Study Of Drapery.
(Sotheby's) $7,700   £4,400

BURRA

EDWARD BURRA – Remenice No. 2 – signed, dated 1926 and inscribed – pencil, watercolour and bodycolour on beige paper – unframed – 11¼ x 9¼in.
(Christie's) $6,429   £3,850

SIMON BUSSY – A Bridge Over A Canal – signed – pastel – 11¼ x 8¼in.
(Christie's) $1,636   £935

PETER JOHAN VALDEMAR BUSCH – A Wooded Winter Landscape With Deer – signed – 38½ x 30¾in.
(Christie's) $1,513   £860

LADY ELIZABETH SOUTHERDEN BUTLER – A Gentleman In A Frock Coat, Standing Reading A Letter In An Interior – signed with monogram and inscribed – on panel – 7¾ x 5in.
(Phillips) $1,280   £800

MILDRED ANNE BUTLER – A Young Girl In A Flower Garden – signed and dated '97 – watercolour heightened with bodycolour – 34 x 51.5 cm.
(Sotheby's) $10,010 £5,720

JAMES E. BUTTERSWORTH – New York From The Bay – signed – oil on canvas – 22 x 36¼in.
(Christie's) $165,000 £92,185

MILDRED ANNE BUTLER – Hard Times: Rooks Feeding In The Snow – signed and dated 1917, and inscribed on the reverse – watercolour heightened with white – 7 x 9¾in.
(Christie's) **$3,465** £1,980

JAMES E. BUTTERSWORTH – Fishing Boats And Windmill – signed, and signed on the reverse – oil on panel – 7¾ x 9¾in.
(Christie's) $8,800 £4,916

THEODORE EARL BUTLER – Valley Farm – signed and dated '07 – oil on canvas – 23¼ x 28¾in.
(Christie's) $60,500 £33,801

THOMAS BUTTERSWORTH – Cutters In A Stiff Breeze Off The Coast – signed – oil on canvas – 38 x 53cm.
(Sotheby's) **$6,054** £3,520

CADEL

HECTOR CAFFIERI – A Lady Gathering Flowers In A Wooded River Landscape – signed – on canvas – 20 x 16in.
(Phillips) $7,040   £4,000

EUGENE CADEL – Scenes Sportifs – signed and dated '18 – oil on canvas – 51.5 x 326.5cm.; and five others.
(Phillips) $5,376   £3,200 Six

HECTOR CAFFIERI – The Fishmarket – signed – watercolour heightened with white – 58.5 x 46cm.
(Sotheby's) $15,400   £8,800

GUSTAVE CAILLEBOTTE – Baigneurs
appretant a plonger, Bords de l'Yerres – signed –
oil on canvas – 46 x 35in.
(Christie's)   **$637,560   £396,000**

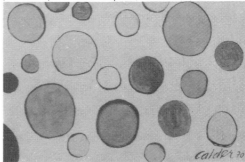

ALEXANDER CALDER – Coloured Circles –
signed and dated '70 – gouache on paper mounted
on canvas – 29 x 43in.
(Christie's)   **$3,603   £1,980**

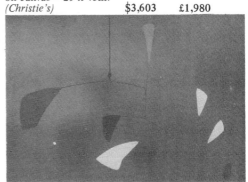

CHRISTIAN CAILLARD – Danseuse au Maillot
rose – signed – oil on board – 28¼ x 12½in.
(Christie's)   **$8,910   £5,500**

ALEXANDER CALDER – One Yellow – signed
with the initials and dated '65 – painted steel –
110 x 150cm.
(Sotheby's)   **$83,248   £47,300**

CALDER

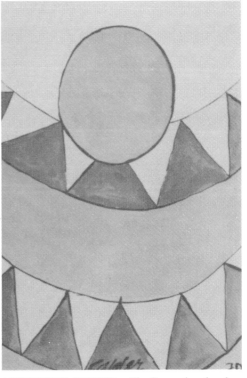

ALEXANDER CALDER – Fleurs Rouges Dans Un Champ Blanc – signed with the monogram – oil on canvas – 81 x 65 cm.
(Sotheby's) **$44,352** **£23,100**

ALEXANDER CALDER – The Sun – signed and dated '70 – gouache on paper – 42½ x 29 in.
(Christie's) **$3,803** **£2,090**

ALEXANDER CALDER – Untitled – signed with initials – mobile of painted sheet metal and rod – 40½ x 55¼ in.
(Christie's) **$128,304** **£79,200**

ALEXANDER CALDER – Composition – signed and dated '71 – gouache on paper – 30¾ x 22¾ in.
(Christie's) **$5,205** **£2,860**

RICARDO ARREDONDO Y CALMACHE – A
Boy Attending Donkeys Before The City Walls –
signed, inscribed and dated 1882 – oil on panel –
25.5 x 21cm.
(Phillips) $3,240 £1,800

KATHERINE CAMERON – Daffodils And
Crocuses – signed – watercolour over pencil –
58.5 x 47.5cm.
(Sotheby's) $3,465 £1,980

P. CAMIO – The Spanish Beauty – signed – 51 x
63in.
(Christie's) $5,445 £3,300

HENRY CALVERT – A Bay Hunter And A Grey
Pony With A Spaniel, Beside A Barn In An
Extensive Wooded Landscape – oil on canvas –
25½ x 33in.
(Phillips) $10,175 £5,500

CHARLES CAMOIN – La Place du Marche,
Toulon – signed – oil on canvas – 25¾ x 31¾in.
(Christie's) $80,960 £50,600

CAMOIN

CHARLES CAMOIN — Nu allonge sur un Lit — signed — oil on canvas — 25½ x 31¾in.
(Christie's) **$28,028 £15,400**

HEINRICH CAMPENDONK — Der Hafen, Ostende
— signed with the initial and dated '35 —
watercolour and pencil on paper — 15½ x 18½in.
(Christie's) **$11,440 £7,150**

HEINRICH CAMPENDONK — Rote Kuh vor
Hausern — signed and dated '13 — oil on canvas
— 12¾ x 15¼in.
(Christie's) **$230,230 £126,500**

BERNARDINO CAMPI, Attributed to – Portrait Of A Gentleman With A Dog – oil on canvas – 129 x 103cm.
(Sotheby's)   **$72,314   £41,800**

FEDERICO DEL CAMPO – A Farmyard Scene, Capri – signed and dated 1881 – on panel – 8 x 4½in.
(Christie's)   **$7,744   £4,400**

FEDERICO DEL CAMPO – A Side Canal, Venice – signed, inscribed and dated 1893 – oil on panel – 19 x 28cm. – and Dusk On The Lagoon – signed and dated.
(Phillips)   **$12,600   £7,000 Two**

ALCESTE CAMPRIANI – Italian Fishermen Mending Their Nets – signed and dated 1900 – 20 x 28in.
(Christie's)   **$4,537   £2,750**

CANADIAN SCHOOL

CANADIAN SCHOOL – View Of Horseshoe Falls, Niagara – signed with monogram, inscribed and dated 1882 – watercolour over traces of pencil heightened with bodycolour – 24¼ x 33¾in.
(Sotheby's) **$1,302** **£704**

CANADIAN SCHOOL, circa 1850 – Timber Yards On The St. Lawrence River – watercolour over pencil with scratching out – 9 x 6¾in.
(Sotheby's) **$936** **£506**

CANADIAN SCHOOL, mid 19th century – Supply Sledges In The Snow – watercolour over pencil heightened with white – 10½ x 20½in.
(Sotheby's) **$2,238** **£1,210 Two**

ELLA DU CANE – Phloxes – watercolour – 17¾ x 11¾in.
(Christie's) **$1,193** **£682**

G. P. CANITZ – Cape Landscape – signed – oil on canvas – 54 x 74cm.
(Sotheby's) **$610** **£330**

CAPULETTI – Le Danseur Escudero – signed – oil on canvas – 55 x 33cm.
(Phillips) **$840** **£500**

CARMINE A. CARBONE – Fenway Skating Party
– signed – oil on canvas – 19¾ x 23¾in.
(Robt. W. Skinner Inc.)   **$550**   **£307**

CARMINE CARBONE – Profile Of A Man –
inscribed and dated 1928 on reverse – oil on
canvas – 21¼ x 17¼in.
(Robt. W. Skinner Inc.)   **$200**   **£121**

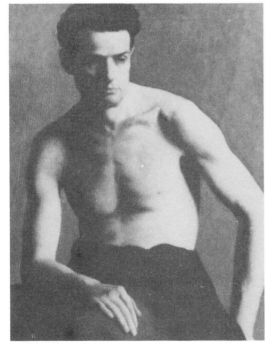

ARTHUR BEECHER CARLES – Abstract –
signed – oil on panel – 16 x 12¾in.
(Christie's)   **$20,900**   **£11,676**

CARMINE CARBONE – Figure Study Of A Young
Man – signed, and inscribed and dated 1929 on
reverse – oil on canvas – 30 x 24in.
(Robt. W. Skinner Inc.)   **$250**   **£151**

SOREN EMIL CARLSEN – Surf Breaking On
Rocks – oil on canvas – 26¼ x 36in.
(Christie's)   **$7,700**   **£4,717**

CARLSEN

SOREN EMIL CARLSEN – The Majestic Sea –
signed – oil on canvas – 30 x 35 in.
(Christie's)   **$30,800**   **£18,871**

JOHN FABIAN CARLSON – Sunlit Grove –
signed, signed again and inscribed – oil on canvas
– 30½ x 40½ in.
(Christie's)   **$12,100**   **£7,413**

JOHN FABIAN CARLSON – River Sentinels –
signed, signed again and inscribed – oil on canvas
– 30 x 40 in.
(Christie's)   **$14,300**   **£8,761**

HENRI CARPENTERO – A Lady With Her Dog In
An Extensive Landscape – signed and dated 1859
– on panel – 19 x 14½ in.
(Christie's)   **$1,839**   **£1,045**

ROSALBA CARRIERA – Portrait Of A Gentleman
– pastel on blue paper laid down on canvas – 580
x 455 mm.
(Sotheby's)   **$14,190**   **£8,250**

MARY STEVENSON CASSATT – Margot In A
Dark Red Costume Seated On A Round-Backed
Chair (La Petite) – signed – pastel on buff
paper – 25½ x 21¼in.
(Christie's) **$660,000 £404,382**

JACOPO CARRUCCI, Called Pontormo – Study
Of A Standing Male Nude, And Part Of Another
Nude Figure – recto – red chalk with touches of
white chalk; Seated Male Nude – verso – red
chalk with touches of white chalk and black chalk
– 388 x 240mm.
(Sotheby's) **$605,440 £352,000**

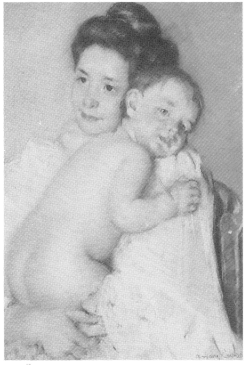

MARY STEVENSON CASSATT – On The Water
– oil on canvas – 23¾ x 28¾in.
(Christie's) **$176,000 £107,835**

MARY STEVENSON CASSATT – Mother Bertha
Holding Her Nude Baby – signed – pastel on
paper – 24½ x 19in.
(Christie's) **$1,045,000 £583,841**

CASSATT

MARY STEVENSON CASSATT − Portrait Of A
Young Girl In A Hat − signed − pastel on paper −
15¼ x 17in.
(Christie's) $132,000   £80,876

ALFRED JOSEPH CASSON − Carson Lake,
Madawaska River Country − signed and inscribed
− oil on board − 12 x 14¾in.
(Sotheby's) $8,954   £4,840

NEVILLE HENRY PENISTON CAYLEY − Fighting White Cranes − inscribed −
watercolour over pencil heightened with bodycolour − 48.5 x 63.5cm. *(Sotheby's)*
$2,645 £1,430

PAUL CEZANNE – Sous-bois – watercolour and
pencil on paper – 12¼ x 18½in.
(Christie's)　　　**$540,540　£297,000**

PAUL CEZANNE – Route Tournante Pres D'Aix
– pencil and watercolour – 47 x 31 cm.
(Sotheby's)　　　**$630,300　£330,000**

PAUL CEZANNE – Baigneurs et Baigneuses –
signed – oil on canvas – 8 x 15¾in.
(Christie's)　　　**$336,490　£209,000**

PAUL CEZANNE – Riviere dans la Plaine – oil on
canvas – 10¾ x 13½in.
(Christie's)　　　**$96,096　£52,800**

PAUL CEZANNE – Baigneur – oil on canvas –
12¾ x 9in.
(Christie's)　　　**$500,500　£275,000**

WILLIAM CHADWICK – A Pewter Mug With
Delphiniums – signed – oil on canvas – 24 x 20in.
(Christie's)　　　**$1,760　£1,085**

CHADWICK

WILLIAM CHADWICK – Laurels At Old Lyme –
signed – oil on canvas – 20 x 24in.
(Christie's)   **$19,800**   **£11,062**

MARC CHAGALL – Les Compagnons De Charlot
– signed twice – gouache and watercolour and pen
and ink – 48 x 63cm.
(Sotheby's)   **$420,200**   **£220,000**

MARC CHAGALL – Jeune Fille au Divan –
signed and dated 1907 – oil on canvas – 29½ x
36½in.
(Christie's)   **$185,955**   **£115,500**

MARC CHAGALL – Le Peintre a la Colombe –
signed – oil on canvas – 45½ x 31¾in.
(Christie's)   **$1,098,020**   **£682,000**

MARC CHAGALL – La Ferme – signed – oil on
canvas – 14½ x 14in.
(Christie's)   **$480,480**   **£264,000**

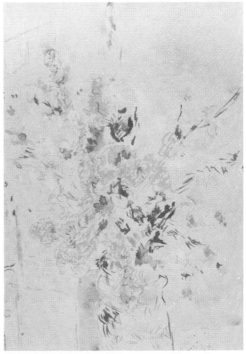

MARC CHAGALL – L'Ete – signed – gouache, watercolour, pastel and brush and black ink on paper – 27 x 19¾in.
(Christie's)   **$264,000   £165,000**

MARC CHAGALL – Nature morte, Fleurs dans un Vase – signed – watercolour heightened with white on paper – 16¾ x 10¾in.
(Christie's)   **$40,040   £22,000**

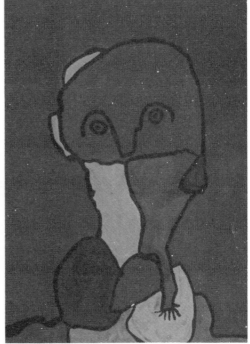

MARC CHAGALL – Le Bouquet illuminant le Ciel – signed, signed on the reverse – oil on canvas – 39¼ x 32in.
(Christie's)   **$109,802   £68,200**

GASTON CHAISSAC – Personnage – signed – oil on canvas – 100.5 x 65cm.
(Sotheby's)   **$34,848   £19,800**

CHAMBERLAIN

JAMES CHARLES – On The Grand Canal –
signed and dated 1892 – oil on canvas – 18 x
14½in.
(Christie's) $10,103   £6,050

WYNN CHAMBERLAIN – Trapped – signed –
tempera on masonite – 32 x 20¼in.
(Christie's) $8,250   £4,609

JOHN CHARLTON – 'The Moon's On The Lake
And The Mist's On The Brae' (MacGregors
Gathering) – signed with initials and dated 1915,
and inscribed on a label attached to the reverse –
pastel – 36 x 28¼in.
(Christie's) $2,310   £1,320

CHARLES CHAPLIN – Portrait d'Une Jeune
Femme – signed – oil on canvas – 44 x 31cm.
(Phillips) $2,700   £1,500

ARMAND CHARNAY — Chateau Morand — signed — 9¾ x 14¼in.
(Christie's)   **$5,808**   **£3,520**

WILLIAM MERRITT CHASE — Venetian Scene — signed — watercolour and pencil on board — 12½ x 9¾in.
(Christie's)   **$16,500**   **£9,218**

WILLIAM MERRITT CHASE — Mrs. Helen Dixon — oil on canvas — 60¼ x 36in.
(Christie's)   **$165,000**   **£101,095**

WILLIAM MERRITT CHASE — Copper Pitcher And Brass Bowl — signed — oil on panel — 14½ x 16in.
(Christie's)   **$8,800**   **£4,916**

WILLIAM MERRITT CHASE — Still Life With Copper Pots — signed — oil on canvas — 23¼ x 39¾in.
(Christie's)   **$16,500**   **£9,218**

CHAVANNES

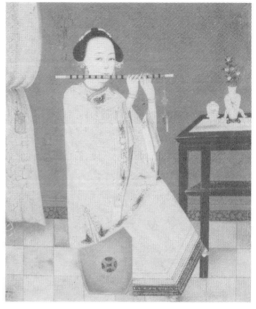

PIERRE PUVIS DE CHAVANNES – La peche –
15 x 12in.
(Christie's) $6,352   £3,850

CHINESE SCHOOL, mid 19th century – A
Chinese Lady Playing A Flute (Ti-Tzu); and A
Seated Chinese Lady – one inscribed on the
reverse – oil on canvas – 59.5 x 46cm.
(Sotheby's) $4,884   £2,640 **Pair**

GIORGIO DE CHIRICO – Piazza d'Italia – signed, and inscribed and signed again on the
reverse – oil on canvas – 15¾ x 29¾in. *(Christie's)* $72,072 £39,600

CHRISTO – Surrounded Islands (Project For
Biscayne Bay, Greater Miami, Florida) – diptych–
signed, inscribed and dated 1982 on the top panel
– top panel–fabric, photograph and coloured
crayon on paper – bottom panel–fabric collage
and coloured crayon on paper – top panel 11¼ x
28¼in.; bottom panel 22¼ x 28¼in.
(Christie's) $29,403 £18,150

CHRISTO – Package On Hand Truck (Project) –
signed and dated 1973 – fabric collage, string,
pencil, black and coloured crayon on board – 28 x
21¾in.
(Christie's) $25,839 £15,950

CHRISTO – 388 Barrels Construction (Project For
Documenta 68 Kassel) – signed, inscribed and
dated '67 – pencil, oil and black chalk on board –
27½ x 21¼in. – on the reverse is a watercolour and
pencil sketch.
(Christie's) $24,024 £13,200

HOWARD CHANDLER CHRISTY – The
American Dream Home – signed and dated 1937 –
oil on canvas – 42¼ x 30¼in.
(Christie's) $3,850 £2,375

CHRISTY

HOWARD CHANDLER CHRISTY – A Seductive Pose – signed and dated 1931 – oil on canvas – 39 x 50¼in. *(Christie's)*   **$16,500 £10,178**

SIR WINSTON CHURCHILL – Villa On Cap Martin – signed with initials – oil on canvas – 24 x 20in.
(Christie's)   **$39,160**   **£22,000**

SIR WINSTON CHURCHILL – Avenue, Trent Park – signed with initials – oil on canvas – 24 x 20in.
(Christie's)   **$31,328**   **£17,600**

LUIGI CIMA – A Girl Feeding Goats In An
Interior – signed – 11¼ x 19in.
(Christie's)   **$9,292**   **£5,280**

ANTONIO CIRINO – Pond Lilies – signed – oil
on board – 8 x 10in.
(Bruce D. Collins)   **$465**   **£262**

ANTONIO CIRINO – Horsedrawn Wagon,
Providence – signed – oil on board – 10 x 12in.
(Bruce D. Collins)   **$990**   **£559**

ANTONIO CIRINO – 'Winter's Mill Stream' –
signed – oil on canvas – 19 x 23in.
(Robt. W. Skinner Inc.)   **$4,750**   **£2,653**

ANTONIO CIRINO – Boat's Lone Sentinel –
signed – oil on canvas – 24 x 30in.
(Bruce D. Collins)   **$4,400**   **£2,485**

ANTONIO CIRINO – Pigeon Cove – signed – oil
on board – 10 x 12in.
(Bruce D. Collins)   **$1,100**   **$621**

CLACK

ARTHUR BAKER CLACK — Sailing Yatchts In A
Continental Harbour — signed — oil on canvas —
46 x 37cm.
(W. H. Lane & Son)   **$1,650**   **£1,000**

GEORGE CLARE — Still Life Of Apples, Plums
And Raspberries; and Still Life Of Apples, Grapes
And Strawberries — signed — oil on canvas — 9½ x
7½in.
(Phillips)   **$4,576**   **£2,600 Two**

MARK LE CLAIRE — A Day At The Races —
signed — oil on canvas — 28 x 23½in.
(Christie's)   **$939**   **£528**

GEORGE CLARE – A Still Life Of Apple Blossom And Violets With Primulas In A Wicker Basket Near A Grassy Knoll, With A Bird's Nest – signed – on canvas – 12 x 10in.
(Phillips)   **$3,040**   **£1,900**

JOHN HEAVISIDE 'WATERLOO' CLARK – Warriors – watercolour over pencil and touches of gum arabic – 14 x 18.5cm.
(Sotheby's)   **$30,525**   **£16,500**

EUGENE CLAUDE – A Still Life With A Wine Flagon, A Basket, Pears, Onions, Cauliflowers, Cabbages, Garlic And A Pumpkin – signed – 31¾ x 39¼in.
(Christie's)   **$7,744**   **£4,400**

JOHN HEAVISIDE 'WATERLOO' CLARK – Climbing Trees – watercolour over pencil with a black line border – 7¼ x 5¼in.
(Sotheby's)   **$34,595**   **£18,700**

EUGENE CLAUDE – A Basket Of Lilac In A Wooded Landscape – signed – 38 x 51in.
(Christie's)   **$16,038**   **£9,900**

CLAUS

EMILE CLAUS – A Young Woman Arranging Flowers – signed – on panel – 8 x 14in.
(Christie's) $17,820 £11,000

PIERRE DE CLAUSADES – Bord de Mer –
signed – oil on canvas – 18¼ x 21¾in.
(Christie's) **$2,138** **£1,320**

EMILE CLAUS – Rencontre d'Apres-Midi –
signed – oil on board – 13½ x 10¼in.
(Christie's) **$6,006** **£3,300**

PIERRE DE CLAUSADES – Ciel de Loire –
signed – oil on canvas – 60 x 91.5cm.
(Phillips) **$5,040** **£3,000**

SIR GEORGE CLAUSEN – Spring – signed – oil on canvas – 20¼ x 16¼in.
(Christie's) $8,817 £5,280

SIR GEORGE CLAUSEN – Gaywood Almshouses, Kings Lynn – signed and dated 1881 – watercolour – 10¼ x 13¾in.
(Christie's) $16,643 £9,350

SIR GEORGE CLAUSEN – Twilight – signed, and signed again and inscribed on the reverse – oil on canvas – 15 x 18in.
(Christie's) $12,512 £7,150

SIR GEORGE CLAUSEN – My Orchard – signed – oil on canvas – 20 x 16in.
(Christie's) $8,662 £4,950

SIR GEORGE CLAUSEN – The Gleaners – signed and dated 1900, and also signed, inscribed and dated – bodycolour over traces of pencil – 43.5 x 34.5cm.
(Phillips) $36,080 £22,000

PAUL JEAN CLAYS – A Harbour Scene With
Numerous Sailing Vessels – signed – 26¾ x 36¼in.
(Christie's)   **$8,910**   **£5,500**

**ALEXANDER BENJAMIN CLAYTON, Attributed
to** – 'Subway Entrance' – signed indistinctly, and
inscribed on reverse – oil on board – 11¾ x 15¾in.
(Robt. W. Skinner Inc.)   **$475**   **£287**

GAD FREDERICK CLEMENT – A Pastoral View,
Near Civita d'Antino – signed – 22 x 27in.
(Christie's)   **$1,179**   **£715**

S. CLEMENTE – Children Outside A House –
signed and dated '82 – on panel – 9 x 5½in.; and
seven others by or attributed to D. Ciragy, Apa and
Jose Rico.
(Christie's)   **$3,267**   **£1,980 Eight**

WINFIELD SCOTT CLIME – Gloucester Wharf –
signed – oil on board – 12 x 16in.
(Bruce D. Collins)   **$935**   **£528**

JEAN COCTEAU – Tete de Profil – signed –
coloured crayon on paper – 13½ x 9¾in.
(Christie's)   **$2,202**   **£1,210**

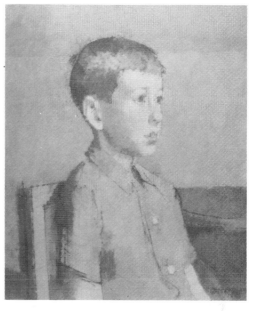

SIR WILLIAM COLDSTREAM – Portrait Of
James – signed and dated 1948 – oil on canvas –
52.5 x 47cm.
(Phillips)   **$3,280**   **£2,000**

FELIX COGEN – Awaiting The Catch – signed –
oil on canvas – 66 x 55cm.
(Phillips)   **$1,800**   **£1,000**

SIR WILLIAM COLDSTREAM – Portrait Of
Fiona – signed – oil on canvas – 61 x 46cm.
(Phillips)   **$2,460**   **£1,500**

COLERIDGE

EMILE COLINUS – Village pres du Port de Garde
– signed – oil on canvas – 54 x 65cm.
(Phillips) $2,016   £1,200

EDWARD COLLIER – A Cartographer's Still Life
– signed and inscribed on a letter, and dated 1698
on hand bill – oil on canvas – 73 x 61.5cm.
(Sotheby's) $22,704   £13,200

F. G. COLERIDGE – Study Of A Boy With His
Catch; and A Girl With A Basket Of Cockles –
watercolour – 12¼ x 8¼in. and 11½ x 8½in.
*(Prudential Fine Art
   Auctioneers)* $810   £500 Pair

CECIL COLLINS – Nocturne – signed and dated
1948, and also signed, inscribed and dated on the
reverse – oil on canvas – 25.5 x 18cm.
(Phillips) $2,145   £1,300

CECIL COLLINS – Pastoral 1950 – signed and dated 1950, and signed, inscribed and dated on a label on the reverse – oil on board – 46 x 61 cm.
(Phillips)   **$3,222   £1,800**

FRANCIS EDWARD COLTHURST – The Carpenter's Shop – signed and dated '96 – oil on canvas – 20 x 30in.
(Christie's)   **$2,939   £1,760**

ROBERT COMBAS – L'homme au cheveau de fleurs – signed, inscribed and dated '82 – acrylic on canvas – unstretched – 49½ x 33¾in.
(Christie's)   **$3,207   £1,980**

CHARLES CONDER – The Pergola – oil on canvas – unframed – 71 x 91cm.
(Phillips)   **$6,232   £3,800**

PHILIP CONNARD – Customs House, Tangier – signed, and also signed and inscribed on the reverse – oil on panel – 31 x 35cm.
(Phillips)   **$2,506   £1,400**

TITO CONTI – Good Morning – signed – 17 x 20in.
(Christie's)   **$3,993   £2,420**

CONTINENTAL SCHOOL

BERYL COOK – Roadside Snack – signed and inscribed on the reverse – oil on panel – 24 x 30in.
(Christie's) $11,022   £6,600

CONTINENTAL SCHOOL, 17th century – The Money Lenders, Interior With Two Figures Seated At A Table Counting Coins And Entering In A Ledger With A Quill Pen, Parakeet At Rear – oil – 37 x 28in.
(Capes, Dunn & Co.) $720   £450

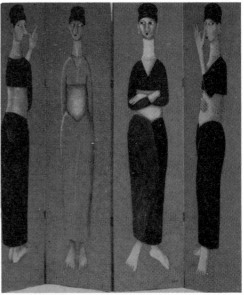

BERYL COOK – Arabian Ladies – four panels – one panel signed – oil on canvas – each panel 67 x 17in.
(Christie's) $5,511   £3,300

CONTINENTAL SCHOOL, 19th century – Mediterranean Street Scene – oil on panel – 7¼ x 10¼in.
(Robt. W. Skinner Inc.) $550   £333

PIERRE OLIVIER JOSEPH COOMANS – Cleopatra – signed and dated 1887 – 9½ x 12¼in.
(Christie's) $1,587   £902

ABRAHAM COOPER – A Saddled Grey Arab Stallion In A Landscape – signed with monogram and indistinctly dated 1820? – oil on canvas – 60 x 75cm.
(Sotheby's) $24,596   £14,300

ALFRED EGERTON COOPER – The Australian – signed, and also signed and inscribed on the reverse – oil on canvas – 36 x 45¼in.
(Phillips) $2,460   £1,500

COLIN CAMPBELL COOPER – Trevi Fountain, Rome – signed – oil on canvas – 42¼ x 35¼in.
(Christie's) $7,700   £4,750

COOPER

COLIN CAMPBELL COOPER – Alcazar Gardens, Seville – signed – oil on canvasboard – 14¾ x 17¾in.
(Christie's) $12,100 £7,464

COLIN CAMPBELL COOPER – Two Women – signed – oil on board – 24½ x 21½in.
(Christie's) $24,200 £14,827

GERALD COOPER – Sunflower Seed No. 2 – signed and inscribed on the reverse – oil on canvas – 30 x 25in.
(Christie's) $4,812 £2,750

THOMAS SIDNEY COOPER – Cattle And Sheep In The Shelter Of A Blasted Tree At A Riverside – signed and dated 1887 – oil on canvas – 24 x 36in.
(Phillips) $9,250 £5,000

THOMAS SIDNEY COOPER – Cattle, Sheep And A Goat Resting By A Tree In An Extensive Marsh Landscape – signed and dated 1854 – on canvas – 35¾ x 48in.
(Phillips) $28,160 £16,000

THOMAS SIDNEY COOPER – Cattle Resting In An Extensive River Landscape – signed and dated 1890 – on panel – 11½ x 15½in.
(Phillips) $4,400 £2,500

THOMAS SIDNEY COOPER – A Cow With Sheep Resting In An Extensive Landscape – signed and dated 1844 – on panel – 10 x 8in.
(Phillips)   **$3,344**   **£1,900**

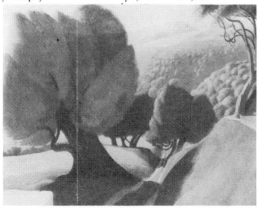

WILLIAM HEATON COOPER – A Hillside Track – signed – oil on canvas – 22¾ x 26¾in.
(Christie's)   **$1,443**   **£825**

WILLIAM SIDNEY COOPER – Cows In A Watermeadow With Church And Village In Background – signed – watercolour – 13 x 19½in.
(Worsfolds)   **$638**   **£380**

CHARLES WEST COPE – Faraway Thoughts – signed with monogram and dated 1880 – oil on panel – 42 x 51cm.
(Sotheby's)   **$5,676**   **£3,300**

JOHN SINGLETON COPLEY – Portrait Of Robert Hooper – oil on canvas – 49¾ x 39¾in.
(Christie's)   **$330,000**   **£186,047**

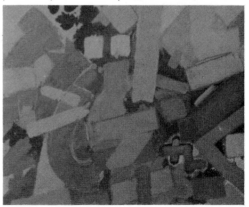

JOHN COPNALL – Small Orange Diamond I – signed, inscribed and dated 1986 on the reverse – acrylic on canvas – unframed – 32 x 32in.
(Christie's)   **$734**   **£440**

CORBUSIER

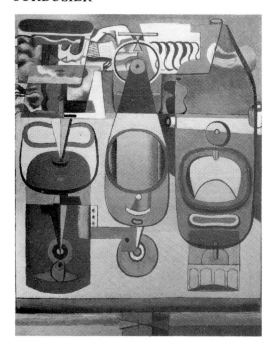

LE CORBUSIER, circa 1926 – Trois Bouteilles – oil on canvas – 100 x 81cm.
(Sotheby's)   **$117,656**   **£61,600**

LE CORBUSIER – La Femme A L'Accordeon Et Le Coureur – signed and dated 1928 – oil on canvas – 130 x 91cm.
(Sotheby's)   **$588,280**   **£308,000**

LE CORBUSIER – Femme Etendue, Vue De Dos – charcoal, pastel and pencil on paper – 21 x 31cm. *(Sotheby's)*   **$4,202 £2,200**

LE CORBUSIER – La Guitare Et Le Mannequin – signed and dated 1927, and signed and dated on the reverse – oil on canvas – 89 x 130.5cm. *(Sotheby's)* **\$745,855 £390,500**

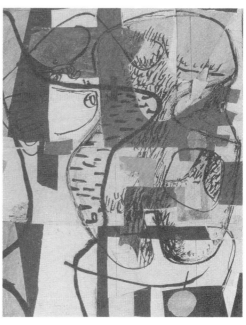

LE CORBUSIER, 1929 – Le Cirque, Femme Et Cheval – oil on canvas – 81 x 65cm. *(Sotheby's)* **\$77,737 £40,700**

LE CORBUSIER – Femme Et Coquillage – signed with the initials and dated '48 – brush and ink, gouache and collage on black paper – 40 x 35.5cm. (Sotheby's) **\$18,909 £9,900**

CORBUSIER

LE CORBUSIER – La Pecheuse d'Huitres d'
Arcachon – signed with the initials – watercolour,
coloured chalk and pen and black ink on paper –
22½ x 19in.
(Christie's) $17,017   £9,350

LOVIS CORINTH – Amaryllis, Kalla und
Flieder – signed and dated 1922 – oil on canvas
– 41½ x 31½in.
(Christie's) $194,810   £121,000

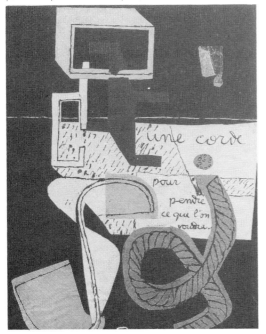

LE CORBUSIER – Une Corde Pour Pendre Ce
Que L'On Voudra – signed with the initials and
dated '63 – watercolour, brush and ink and
collage on paper – 94 x 72cm.
(Sotheby's) $33,616   £17,600

**CORNEILLE (CORNELIUS GUILLAUME VAN
BEVERLOO)** – Les Amoureux – signed and dated
'81 – acrylic on paper mounted on canvas – 25¾
x 19¾in.
(Christie's) $9,009   £4,950

JEAN BAPTISTE CAMILLE COROT – Fermiere agenouillee cueillant des Pissenlits – signed – oil on canvas – 8¾ x 12¾in.
(Christie's)   **$91,520**   **£57,200**

JEAN BAPTISTE CAMILLE COROT – Semur, le Chemin de l'Eglise – signed – oil on panel – 16½ x 13in.
(Christie's)   **$130,130**   **£71,500**

CARLO CORRADINI – A Musical Interlude – signed – 18 x 20¼in.
(Christie's)   **$8,712**   **£4,950**

JOSE CORRAL – A Spanish Interior – signed and dated 1917 – 65 x 61½in.
(Christie's)   **$6,171**   **£3,740**

EDOUARD CORTES – The Porte St. Martin, And The Porte St. Denis, Paris – signed – 10½ x 18¼in.
(Christie's)   **$16,456**   **£9,350**

EDOUARD CORTES – Cafe de la Paix, Paris – signed – 13 x 18in.
(Christie's)   **$11,616**   **£6,600**

CORWIN

CHARLES ABEL CORWIN – A Summer Day –
signed – pastel on canvas – 20 x 16in.
(Christie's) **$4,400 £2,714**

LORENZO COSTA – The Mystic Marriage Of
Saint Catherine With God The Father And
Musician Angels – oil on panel – 61.5 x 52.5cm.
(Sotheby's) **$171,270 £99,000**

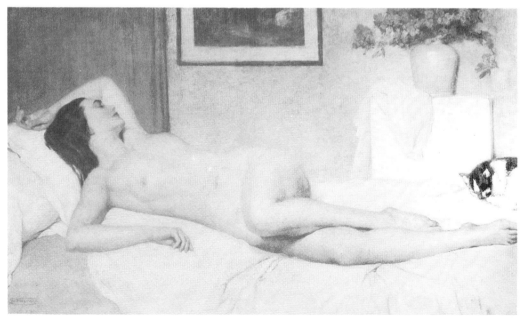

JEAN COTTENET – A Nude Reclining Full Length On A Bed – signed – 42 x 72in.
(Christie's) **$12,705 £7,700**

WILLIAM COTTON – Golden Helmet – signed –
oil on canvas – 26 x 20in.
(Christie's) $2,860   £1,764

WILLIAM COTTON – Dr. Nicholas Murray
Butler – signed – pastel on board – 9¼ x 12¼in.
(Christie's) $660   £407

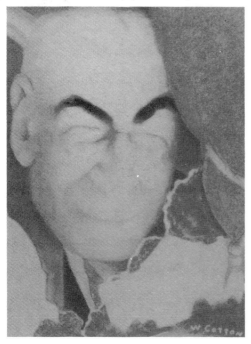

WILLIAM COTTON – Bernard Baruch – signed
– pastel on board – 9¼ x 12in.
(Christie's) $990   £610

WILLIAM COTTON – Frances Perkins – signed
– pastel on board – 12¼ x 9¼in.
(Christie's) $1,100   £678

COULDERY

HORATIO HENRY COULDERY – The Mischief Makers – signed – oil on canvas – 13½ x 17½in. *(Phillips)* $6,160 £3,500

HORATIO HENRY COULDERY – The Little Mischief Makers – signed, and also inscribed – on canvas – 18 x 24in.
(Phillips) $7,680 £4,800

HORATIO HENRY COULDERY – Two Pugs With A Kitten – signed and dated 1880 – oil on canvas – 31 x 40.5cm.
(Sotheby's) $14,190 £8,250

RENE COULON – Ile Brehat – signed – oil on canvas – 65 x 100.5cm.
(Phillips) $2,688   £1,600

GUSTAVE COURBET – Nature morte aux Poires et Pommes – signed with initials – oil on panel – 13¼ x 17¼in.
(Christie's) $79,200   £49,500

SIR NOEL COWARD – Portofino – signed – oil on canvas – 28 x 22in.
(Christie's) $45,500   £26,000

GUSTAVE COURBET and MARCEL ORDINAIRE – La Cascade de Hauteville au-dessus de la Tour de Peliz – signed and dated '75 – oil on canvas – 18 x 15in.
(Christie's) $23,166   £14,300

SIR NOEL COWARD – Unloading On The Quay, Jamaica – signed – oil on canvas – 16 x 11¾in.
(Christie's) $45,500   £26,000

COWARD

SIR NOEL COWARD – The Harbour, Portofino – signed – oil on canvas – 16 x 20in. *(Christie's)*
$24,500 £14,000

SIR NOEL COWARD – A Road In Jamaica –
signed – oil on canvas – 23¾ x 17¾in.
(Christie's)   **$24,500   £14,000**

SIR NOEL COWARD – The Gardener At Firefly,
Jamaica – signed – oil on canvas – 18 x 14in.
(Christie's)   **$13,125   £7,500**

SIR NOEL COWARD – The Pond At Golden-
hurst Farm, Kent – signed – oil on canvas –
16 x 20in.
(Christie's) $15,750 £9,000

SIR NOEL COWARD – The White Cliffs Of
Dover – signed – oil on canvas – 16 x 18in.
(Christie's) $21,000 £12,000

SIR NOEL COWARD – Loading A Cargo Ship, Jamaica – signed – oil on canvas – 24 x
30in. *(Christie's)* $63,000 £36,000

COX

DAVID COX – 'Hereford' With Figures And Animals In Front Of Woodland In The Foreground – signed and dated 1850 – watercolour – 8 x 11¾in.
(Hobbs & Chambers)   **$2,250**   **£1,250**

PERCY R. CRAFT – Winter In Tiberias – signed, and label attached to stretcher – oil on canvas – 50 x 59.5cm.
(Sotheby's)   **$1,831**   **£990**

JAMES HUMBERT CRAIG – Sheef Haven, County Donegal – signed and inscribed on the reverse – oil on canvas – 15 x 20in.
(Christie's)   **$2,571**   **£1,540**

DAVID COX – A Welshwoman – watercolour over black chalk – 17.5 x 11.5cm.
(Phillips)   **$3,894**   **£2,200**

FREDERICK SCHILLER COZZENS – Kill Van Kull, Morning On The Hudson – signed and dated '83, and signed again and inscribed on the reverse – watercolour on paper – 10¼ x 14in.
(Christie's)   **$8,250**   **£5,089**

JAMES HUMBERT CRAIG – Dungloe In The Rosses – signed, and signed again and inscribed on the reverse – oil on canvas – 20 x 24in.
(Christie's)   **$5,143**   **£3,080**

JAMES HUMBERT CRAIG – A Mountainous Landscape – signed – oil on canvas – 20 x 24in.
(Christie's) $4,776   £2,860

BRUCE CRANE – A River Landscape – signed – watercolour over pencil heightened with bodycolour – 13¾ x 20¾in.
(Sotheby's) $1,119   £605

ROBERT BRUCE CRANE – The Hills – signed – oil on canvas – 46¼ x 45¼in.
(Christie's) $28,600   £17,523

RALSTON CRAWFORD – Anchor – signed and dated 1939, and dated again and inscribed on the reverse – watercolour and pen and ink on paper – 11 x 15½in.
(Christie's) $2,200   £1,229

LIONEL TOWNSEND CRAWSHAW – A Mid-Summer Evening – signed, and signed again and inscribed on a label on the reverse – oil on panel – 8¾ x 11½in.
(Christie's) $924   £528

JOHN CRAXTON – Willow – signed and dated '44 – watercolour and gouache – 16¼ x 20¾in.
(Christie's) $1,653   £990

JOHN MANSFIELD CREALOCK – The Red Sofa – signed, and also signed, inscribed and dated 1912 on the reverse – oil on canvas – unframed – 130 x 96cm.
(Phillips) $7,872   £4,800

CRESWICK

JASPER FRANCIS CROPSEY – Autumn Splendor – signed and dated 1888 – oil on canvas – 22¼ x 28in.
(Christie's)   **$38,500**   **£21,509**

THOMAS CRESWICK – Figures In An Extensive Landscape At Grandaia, Lake Lugano – signed with monogram, and also signed and inscribed – on metal – 10½ x 7½in.
(Phillips)   **$1,920**   **£1,200**

HENRI EDMOND CROSS – Le Lac du Bois de Boulogne – signed – oil on canvas – 25¾ x 32in.
(Christie's)   **$602,140**   **£374,000**

JOHN DE CRITZ, Studio of – Portrait Of James I Of England, James VI Of Scotland – oil on panel – 45 x 34½in.
(Phillips)   **$62,900**   **£34,000**

HENRI EDMOND CROSS – Les Petits Montagnes Mauresques –'signed and dated '09 – oil on canvas – 18¼ x 24in.
(Christie's)   **$114,400**   **£71,500**

HENRI EDMOND CROSS – Portrait de Seurat –
signed with monogram – oil on canvas – 41.5 x
33cm.
(Phillips)   **$7,560   £4,500**

CHARLES COURTNEY CURRAN – On The
Summit – signed and dated 1932, and signed
with initials on the reverse – oil on masonite –
30 x 25in.
(Christie's)   **$7,700   £4,717**

TERENCE CUNEO – Spanish Street Scene –
signed and dated '59 – oil on canvasboard – 23½
x 19½in.
(Christie's)   **$2,153   £1,210**

CHARLES COURTNEY CURRAN – Walking On
The Cliff – signed, dated 1935 and inscribed, and
signed again and inscribed on the reverse – oil on
masonite – 16 x 12in.
(Christie's)   **$1,650   £1,017**

DABO

LEON DABO – The Thames Near Richmond –
signed, and inscribed on the reverse – oil on
canvas – 15 x 23¼in.
(Christie's)   **$8,800**   **£4,916**

LEON DABO – Study Of Flowers – signed, and
signed again, dated 1929 and inscribed on the
reverse – oil on board – 20 x 15¾in.
(Christie's)   **$1,100**   **£678**

LEON DABO – Inlet – signed – oil on canvas –
24½ x 34in.
(Christie's)   **$18,700**   **£11,457**

MICHAEL DAHL, Circle of – A Portrait Of
Annabella Norwich – oil on canvas – 50 x 40in.
(Phillips)   **$2,775**   **£1,500**

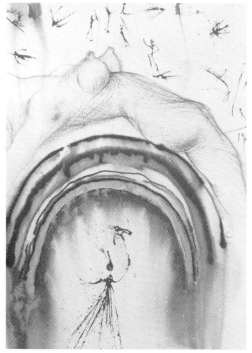

SALVADOR DALI – Femme nue sur un Arc en
Ciel – signed and dated 1968 – watercolour, pen
and black ink and charcoal on paper – 29½ x
21½in.
(Christie's)   **$56,320**   **£35,200**

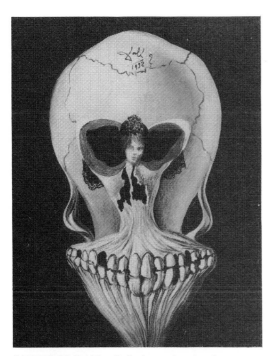

SALVADOR DALI − Ballerine − signed and
dated 1932 − oil on canvas − 9¾ x 7¾in.
(Christie's) $66,880   £41,800

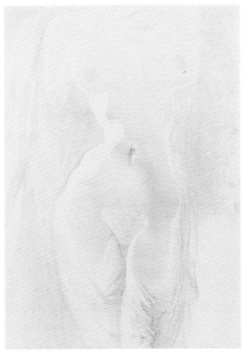

SALVADOR DALI − Aphrodite voilee − signed
and dated 1974 − red chalk on paper − 40¼ x
27½in.
(Christie's) $40,480   £25,300

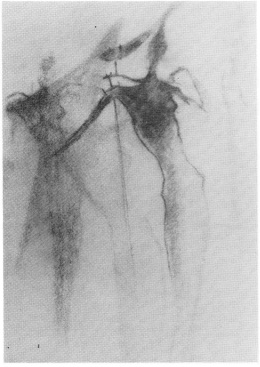

SALVADOR DALI − Nus aux Bras mous − signed
− charcoal on paper − 21¾ x 15½in.
(Christie's) $5,280   £3,300

BARTHOLOMEW DANDRIDGE, Studio of − A
Portrait Of A Dandy Standing Three-Quarter
Length Wearing A Green Coat And Red Gown −
oil on canvas − 29¾ x 25¼in.
(Phillips) $5,180   £2,800

DANIELS

WILLIAM DANIELS – Portrait Of The Artist,
Half Length, Wearing Brown Jacket And Hat And
Holding A Musket – oil on canvas – 89 x 69.5cm.
(Sotheby's)   **$6,622**   **£3,850**

FRANCESCO D'ANTONIO – The Madonna And
Child With Angels – tempera on panel – 94 x
57cm.
(Sotheby's)   **$137,016**   **£79,200**

LEON MARIE CONSTANT DANSAERT – A
Young Girl Seated In A Chair With Her Doll –
signed, inscribed and dated 1892 – on panel –
10½ x 8in.
(Christie's)   **$1,179**   **£715**

ANDREW MICHAEL DASBURG – Souvenir
From Maine – signed, dated 1913 and inscribed
on the reverse – oil on board – 6½ x 9½in.
(Christie's)   **$14,300**   **£8,761**

M. DASSO – In The Garden – signed and dated 1913 – 43 x 43in.
(Christie's) $19,602   £12,100

ANDREW MICHAEL DASBURG – Still Life – signed – oil on canvas laid down on board – 16¼ x 13in.
(Christie's) $82,500   £50,547

ANDREW MICHAEL DASBURG – Still Life With Flowers – oil on canvas – 20¼ x 16¼in.
(Christie's) $9,900   £6,065

RANDALL DAVEY – Rosie – signed – oil on canvas – 30 x 20¼in.
(Christie's) $4,400   £2,458

DAVEY

RANDALL DAVEY – Portuguese Grandmother –
oil on canvas – 35½ x 27½in.
(Christie's)   **$13,200**   **£7,374**

ARTHUR E. DAVIES – Wroxham Bridge, Norfolk
– signed – watercolour – 12 x 16in.
(Messrs. G. A. Key)   **$764**   **£420**

LOUIS DAVID – Portrait Of Mademoiselle
Guimard As Terpsichore – oil on canvas – 195.5
x 120.5cm.
(Sotheby's)   **$380,600**   **£220,000**

DAVID DAVIES – Fishing Boats In A Harbour –
signed – watercolour over pencil – 27 x 21cm.
(Sotheby's)   **$1,628**   **£880**

CHARLES HAROLD DAVIS – Golden Trees –
signed and inscribed – oil on canvas – 12 x 16in.
(Christie's)   **$12,100**   **£7,413**

EDGAR DEGAS – Mlle. Becat aux Ambassadeurs
– signed on the reverse – oil on tile – 8 x 8in.
(Christie's) $202,400   £126,500

STUART DAVIS – Chinatown – signed and
dated 1912 – oil on canvas – 37 x 30in.
(Christie's) $44,000   £29,958

MAURICE DECAMPS – Roses – signed – oil on
canvas – 46 x 55cm.
(Phillips) $2,016   £1,200

JOSEPH DECKER – Collecting Nuts – signed and
dated 1899 – oil on canvas – 14 x 17¾in.
(Christie's) $11,000   £6,145

EDGAR DEGAS – Apres Le Bain, Femme S'
Essuyant – charcoal – 64 x 39cm.
(Sotheby's) $105,050   £55,000

DEGAS

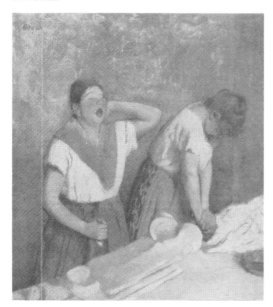

EDGAR DEGAS – Les Blanchisseuses (Les Repasseuses) – signed – oil on canvas – 32 x 30in.
(Christie's) $13,613,600   £7,480,000

EDGAR DEGAS – Jeune Fille assise appuyee au Dossier d'un Fauteuil – oil on cradled panel – 27½ x 19¼in.
(Christie's) $280,280   £154,000

EDGAR DEGAS – Homme nu debout – recto – pencil on paper; Femme nue assise – verso – pencil on paper – 23½ x 17¾in.
(Christie's) $20,020   £11,000

EDGAR DEGAS – Femme a sa Toilette – charcoal on paper – 23¾ x 18¼in.
(Christie's) $65,120   £40,700

EUGENE DELACROIX – Selle et Harnachement Marocain – watercolour and pencil on paper – 5½ x 8¾in.
(Christie's) $2,802 £1,540

SONIA DELAUNAY – 'Pneu Pinelli' – signed – coloured crayons – 19 x 26cm.
(Sotheby's) $25,212 £13,200

SONIA DELAUNAY – Danseuse – gouache – 26 x 18cm.
(Sotheby's) $23,111 £12,100

SONIA DELAUNAY – Danseuse – signed and dated 1917 – coloured crayons and gouache – 41 x 29cm.
(Sotheby's) $23,111 £12,100

PAUL DELVAUX – Nu – signed and dated '48 – brush and indian ink, watercolour and wash – 29.6 x 37.7cm.
(Sotheby's) $32,565 £17,050

PAUL DELVAUX – Nu a l'Eventail – signed and inscribed – gouache and black ink on paper – 7¾ x 4¼in.
(Christie's) $4,004 £2,200

DELVAUX

PAUL DELVAUX – La Prisonniere or La Prisonniere II – signed and dated '6-42 – oil on panel – 32¼ x 41¾in. *(Christie's)* $513,590   £319,000

CHARLES DEMUTH – Aunt Ellen – signed, dated 1910 and inscribed – watercolour, pen and black ink and pencil on paper – 8¾ x 5¾in. *(Christie's)* $12,100   £7,413

CHARLES HENRY DEMUTH – Flowers – watercolour and pencil on paper – 13¼ x 10¼in. *(Christie's)* $11,000   £6,145

CHARLES HENRY DEMUTH – Revue In Paris –
watercolour on paper – 10½ x 8in.
(Christie's)   **$4,950**   **£2,765**

ANDRE DERAIN – Genevieve – signed – oil on
canvas – 23 x 19in.
(Christie's)   **$12,474**   **£7,700**

ANDRE DERAIN – Nature morte aux Poissons – signed on reverse – oil on canvas – 21¼
x 28¾in. *(Christie's)*   **•$120,120**   **£66,000**

DERAIN

ANDRE DERAIN – Village de Provence – signed – oil on canvas – 13 x 16in.
(Christie's) $19,602 £12,100

ANDRE DERAIN – Tete de Femme – signed – oil on canvas – 10 x 9¾in.
(Christie's) $8,910 £5,500

GABRIEL DESCHAMPS – Le Chemin du Village – signed – oil on canvas – 45.5 x 65cm.
(Phillips) $2,016 £1,200

EUGENE DESHAYES, Attributed to – Figures By A River Before A Medieval French Village – oil on panel – 24 x 34.5cm.
(Phillips) $576 £320

ALEXANDRE FRANCOIS DESPORTES – A Still Life Of A Partridge With Prunus And A Branch Of Orange Blossom In A Kangxi Blue And White Porcelain Bowl – oil on canvas – 52 x 60cm.
(Sotheby's) $78,023 £45,100

ANTHONY DEVAS – Seated Nude, Half Length – signed – oil on canvas – 24 x 20in.
(Christie's) $2,020 £1,210

CHARLES MELVILLE DEWEY – Sailboats –
signed and dated '71 – watercolour on paper –
5¾ x 9½in.
(Christie's)   **$7,150   £4,380**

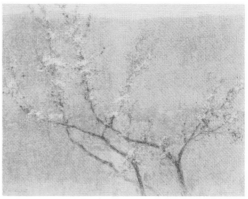

WYNFORD DEWHURST – A Branch Of Apple
Blossom – signed – oil on canvas – 19¾ x 28½in.
(Christie's)   **$4,235   £2,420**

WYNFORD DEWHURST – Autumn Morning
Heatherland – signed – oil on canvas – 17¼ x
21½in.
(Christie's)   **$1,443   £825**

WYNFORD DEWHURST – Lake Geneva – signed
– oil on panel – 10¼ x 13¼in.
(Christie's)   **$616   £352**

THOMAS WILMER DEWING – An Elegant Lady
– signed and dated '22 – pastel on brown paper
laid down on board – 10½ x 7¼in.
(Christie's)   **$46,200   £25,811**

DICKSEE

PIERRE JAQUES DIERCKX – The Little
Helpers – signed – 23 x 29in.
(Christie's) **$6,776** **£3,850**

THOMAS FRANCIS DICKSEE – Portrait Of A
Girl – signed and dated '86 – oil on canvas – 55 x
40.5cm.
(Sotheby's) **$15,136** **£8,800**

ADELHEID DIETRICH – Still Life With Peach,
Grapes And Rosehips – signed and dated 1865 –
oil on canvas – 8¾ x 10¼in.
(Christie's) **$11,000** **£6,739**

JACOB VAN DIEGHEM – Sheep And Poultry In
A Landscape; and Sheep And Poultry In A Barn –
signed and dated 1880 – oil on panel – 24 x 17cm.
(Phillips) **$1,656** **£920 Pair**

WILHELM VON DIEZ – Horsemen Fording A
River – signed and dated '89 – on board – 11½ x
16¼in.
(Christie's) **$1,452** **£880**

JIM DINE — Desire (A Study) — signed and dated 1981 — watercolour, black ink, chalk and paper collage on three sheets of paper — 39 x 83in. *(Christie's)* **$32,032 £17,600**

BURGOYNE DILLER — First Theme — oil on canvas — 50¼ x 50¼in. *(Christie's)* **$35,200 £19,666**

JESSICA DISMOOR — Les Baux, Provence — oil on panel — 12¾ x 16in. *(Christie's)* **$2,571 £1,540**

OTTO DIX — Winterlandschaft mit Mond or Winterbrand im Hegau — signed with monogram and dated 1935 — oil on board — 23½ x 31½in. *(Christie's)* **$96,800 £60,500**

DOBSON

FRANK DOBSON – Pollarded Willows By A Stream, Hampshire – signed and dated '40 – gouache, watercolour, brush and black ink – 13½ x 19¼in.
(Christie's)   **$1,058**   **£605**

FRANK DOBSON – The Hampshire Wagon – signed and dated '44 – watercolour, gouache, brush and black ink – 13¾ x 17¾in.
(Christie's)   **$1,155**   **£660**

FRANK DOBSON – Landscape With A Fence – watercolour, gouache, brush and black ink – 13¾ x 17½in.
(Christie's)   **$673**   **£385**

FRANK DOBSON – Head Of A Girl – pastel – 20 x 14½in.
(Christie's)   **$481**   **£275**

STEVEN DOHANOS – No Passing – signed – gouache on board – 26¼ x 20in.
(Christie's)   **$8,800**   **£5,428**

JEAN GABRIEL DOMERGUE – Portrait de
Femme – signed and dated '33 – oil on panel –
21¾ x 18in.
(Christie's) $1,782   £1,100

KEES VAN DONGEN – La Femme Orientale –
signed – oil on canvas – 39¼ x 31¾in.
(Christie's) $800,800   £440,000

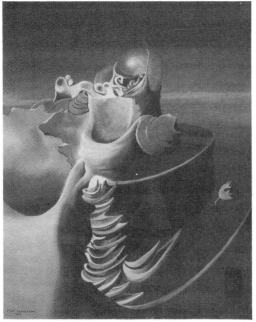

OSCAR DOMINGUEZ – Le Dimanche – signed
and dated 1938, and inscribed on the reverse –
oil on canvas – 23¾ x 19¼in.
(Christie's) $42,240   £26,400

KEES VAN DONGEN – Deshabille debout –
signed – oil on canvas – 25½ x 21¼in.
(Christie's) $318,780   £198,000

DONGEN

KEES VAN DONGEN – Odalisque couchee –
signed – oil on board – 21 x 27¾in.
(Christie's)   **$320,320   £176,000**

KEES VAN DONGEN – Les Elegantes A
Deauville – signed and inscribed – watercolour and
coloured crayons – 67 x 54cm.
(Sotheby's)   **$100,848   £52,800**

KEES VAN DONGEN – Les Voiliers, Rotterdam
– signed – oil on canvas – 21¼ x 17¾in.
(Christie's)   **$110,110   £60,500**

DELAPOER DOWNING – 'Marriage In The Fleet' – signed and dated '98 – on canvas – 37
x 52.5in. *(Phillips)*   **$5,280 £3,000**

WILLIAM DRING – Summer – signed – oil on canvas – 76 x 81cm. *(Phillips)*
$14,760 £9,000

MALCOLM DRUMMOND – The Black Book
Trials – oil on canvas – 20 x 16in.
(Christie's) $2,204   £1,320

J. T. DRYSDALE – Edgware Road Looking
Towards Marble Arch – signed and dated 1899 –
oil on canvas – 64 x 76cm.
(Sotheby's) $9,460   £5,500

DUBUFFET

JEAN DUBUFFET − Vache bleue et rouge −
signed and dated '43 − oil on panel − 24¾ x 29¾in.
(Christie's) **$220,220 £121,000**

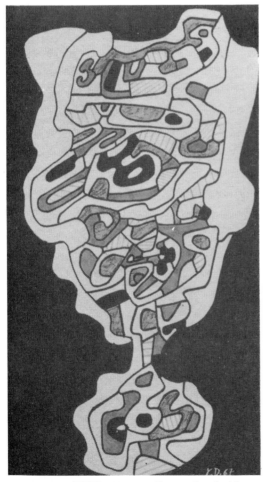

JEAN DUBUFFET − Chameau entrave − signed
and dated '48 − gouache on paper − 12¾ x 9½in.
(Christie's) **$14,960 £9,350**

JEAN DUBUFFET − Le verre d'eau − signed with
initials and dated '67 − felt-tip pen and paper
collage on paper − 13½ x 8¾in.
(Christie's) **$16,016 £8,800**

JEAN DUBUFFET − Papa Flumette (Portrait) −
signed and dated '67, and signed and dated on the
reverse − vinyl on canvas − 100 x 81cm.
(Sotheby's) **$221,760 £115,500**

JEAN DUBUFFET – Empressements – signed
with initials and dated '80, and also signed,
inscribed and dated on the reverse – acrylic on
canvas – 39¼ x 31¾in.
(Christie's) $115,830 £71,500

T. DUDLEY – River Scene With Figures, Barges
etc. – signed – watercolour – 10 x 14in.
(Messrs. G. A. Key) $491 £270

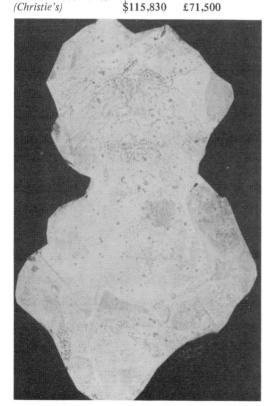

CLEMENTINE HELENE DUFAU – A Moorish
Beauty – signed – 36 x 47½in.
(Christie's) $6,897 £4,180

JEAN DUBUFFET – Dame abondante – signed
and dated '54 – collage and gouache on paper –
17¾ x 11¼in.
(Christie's) $23,023 £12,650

JEAN DUFY – Preilly-sur-Claisse, Normandie –
signed – oil on canvas – 20 x 25¾in.
(Christie's) $15,147 £9,350

DUFY

JEAN DUFY – Le Pont dans la Ville – signed and dated 1922 – watercolour and pencil on paper – 15¾ x 21¾in.
(Christie's) $4,928   £3,080

RAOUL DUFY – Bouquet de Fleurs – signed – watercolour on paper – 19 x 25in.
(Christie's) $73,920   £46,200

RAOUL DUFY – La Maison dans les Arbres – signed – oil on canvas – 29¾ x 23½in.
(Christie's) $90,090   £49,500

RAOUL DUFY – Le Champs De Course D'Ascot – signed – gouache and watercolour – 48 x 63cm. *(Sotheby's)* $136,565 £71,500

RAOUL DUFY – La Baie de Nice; Le Jardin de la Residence – signed – watercolour on paper laid on canvas – 26 x 19¾in. *(Christie's)* **$61,600 £38,500**

RAOUL DUFY – Le Pin – signed – oil on canvas – 28¾ x 36¼in.
(Christie's) **$190,190 £104,500**

RAOUL DUFY – Le Paddock a Deauville – signed and dated – oil on canvas – 25¾ x 31¾in.
(Christie's) **$159,390 £99,000**

DUGDALE

THOMAS C. DUGDALE – Female Nude – signed – oil on canvas – 35½ x 30¼in.
(Christie's)   **$6,853**   **£3,850**

ADOLFO DUMINI – It's Mine – signed – 23 x 17¼in.
(Christie's)   **$4,065**   **£2,310**

FRANK VINCENT DUMOND – New Thorn Bush Pool, Margaree, Nova Scotia – signed and inscribed – oil on canvas – 24¼ x 30in.
(Christie's)   **$4,950**   **£3,032**

CHARLES DUKES – The Reading Lesson – signed – on canvas – 27½ x 21in.
(Phillips)   **$3,872**   **£2,200**

FRANK VINCENT DUMOND – A Salmon Fisherman In The North River – signed and inscribed – oil on canvas – 23¾ x 30¼in.
(Christie's)   **$2,860**   **£1,752**

RONALD OSSORY DUNLOP – The Unadopted
Road, Sussex – signed – oil on canvas – 63.5 x
76cm.
(Phillips)   **$1,023**   **£620**

JULES DUPRE – A Village Street – signed – oil
on canvas – 35 x 27.5cm.
(Phillips)   **$1,440**   **£800**

W. HERBERT ('BUCK') DUNTON – The Trapper
– signed – oil on canvas – 28¼ x 22¼in.
(Christie's)   **$22,000**   **£12,291**

JOHANNES BERTHOLOMAUS DUNTZE – An
Alpine Lakeside Town At Dusk – signed and
dated 1861 – 66 x 95cm.
(Phillips)   **$14,400**   **£8,000**

MICHAEL DUREUIL – La Porte ouverte –
signed and dated '54, and inscribed on the reverse
– oil on canvas – 41 x 33cm.
(Phillips)   **$924**   **£550**

DURRIE

GEORGE HENRY DURRIE – Miles To Salem –
signed and dated 1862 – oil on board – 12 x
20¼in.
(Christie's) $71,500   £39,947

GEORGE HENRY DURRIE – View Of
Westville – oil on canvas – 25¾ x 36¼in.
(Christie's) $60,500   £33,801

GEORGE HENRY DURRIE – Summer Farm
Scene; and Winter Farmyard And Travelers – the
first signed with initials – oil on board – 13¼ x
16½in.
(Christie's) $77,000   £43,019 **Pair**

GEORGE HENRY DURRIE – Stream Fishing –
signed and dated 1856 – oil on canvas – 30¼ x
25¼in.
(Christie's) $16,500   £9,218

DUTCH SCHOOL – A Frozen River Scene With
Skaters – 18¾ x 29in.
(Christie's) $5,808   £3,300

DUTCH SCHOOL, 17th century – 'Portrait Of A
Lady' – dated 1629 – oil on panel – 29 x 20¾in.
(Robt. W. Skinner Inc.) **$1,800** **£1,005**

FRANK DUVENECK – Peasant Girl –
watercolour and pencil on paper – 18¾ x 13¼in.
(Christie's) **$3,300** **£2,035**

PIERRE DUTEUTRE – La Galette des Rois –
signed – oil on canvas – 55 x 46cm.
(Phillips) **$369** **£220**

SIR ANTHONY VAN DYCK – Portrait Of A
Lady, Said To Be The Marchesa Di Serra – oil on
canvas – 71 x 59cm.
(Sotheby's) **$121,792** **£70,400**

DYCK

SIR ANTHONY VAN DYCK, After – The Three Eldest Children of Charles I – oil on canvas – 129 x 149cm.
(Sotheby's)   **$16,082**   **£9,350**

H. ANTHONY DYER – St. Marguerite, Normandy – watercolour – 7 x 10in.
(Bruce D. Collins)   **$264**   **£149**

H. ANTHONY DYER – Tiverton – signed – watercolour – 8 x 10in.
(Bruce D. Collins)   **$330**   **£186**

H. ANTHONY DYER – Venetian Entrance – signed – watercolour – 14 x 11in.
(Bruce D. Collins)   **$1,320**   **£745**

MARCEL DYF – Clodine a la Toilette – signed – oil on canvas – 24¾ x 20½in.
(Christie's)   **$14,014**   **£7,700**

MARCEL DYF – Le Dessert – signed – oil on canvas – 23½ x 28¾in. *(Christie's)*
$19,602 £12,100

MARCEL DYF – Les Danseurs – signed – oil on
canvas – 21½ x 18in.
(Christie's)   **$2,402   £1,320**

MARCEL DYF – Fille a la Mandoline devant un
Miroir – signed – oil on canvas – 28¾ x 23¾in.
(Christie's)   **$19,602   £12,100**

DYF

MARCEL DYF – Village d'Arzon – signed – oil
on canvas – 18¼ x 22in.
(Christie's)   **$16,016**   **£8,800**

MARCEL DYF – Gitane a l'Echarpe – signed –
oil on canvas – 28 x 23in.
(Christie's)   **$13,365**   **£8,250**

MARCEL DYF – Le Champ de Ble – signed – oil
on canvas – 23½ x 29in.
(Christie's)   **$9,266**   **£5,720**

MARCEL DYF – Jeune Fille blonde au Chapeau
noir – signed – oil on canvas – 21¾ x 18in.
(Christie's)   **$3,207**   **£1,980**

GEORGE EARL – The Warrener's Friends
'Vulcan' And 'Fly' – signed and dated 1878 – oil
on canvas – 122 x 152.5cm.
(Sotheby's)   **$16,649**   **£9,680**

MAUD EARL – Yorkies – signed – 26¼ x 32¼in.
(Christie's) **$8,349** **£5,060**

THOMAS EARL – 'Ham', A West Highland
Terrier – signed and inscribed – 25 x 30in.
(Christie's) **$4,719** **£2,860**

MAUD EARL – Mastiffs On The Alert – signed
– 26 x 32¼in.
(Christie's) **$13,612** **£8,250**

SIR ALFRED EAST – Gold – signed – oil on
canvas – 76.5 x 102cm.
(Phillips) **$6,265** **£3,500**

MAUD EARL – 'Spring', A Lurcher In A
Landscape – signed, inscribed and dated 1905 –
30 x 40in.
(Christie's) **$10,890** **£6,600**

CHARLES WARREN EATON – Sentinel Pines –
signed, and signed again, dated 1931 and inscribed
on the reverse – oil on canvas – 28¼ x 30¼in.
(Christie's) **$5,500** **£3,392**

EATON

CHARLES WARREN EATON – Winter Woods – signed, and signed again and inscribed on an old label attached to the stretcher – oil on canvas – 30 x 28in.
(Christie's) $6,600   £4,071

CHARLES WARREN EATON – Melting Snow – signed, and signed again and inscribed on the reverse – oil on canvas – 30¼ x 28¼in.
(Christie's) $14,300   £7,989

CHARLES WARREN EATON – A Starry Night – signed – pastel on paper laid down on board – 21½ x 17¾in.
(Christie's) $1,980   £1,221

JOSE ECHENA – The Favourite Of The Harem Endangered – signed and inscribed? – 25½ x 41in.
(Christie's) $14,520   £8,800

CHRISTOFFER WILHELM ECKERSBERG – A Gentleman Inspecting Ruins In The Colosseum With The Arch Of Constantine Beyond – 17 x 13½in.
(Christie's) $74,844   £46,200

FREDERIC E. VIPONT EDE – Cattle Watering By A River – signed – oil on canvas – 32½ x 56in.
(Christie's) $3,306   £1,980

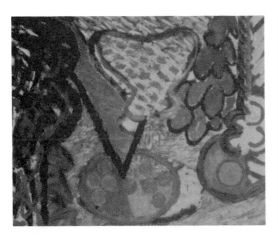

JOHN EDWARDS – Japanese Salad – signed, inscribed and dated 1982/83 on the reverse – oil on canvas – unframed – 48 x 60½in.
(Christie's) $771 £462

LIONEL EDWARDS – The New Forest Fox Hounds – signed and dated 1912 – watercolour, bodycolour and pencil – 20 x 31in.
(Christie's) $40,414 £24,200

LIONEL EDWARDS – Huntsman On A Bay Hunter In A Landscape – signed – oil on canvas – 50 x 60¼in. *(Christie's)* $27,412 £15,400

EDWARDS

LIONEL EDWARDS – Coming On To The Course, Sandown Park – signed – watercolour and bodycolour on paper – 14½ x 10½in.
(Christie's) **$16,533** **£9,900**

DANIEL THOMAS EGERTON – The Cross At Bernardes, Zacatecas, Mexico; Near Cienega Mata, Mexico; and Near Santiago, Mexico – three on two sheets – inscribed – watercolour over pencil – 21.5 x 16cm.
(Sotheby's) **$1,180** **£638 Two**

WILLIAM MAW EGLEY – Home–The Return – signed and dated 1866 – oil on canvas – 76 x 125cm.
(Sotheby's) **$9,460** **£5,500**

ROGELIO EGUSQUIZA – A Moment's Thought – signed and dated 1883 – on panel – 36 x 26in.
(Christie's) **$18,150** **£11,000**

REINHOLD MAX EICHLER – Mai morgen – signed, and signed and inscribed on the reverse – 33 x 39in.
(Christie's) **$2,268** **£1,375**

WILLY EISENCHITZ – Jour d'Orage – signed – oil on canvas – 54 x 73cm.
(Phillips)   **$3,024**   **£1,800**

WILLY EISENCHITZ – Landschaft bei Drom – signed and dated 1927 – oil on canvas – 27 x 36¼in.
(Christie's)   **$6,406**   **£3,520**

GEORGE SAMUEL ELGOOD – The Old Post Office, Ditton – signed – watercolour – 25.5 x 23cm.
(Phillips)   **$5,664**   **£3,200**

TRISTRAM A. ELLIS – An Arab Caravan Departing – signed and dated 1881 – watercolour over pencil – 58.5 x 89cm.
(Sotheby's)   **$3,080**   **£1,760**

CHARLES EDOUARD ELMERICH – The Travelling Circus – signed – 32¼ x 23½in.
(Christie's)   **$4,840**   **£2,750**

FREDERICK WILLIAM ELWELL – Interior With Welsh Dresser – signed on the reverse – oil on canvas – 64 x 76cm.
(Phillips)   **$742**   **£450**

EMMS

JOHN EMMS – A Boy And His Retrievers With The Day's Bag, Resting On A Country Lane – signed – on canvas – 18 x 24in.
(Phillips) **$9,280** **£5,800**

JOHN EMMS – Stable Mates – signed and dated '80 – on canvas – 15½ x 20in.
(Phillips) **$4,048** **£2,300**

JOHN EMMS – Two St. Bernard Dogs – signed – oil on canvas – 35 x 27in.
(Prudential Fine Art Auctioneers) **$3,888** **£2,400**

THOMAS ENDER – A Neapolitan Coastal Landscape With Figures Unloading Boats And Vesuvius Beyond – signed – 15¼ x 21½in.
(Christie's) **$7,744** **£4,400**

ENGLISH PRIMITIVE, mid 19th century – A Farm Scene, With Poultry, Pigs, Horses, Cattle And A Dog – watercolour with pen and coloured inks – 38 x 48cm.
(Sotheby's) **$1,513** **£880**

ENGLISH PROVINCIAL SCHOOL, circa 1840 – A Gentleman Farmer With His Prize Hereford Ox – oil on canvas – 59.5 x 86.5cm.
(Sotheby's) **$26,488** **£15,400**

ENGLISH SCHOOL

ENGLISH PROVINCIAL SCHOOL, 1841 –
Portrait Of Quartermaster J. Kirk Of The
Leicestershire Yeomanry, Mounted On His Charger
With An Encampment Beyond – inscribed and
dated 1841 – oil on canvas – 62 x 53cm.
(Sotheby's)   **$2,838**   **£1,650**

ENGLISH PROVINCIAL SCHOOL, circa 1844 –
A Prize Hog, The Property Of Charles, Lord
Western, In A Landscape – inscribed on the
reverse – oil on canvas – 30 x 40cm.
(Sotheby's)   **$17,028**   **£9,900**

ENGLISH PROVINCIAL SCHOOL, 19th century
– A Gentleman Farmer With His Prize Cow –
watercolour over pencil – 42 x 54cm.
(Sotheby's)   **$1,229**   **£715**

ENGLISH SCHOOL, 1616 – Portrait Of A Lady,
Said To Be Margaret, Daughter Of William, Lord
Conyers – inscribed and dated 1616 – oil on
panel – 148.5 x 99cm.
(Sotheby's)   **$18,920**   **£11,000**

ENGLISH SCHOOL, circa 1790 – A View Of
Pope's Villa On The River Thames At Twickenham
– oil on canvas – 16½ x 23½in.
(Phillips)   **$3,515**   **£1,900**

ENGLISH SCHOOL

ENGLISH SCHOOL, 18th century – Group Of Figures And A Dog, Darkened Sky Background – oil – 11in. diam.
(Capes, Dunn & Co.)　　**$1,520**　　**£950**

ENGLISH SCHOOL, circa 1830 – The Lord Mayor Disembarking At Blackfriars Bridge – pencil and watercolour – 19 x 27in.
(Christie's)　　**$3,080**　　**£1,760**

ENGLISH SCHOOL, 1836 – Quebec From Point Levi – inscribed – pencil – 9¼ x 14½in.
(Sotheby's)　　**$814**　　**£440**

ENGLISH SCHOOL, circa 1850 – Whipcrack The Celebrated Ratter – pencil and watercolour – 25.5 x 35.5cm.
(Sotheby's)　　**$529**　　**£308**

ENGLISH SCHOOL, 19th century – Extensive Wooded Landscape With Stream And Tower Boy With Dog Seated By Path In Foreground – oil – 37 x 46½in.
(Capes, Dunn & Co.)　　**$1,600**　　**£1,000**

ENGLISH SCHOOL, mid 19th century – View Of Constantinople; and Sultan's Valley And The Bospherous – one inscribed on the reverse – watercolour over pencil heightened with bodycolour – one oval, 20 x 26.5cm. and the other, 20 x 30cm.
(Sotheby's)　　**$5,291**　　**£2,860 Two**

ENGLISH SCHOOL, mid 19th century – Shipping In Table Bay, Cape Town – indistinctly signed – oil on canvas – 52 x 68cm.
(Sotheby's) $4,070   £2,200

ENGLISH SCHOOL, late 19th century – Merchants In A Town Square – oil on canvas – 44.5 x 60cm.
(Sotheby's) $1,628   £880

ENGLISH SCHOOL, circa 1930 – Seated Dancer – indistinctly signed – oil on canvas – 24 x 18in.
(Christie's) $1,155   £660

JOHN JOSEPH ENNEKING – Forest Brook – oil on canvas – 20 x 24in.
(Christie's) $4,950   £3,053

ENGLISH SCHOOL, late 19th century – Constantinople – watercolour over traces of pencil heightened with touches of white and gum arabic – 23.5 x 37cm.
(Sotheby's) $3,256   £1,760

JAMES ENSOR – Nature morte au Perroquet – signed and dated '89 – oil on canvas – 23½ x 29½in.
(Christie's) $425,040   £264,000

EPSTEIN

SIR JACOB EPSTEIN – Study Of Jackie, The
Artist's Son – signed – pencil – 23 x 18in.
(Christie's) **$1,469** **£880**

SIR JACOB EPSTEIN – Roses – signed – gouache
and pencil – 17 x 22¼in.
(Christie's) **$2,887** **£1,650**

SIR JACOB EPSTEIN – Study Of Kathleen –
signed – watercolour and pencil – 17¾ x 23in.
(Christie's) **$3,490** **£2,090**

SIR JACOB EPSTEIN – Portrait Of Jackie, The
Artist's Son – signed – soft pencil – 22 x 17in.
(Christie's) **$1,386** **£792**

SIR JACOB EPSTEIN – Study Of A Child
Sucking Its Thumb – signed – pencil – 25 x 20in.
(Christie's) **$1,010** **£605**

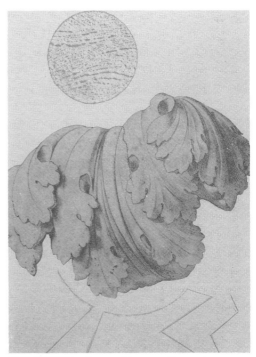

VASSILY ERMILOV – Match Box – painted
wood relief on panel – 18¾ x 14¼in.
(Christie's)   **$38,038   £20,900**

MAX ERNST – Composition – collage and
coloured crayon – 47 x 37.5cm.
(Sotheby's)   **$15,757   £8,250**

MAX ERNST – Ohne Titel (Raisins) – signed and
dated 1925 – oil on canvas – 31¾ x 25¾in.
(Christie's)   **$420,420   £231,000**

MAX ERNST – Composition – collage and
coloured crayons – 47 x 37.5cm.
(Sotheby's)   **$15,757   £8,250**

ERNST

MAX ERNST – Les Aveugles dansent la Nuit –
signed and dated '56, signed, dated and inscribed
on the reverse – oil on canvas – 77¼ x 45 in.
(Christie's) **$354,200 £220,000**

RICHARD EURICH – High Tide, Lyme Regis –
signed and dated '74, and signed again, inscribed
and dated on the reverse – oil on canvas – 10 x
18 in.
(Christie's) **$866 £495**

EUROPEAN SCHOOL – A Fresh Fowl – oil on tin
– 10 x 8½ in.
(Bruce D. Collins) **$715 £403**

EUROPEAN SCHOOL – Perusing The News – oil
on canvas – 10 x 8 in.
(Bruce D. Collins) **$297 £167**

EUROPEAN SCHOOL, 19th century – Roosters
And Hens In Farmyard – signed – oil on canvas –
17 x 32 in.
(Bruce D. Collins) **$2,750 £1,553**

ADRIANUS EVERSEN – A Dutch Street Scene – signed, and signed and inscribed on a label on the reverse – on panel – 24¼ x 31¾in.
(Christie's) **$36,300** **£22,000**

JAN EVERSON – Still Life With Wine And Cheese – signed and dated 1962 – oil on canvas – 51 x 71cm.
(Phillips) **$8,736** **£5,200**

DE SCOTT EVANS – The Grandfather Clock – signed and dated '90 – oil on canvas – 30 x 20in.
(Christie's) **$3,300** **£2,035**

PHILIP EVERGOOD – The Necklace – signed – pen and black ink and pencil on paper – 20½ x 16½in.
(Christie's) **$1,100** **£678**

FABIO FABBI – The Slave-Trader – signed – 46½ x 33in.
(Christie's) **$10,648** **£6,050**

FABECK

ALICE FANNER – The Tow Path At Richmond –
signed – oil on canvas – 71 x 91cm.
(Phillips)   **$3,116**   **£1,900**

F. DE FABECK – A Beauty – signed, inscribed
and dated 1888 – oil on board – 5 x 3¾in.
(Christie's)   **$816**   **£495**

JAMES FAIRMAN – Hudson River – signed – oil
on canvas – 31¼ x 52¼in.
(Christie's)   **$12,100**   **£6,760**

ISTVAN FARKAS – On The Terrace, Pimeno –
signed and dated '35 – watercolour and pencil on
paper – 11½ x 10in.
(Christie's)   **$801**   **£495**

ANTON FAISTAUER – Bouquet de Fleurs –
signed and dated 1924 – oil on canvas – 88 x
60cm.
(Phillips)   **$5,040**   **£3,000**

HENRY F. FARNY – The Water Carriers –
signed and dated '88 – watercolour, gouache,
pen and black ink on paper – 8¼ x 16¼in.
(Christie's)   **$15,400**   **£9,435**

HENRY F. FARNY − Fish Traps − signed and dated '95 − gouache and watercolour on paper − 9¾ x 19¼in.
(Christie's) **$13,200 £7,374**

GEORGES FAUVEL − Hounds In A Wood − signed and dated 1896 − 56 x 47in.
(Christie's) **$7,260 £4,400**

R. FAVELLE − Off To War − signed − on panel − 9¾ x 12¾in.
(Christie's) **$2,323 £1,320**

HENRY F. FARNY − Approaching Enemy − signed and dated 1905 − gouache on paper laid down on board − 9½ x 5½in.
(Christie's) **$3,300 £2,035**

HILDA FEARON − The Picture Book − signed and dated 1911 − oil on canvas − 29½ x 24½in.
(Christie's) **$4,601 £2,585**

FEDDEN

MARY FEDDEN — Still Life With Figs — signed and dated 1985 — oil on canvas — 51 x 41cm.
(Phillips) $495 £300

CONRAD FELIXMULLER — Kunstler mit Modell — verso — signed and dated 1934 — oil on canvas — 29¾ x 31¾in.; Das Blumenmadchen — recto — signed and dated '25 — 31½ x 33½in.
(Christie's) **$123,970 £77,000**

CONRAD FELIXMULLER — Stilleben mit Blumen und Katze — signed, and signed again and dated 1925 on the reverse — oil on canvas — 34¼ x 30¼in.
(Christie's) $76,076 £41,800

GABRIEL JOSEPH MARIE AUGUSTIN FERRIER — An Auburn-Haired Beauty — signed — 25½ x 21¼in.
(Christie's) **$3,872 £2,200**

RAINER FETTING – Homage a Monory –
signed, inscribed and dated '78 on the reverse –
acrylic on canvas – 74¾ x 47½in.
(Christie's)   **$8,910   £5,500**

ROBERT FIELD – Portrait Of A Naval Officer,
Half Length, Wearing Undress Uniform – signed
and dated 1818 – oil on canvas – 29¾ x 23¾in.
(Sotheby's)   **$13,838   £7,480**

RAINER FETTING – Mann in der Dusche (rot I)
– signed, inscribed and dated '81 on the reverse –
acrylic on canvas – 98¼ x 63in.
(Christie's)   **$19,602   £12,100**

SIR SAMUEL LUKE FILDES – Sweet Seventeen
– signed – on canvasboard – 16 x 13in.
(Phillips)   **$1,248   £780**

FILOSA

GIOVANNI B. FILOSA – On The Balcony –
signed – watercolour on paper – 22 x 16in.
(Robt. W. Skinner Inc.) **$1,000** **£558**

LEONOR FINI – Margot Fonteyn et son Amie –
signed – oil on canvas – 21¾ x 18¼in.
(Christie's) **$70,400** **£44,000**

LEONOR FINI – L'Essayage – signed and signed
again – oil on canvas – 45¾ x 35in.
(Christie's) **$91,520** **£57,200**

LAURA MARGARET FISHER – Young Woman
Holding A Bowl Of Roses – signed – oil on canvas
– 24 x 17½in.
(Christie's) **$2,310** **£1,320**

MARK FISHER – Ruins On The Coast Of
Provence – signed – oil on canvas – 25 x 29in.
(Christie's) $4,307   £2,420

FREDERICK R. FITZGERALD – Istanbul From
The Bosphorous – signed and dated 1910 – oil on
canvas – 66 x 106.5cm.
(Sotheby's) $22,385   £12,100

MARK FISHER – The Mill Stream – signed and
dated '96 – oil on canvas – 17¾ x 25½in.
(Christie's) $1,925   £1,100

CLAUDE FLIGHT – Landscape Study For Oil –
signed – watercolour and pencil – 6 x 8in.
(Christie's) $1,116   £638

PAUL FISHER – Evening In A Copenhagen
Street – signed – oil on panel – 20 x 25cm.
(Phillips) $3,600   £2,000

CLAUDE FLIGHT – Swimming: The Start Of The
Race – signed, and signed again and inscribed –
oil on canvas – 18 x 24in.
(Christie's) $8,223   £4,620

FLINT

SIR WILLIAM RUSSELL FLINT – 'The Bathers', Nude Females On A River Bank – signed and dated 1909 on the reverse – watercolour – 16½ x 18cm.
(W. H. Lane & Son) **$544** **£330**

SIR WILLIAM RUSSELL FLINT – Cecilia – signed, and signed, inscribed and dated 1956 on the reverse – watercolour.
(Christie's) **$23,496** **£13,200**

SIR WILLIAM RUSSELL FLINT – Study Of A Nude – signed – coloured chalks – 9¾ x 6¾in.
(Christie's) **$2,153** **£1,210**

SIR WILLIAM RUSSELL FLINT – Cynthia – signed – gouache – 25¼ x 29¼in.
(Christie's) **$39,160 £22,000**

SIR WILLIAM RUSSELL FLINT – Two Models
And A Mirror – signed, and signed again, inscribed
and dated on the reverse – tempera – 24¾ x
20¼in.
(Christie's) **$56,782 £31,900**

SIR WILLIAM RUSSELL FLINT –
Alexandrine And Josette, On The River Gard,
Languedoc, South France – signed, and signed
again and inscribed on the reverse – watercolour –
19¼ x 26¾in.
(Christie's) **$44,088 £26,400**

SIR WILLIAM RUSSELL FLINT – Denise –
signed, and signed again with initials and dated
'62 on the reverse – red chalk – 8½ x 13½in.
(Christie's) **$5,511 £3,300**

SIR WILLIAM RUSSELL FLINT – Study In
Sepia – signed – chalk on buff paper – 31 x
22.5cm.
(Phillips) **$4,654 £2,600**

SIR WILLIAM RUSSELL FLINT – The Bath Of
Susanna, Chateau de St. Privat, Languedoc –
signed – watercolour – 14¼ x 21½in.
(Christie's) **$25,718 £15,400**

FLORENTINE SCHOOL

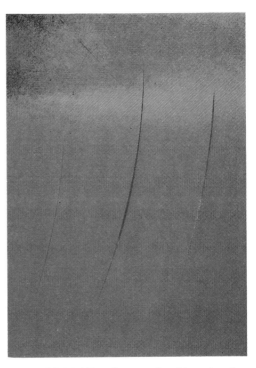

FLORENTINE SCHOOL, 17th century — St. Agnes — 28 x 24¾in.
(Phillips)   **$14,560**   £8,000

LUCIO FONTANA — Concetto Spaziale — signed and inscribed on the reverse — waterpaint on canvas — 92.5 x 72.7cm.
(Sotheby's)   **$105,600**   £55,000

CHARLES E. FLOWER — The King's Manor Garden At East Hendred — signed — pencil and watercolour heightened with white — 13¼ x 10¾in.
(Christie's)   **$1,732**   £990

LUCIO FONTANA — Concetto Spaziale — signed and inscribed on the reverse — waterpaint on canvas — 65 x 54cm.
(Sotheby's)   **$54,208**   £30,800

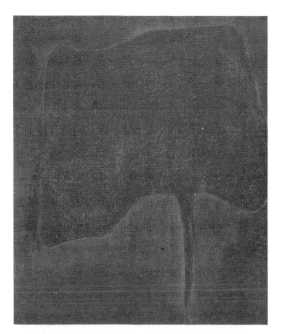

LUCIO FONTANA – Concetto Spaziale – pastel
and collage on canvas – 39¼ x 31½in.
(Christie's). **$120,120   £66,000**

ELIZABETH ADELA STANHOPE FORBES –
Autumn Leaves – signed – watercolour and
bodycolour over black chalk – 26 x 18.5cm.
(Phillips) **$7,380   £4,500**

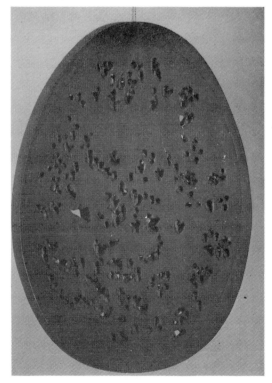

LUCIO FONTANA – Fine di Dio – signed on the
reverse – oil on canvas – 70¼ x 48½in.
(Christie's) **$178,200   £110,000**

ELIZABETH ADELA STANHOPE FORBES – A
Wayside Chapel – signed – oil on canvas – 46 x
35.5cm.
(Phillips) **$2,640   £1,600**

FORBES

STANHOPE ALEXANDER FORBES – The
Barn – signed and dated 1914 – oil on canvas –
30½ x 24½in.
(Christie's) $17,451 £10,450

STANHOPE A. FORBES – Girl Dressed In Blue,
Rowing A Boat On A Wooded River – signed –
oil on panel – 35 x 26cm.
(W. H. Lane & Son) $3,630 £2,200

STANHOPE A. FORBES – Two Boys – signed –
oil on canvas laid down on board – 25.5 x 20cm.
(Phillips) $7,872 £4,800

STANHOPE ALEXANDER FORBES – The Rose
Garden – signed and dated 1915 – oil on canvas –
unframed – 76 x 61cm.
(Phillips) $32,220 £18,000

STANHOPE ALEXANDER FORBES – The Artist's House At Higher Fangan Overlooking Mount's Bay – signed – oil on panel – 12¾ x 9¼in.
(Christie's) $3,916   £2,200

MYLES BIRKET FOSTER – The Entrance To The Ducal Palace, Venice – signed with monogram – watercolour over pencil heightened with bodycolour – 29 x 22cm.
(Sotheby's) $8,085   £4,620

WILLIAM BANKES FORTESCUE – Village Gossip – signed – oil on canvas – 24 x 18in.
(Christie's) $27,718   £15,400

TSUGUHARU FOUJITA – Le Chat Endormi – signed, signed again and dated 1927 – pen and ink and wash – 20 x 24.8cm.
(Sotheby's) $28,363   £14,850

FOUJITA

TSUGUHARU FOUJITA – Portrait De Jeune
Fille Au Bonnet Blanc – signed – pen and ink,
watercolour and gouache laid down on card – 17.9
x 14cm.
(Sotheby's) **$33,616 £17,600**

TSUGUJI FOUJITA – Petite Fille au Chat –
signed and dated – watercolour, pen and ink on
paper – 8¾ x 6½in.
(Christie's) **$60,060 £33,000**

TSUGUHARU FOUJITA – Mere Et Enfant –
signed and inscribed – pen and ink and watercolour
– 28 x 21cm.
(Sotheby's) **$79,838 £41,800**

TSUGUJI FOUJITA – Maternite – signed, and
signed and dated '52 on the reverse – oil on canvas
– 13 x 9¼in.
(Christie's) **$146,146 £80,300**

HENRY CHARLES FOX − River Scene, Figures
On Stone Bridge, Barge In Foreground − signed
and dated 1879 − watercolour − 17½ x 28in.
*(Barbers Fine Art
    Auctioneers)* **$2,275** **£1,300**

TSUGUJI FOUJITA − Nu aux Bras leves −
signed and dated 1925 − thinned oil on canvas
− 25¼ x 17½in.
(Christie's) **$300,300** **£165,000**

ESTEBAN FRANCES − Trompe l'Oeil −
watercolour and thinned oil on paper − 18¼ x
13½in.
(Christie's) **$2,494** **£1,540**

TSUGUJI FOUJITA − Jeune Garcon a la Poupee
− signed and dated 1926 − watercolour, pen and
ink on paper − 13¼ x 10¼in.
(Christie's) **$80,080** **£44,000**

JOHN F. FRANCIS − A Basket Of Cherries −
signed and dated 1868 − oil on canvas − 10½ x
13¾in.
(Christie's) **$71,500** **£43,808**

FRENCH

JARED FRENCH – Chess And Politics – signed – oil on canvas – 21¾ x 26 in.
(Christie's) **$60,500** **£37,068**

FRENCH SCHOOL, circa 1670 – A Lady, Possibly Mme De Montespan, Surrounded By Treasures – gouache on vellum, heightened with gold – 275 x 475mm.
(Sotheby's) **$49,192** **£28,600**

FRENCH SCHOOL, late 18th century – Views Of Ceylon–Pt de Trinquemalaye; Entre d'of Timbourque; and Trinquabare – inscribed – watercolour with pen and black ink – 24.5 x 50cm.
(Sotheby's) **$1,526** **£825 Three**

FRENCH SCHOOL, 1840 – A Chateau On The Banks Of A River – 9 x 15 in.
(Christie's) **$1,633** **£990**

FRENCH SCHOOL, circa 1880 – The Afternoon
Stroll – with signature – 22 x 15in.
(Christie's)   **$1,839**   **£1,045**

EMILE FRIANT – In The Studio – signed and
dated '85 – on panel – 10½ x 8¼in.
(Christie's)   **$9,266**   **£5,720**

WASHINGTON F. FRIEND – On The Ottawa –
signed and inscribed – watercolour heightened
with white on brown paper – 8¾ x 15in.
(Sotheby's)   **$1,058**   **£572**

ROGER DE LA FRESNAYE – Le Medecin Chef –
signed and inscribed – pencil – 29 x 23cm.
(Phillips)   **$1,344**   **£800**

HARRY FRIER – A Thatched Cottage At The
Waters Edge – signed and dated 1902 –
watercolour – 11½ x 20½in.
(Greenslade & Co.)   **$888**   **£480**

HARRY FRIER – A Thatched Entrance Lodge –
signed and dated 1897 – watercolour – 6¼ x 10in.
(Greenslade & Co.)   **$832   £450**

HARRY FRIER – Cottages At The Waters Edge
With High Cliffs Beyond – signed and dated 1913
– watercolour – 8¾ x 12in.
(Greenslade & Co.)   **$296   £160**

FREDERICK CARL FRIESEKE – Summer Reading – signed and dated 19'2 – oil on
canvas – 36¼ x 36¼in. *(Christie's)*   **$264,000 £147,496**

FREDERICK CARL FRIESEKE – The Open
Window – signed – oil on canvas – 51½ x 40in.
(Christie's)   **$825,000   £505,477**

DAME ELIZABETH FRINK – Birdman – signed
and dated '61 – charcoal – 30 x 22in.
(Christie's)   **$1,347   £770**

FREDERICK CARL FRIESEKE – Intermezzo –
signed – oil on canvas – 36 x 28¾in.
(Christie's)   **$132,000   £73,748**

DAME ELIZABETH FRINK – Study For
Sculpture, Birdman – signed and dated '62 –
charcoal – 29½ x 21½in.
(Christie's)   **$1,925   £1,100**

FRITH

WILLIAM POWELL FRITH – Shelley And Mary Wolstencraft – signed and dated 1877 – on canvas – 20 x 15in.
(Phillips) $2,992   £1,700

TERRY FROST – Red And Black (Lincoln) – signed and dated '67 on the reverse, and signed and inscribed – oil on canvas – 72 x 52in.
(Christie's) $7,715   £4,620

WILLIAM POWELL FRITH and RICHARD ANSDELL – A Lady With A Tame Faun – oil on canvas – 56 x 48cm.
(Sotheby's) $9,838   £5,720

ROGER FRY – Study For 'The Round Table', 1920 – signed, inscribed and dated 1923 on the reverse – oil on board – 34 x 27cm.
(Phillips) $9,512   £5,800

CHARLES FUCHS – Woman With Mandolin –
signed – oil on canvas laid down – 22 x 17in.
(Bruce D. Collins) **$220** **£124**

GEORGES DE LA FUENTE – On The Seine In
Winter – signed – 19 x 25in.
(Christie's) **$6,171** **£3,740**

EDMUND G. FULLER – Saturday Afternoon –
signed, and signed again and inscribed on the
reverse – oil on panel – 15¼ x 12in.
(Christie's) **$1,837** **£1,100**

ERNST FUCHS – Gefahrtin der Konigin der Nacht
– signed, dated 1969 and inscribed, and signed
again – pastel and gouache on paper – 11 x 8¼in.
(Christie's) **$3,603** **£1,980**

HELENE FUNKE – Girl With Toys – signed and
dated 1925 – oil on canvas – 85 x 80cm.
(Phillips) **$840** **£500**

GABRINI

PIETRO GABRINI – Harvesters In The Roman Campagna – signed and inscribed – 26 x 51½in. *(Christie's)*   **$9,075 £5,500**

HARRY LAWRENCE GAGE – Tug Boats – signed and dated '36 – oil on board – 15 x 19in. *(Bruce D. Collins)*   **$742   £419**

EUGENE GALIEN-LALOUE – A Parisian Street Scene – signed – unframed – 25 x 45in. *(Christie's)*   **$28,512   £17,600**

EUGENE GALIEN-LALOUE – Place du Theatre Francais, Paris – signed, inscribed and dated 1902 – 35 x 54in. *(Christie's)*   **$53,460   £33,000**

FRANCOIS GALL – Les Fleurs d'Ete – signed – oil on canvas – 79 x 63.5cm. *(Phillips)*   **$5,376   £3,200**

GERARD GAROUSTE – Untitled – signed and
dated '82 – pen and charcoal on joined paper –
48 x 56½in.
(Christie's) $3,203   £1,760

EDOUARD LEON GARRIDO – Les Grands
Boulevards, Paris – signed – on panel – 9½ x 7in.
(Christie's) $9,075   £5,500

ALBERT EUGENE GALLATIN – Abstract –
signed and dated 1939 on the reverse – oil on
canvas – 24¼ x 17¼in.
(Christie's) $20,900   £11,676

MAURO GANDOLFI – Three Ladies, Head And
Shoulders – black and red chalk – 185 x 235mm.
(Sotheby's) $12,865   £7,480

NORMAN GARSTIN – A Farmer And His
Daughter – signed and dated 1889, and also
signed and dated on the reverse – oil on canvas –
63.5 x 46cm.
(Phillips) $3,116   £1,900

GARSTIN

PAUL GAUGUIN – Route de Rouen – gouache on silk – 6¼ x 22 in.
(Christie's)   **$150,150**   **£82,500**

NORMAN GARSTIN – The Butt And Oyster Inn, Pinn Mill, Suffolk – signed and inscribed on the reverse – watercolour – 14¾ x 18¼ in.
(Christie's)   **$2,755**   **£1,650**

ROBERT DAVID GAULEY – Intervale, New Hampshire – signed, dated 1894 and signed again on the reverse – oil on canvas – 18 x 24 in.
(Christie's)   **$3,520**   **£2,156**

GEORGE HOWELL GAY – Full Tide – signed – watercolour – 24 x 36½ in.
(Bruce D. Collins)   **$1,650**   **£932**

PAUL GAUGUIN – Jeune Fille Nue, Assise Au Bord D'Un Lit – signed – pastel – 48.5 x 31.5 cm.
(Sotheby's)   **$441,210**   **£231,000**

GEORGE HOWELL GAY – Sunset Surf – signed – oil on canvas – 25 x 30 in.
(Bruce D. Collins)   **$1,870**   **£1,056**

LUCIEN GENIN – Le Restaurant Le Coucou –
signed and inscribed – gouache on paper – 13¼
x 16¼in.
(Christie's) **$1,401** **£770**

WALTER GAY – Man At A Loom – signed – oil
on board – 16¼ x 12¾in.
(Robt. W. Skinner Inc.) **$900** **£502**

LUCIEN GENIN – Bateau Lavoir au Bord de la
Seine – signed and inscribed – gouache on paper
– 13½ x 16¼in.
(Christie's) **$1,401** **£770**

FRITZ GENUTAT – In The Harem – signed and
dated 1911 – 67 x 43½in.
(Christie's) **$10,067** **£5,720**

GERARD

THEODORE GERARD – Le rendez-vous – signed
– 18½ x 15¼in.
(Christie's)   **$4,840**   **£2,750**

THEODORE GERARD – The Cottage Steps –
signed and dated '61, and signed on the reverse –
on panel – 32½ x 22½in.
(Christie's)   **$23,166**   **£14,300**

GERMAN SCHOOL, circa 1500 – Portrait Of A Lady – oil on panel – 44 x 32.5cm.; the reverse of
the panel painted with the arms of the sitter. *(Sotheby's)*   **$18,649 £10,780**

JEAN LEON GEROME – Un bain maure – signed
– 31 x 26in.
(Christie's) $267,300 £165,000

MARCUS GHEERAERTS, The Younger, Circle of
– A Portrait Of Robert Devereux, 2nd Earl Of
Essex.
(Phillips) $11,100 £6,000

MARK GERTLER – Portrait Of A Man With A
Mexican Blanket Over His Shoulder – signed – oil
on canvas – 20 x 16in.
(Christie's) $9,790 £5,500

ANGELOS GIALLINA – A Peasant Sitting Near
The Sea – signed and dated '94 – watercolour
over pencil – 32 x 16cm.
(Sotheby's) $3,459 £1,870

GIOVANNI GIANI – A South Italian Street Scene
– signed – 10¾ x 16¼in.
(Christie's)　　　　　$4,259　　£2,420

J. GIARDIELLO – Fishermen Hauling Nets –
signed – 29 x 40½in.
(Christie's)　　　$3,630　　£2,200

SANFORD ROBINSON GIFFORD – A Sketch
On The Roman Campagna – oil on canvas laid
down on panel – 3½ x 7¼in.
(Christie's)　　　$17,600　　£10,783

CLARENCE-MONTFORT GIHON – Rue de
Vaugirard, Paris – signed and dated '95 – oil on
canvas – 12¼ x 8¼in.
(Christie's)　　　$1,320　　£808

JUAN ANTONIO BENLLIURE Y GIL — Portrait Of An Old Man, Wearing A Brown Coat With Three Women Behind Him — signed and inscribed — 22¾ x 14½in.
(Christie's) $2,722 £1,650

JUAN ANTONIO BENLLIURE Y GIL — Portrait Of A Bearded Old Man Wearing A Brown Coat With Two Women And A Boy Behind Him — signed and inscribed, and inscribed and dated 1869 on the reverse — 22¾ x 17in.
(Christie's) $2,722 £1,650

EUGENE GILBAULT — Grapes And Peaches On A Mossy Bank — signed and dated 1885 — on panel — 13 x 11in.
(Christie's) $3,650 £2,200

CHARLES GINNER — Boscastle Harbour — signed — oil on canvas — 20 x 27in.
(Christie's) $20,207 £12,100

CHARLES GINNER — The Village Of Suffolk, Near Belfast — signed — watercolour, pen and ink — 9½ x 13¼in.
(Christie's) $5,878 £3,520

GLACKENS

WILLIAM J. GLACKENS – Beach Scene –
pastel on paper – 12 x 17¼in.
(Christie's) **$11,000 £6,739**

WILLIAM J. GLACKENS – New Hampshire
Boarding House – oil on canvas – 12¼ x 15½in.
(Christie's) **$28,600 £17,523**

WILLIAM J. GLACKENS – Terraced Hills, Venice
– oil on canvas – 20 x 24in.
(Christie's) **$46,200 £25,811**

WILLIAM J. GLACKENS – Washington Square –
pastel on brown paper – 15¼ x 16¼in.
(Christie's) **$19,800 £11,062**

JOHN HAMILTON GLASS – A Figure On A Path
In An Extensive Landscape, Above Blyth – signed,
and inscribed on the reverse – 8½ x 11¾in.
(Phillips) **$800 £500**

HUGH DE TWENEBROKES GLAZEBROOK –
Portrait Of Rosaline – signed – on canvas – 22½
x 16½in.
(Phillips) **$8,320 £5,200**

WILFRED GABRIEL DE GLEHN – Apollo And
Daphne – signed – oil on canvas – 28¼ x 36¼in.
(Christie's) **$4,592** **£2,750**

WILFRED GABRIEL DE GLEHN – Santa Maria
della Salute, Venice – signed, inscribed and dated
– watercolour – 15¾ x 19¾in.
(Christie's) **$6,980** **£4,180**

WILFRED GABRIEL DE GLEHN – Figures In A
Garden At Cannes – signed – oil on canvas – 25 x
30in.
(Christie's) **$25,718** **£15,400**

WILFRED GABRIEL DE GLEHN – Night –
signed and dated 1897 – on panel – 28 x 22in.
(Christie's) **$16,929** **£10,450**

ALFRED AUGUSTUS GLENDENING – Cattle
Watering In A Wooded River Landscape – signed –
on canvas – 15 x 29in.
(Phillips) **$4,576** **£2,600**

ALFRED AUGUSTUS GLENDENING, Jnr. – On
The Avon At Stratford – signed with monogram
and dated 1885 – oil on canvas – 51 x 76cm.
(Sotheby's) **$39,732** **£23,100**

GODWARD

JOHN WILLIAM GODWARD – A Classical Beauty
– signed and dated 1909 – 13½ x 11½in.
(Christie's)   **$12,474   £7,700**

MARY GODWIN – St. Vincent's Rock Hotel,
Clifton, Bristol – oil on canvas – 21 x 17in.
(Christie's)   **$2,020   £1,210**

VINCENT VAN GOGH – Girl Kneeling – signed – black chalk and pencil on paper – 17¾
x 23½in. *(Christie's)*   **$126,720 £79,200**

VINCENT VAN GOGH – Le Perroquet vert – oil on canvas laid on panel – 19 x 17in.
(Christie's) $200,200   £110,000

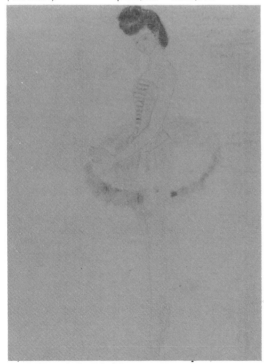

NATALIA GONTCHAROVA – La Danseuse; Carnaval – signed with initials and inscribed – coloured crayons and pencil on paper – 12¼ x 9¼in.
(Christie's) $1,158   £715

NATALIA GONTCHAROVA – Danseuse Espagnole – signed with initials – watercolour and pencil on paper – 12½ x 8½in.
(Christie's) $677   £418

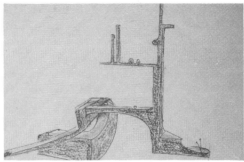

JULIO GONZALEZ – Personnage allonge – pencil, pastel, pen and ink on paper – 7½ x 10in.
(Christie's) $9,009   £4,950

ARTHUR CLIFTON GOODWIN – In The Public Gardens, Boston – signed and dated '04 – oil on canvas – 18 x 25¼in.
(Christie's) $26,400   £16,286

ARTHUR CLIFTON GOODWIN – New York Waterfront – signed, dated 1925 and inscribed on the reverse – oil on canvas – unframed – 30¼ x 36¼in.
(Christie's) $6,600   £4,071

H

GOODWIN

ARTHUR CLIFTON GOODWIN – New York
With Flags – signed and inscribed – pastel on
board – 21 x 17in.
(Christie's)   **$19,800   £12,214**

HORYU GOSEDA – In A Japanese Garden –
signed with monogram – 27¾ x 20½in.
(Christie's)   **$3,630   £2,200**

SPENCER FREDERICK GORE – Mornington Crescent – oil on canvas – 16 x 20in.
          (Christie's)   **$62,458   £37,400**

HENRYK GOTLIB – The Rider – signed – oil on canvas – 25 x 20in.
(Christie's)   **$616**   **£352**

SYLVIA GOSSE – The Elder Sister – signed, and signed again and inscribed on the reverse – oil on canvas – 42 x 24in.
(Christie's)   **$5,874**   **£3,300**

THOMAS COOPER GOTCH – The Coral Necklace – signed with monogram and dated '04 – oil on panel – 42 x 37.5cm.
(Phillips)   **$1,485**   **£900**

WALTER G. GOULD – Henry Clay – signed – oil on canvas – 34¼ x 27in.
(Christie's)   **$2,860**   **£1,764**

GRABACH

JOHN R. GRABACH – The Last Stand – signed
– oil on canvas – 36 x 42in.
(Christie's) $8,800   £5,391

PHILIPP GRAF – Wolfsberg (Chiemgau) – signed
and inscribed – 27½ x 39¼in.
(Christie's) $21,384   £13,200

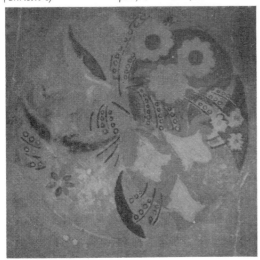

DUNCAN GRANT – Design For A Carpet –
signed, dated '36 and inscribed – oil on card –
27½ x 27½in.
(Christie's) $6,245   £3,740

DUNCAN GRANT – Chrysanthemums In A Vase
– signed and dated '51 – oil on canvas – 24 x
20in.
(Christie's) $2,388   £1,430

DUNCAN GRANT – Old Bill – signed and dated
'30 – oil on canvas – 76 x 51cm.
(Phillips) $3,444   £2,100

DUNCAN GRANT – Oranges And A Jug On A Table – signed and dated '60 – oil on canvas – 17¾ x 14in.
(Christie's) $5,511   £3,300

DUNCAN GRANT – Paul Roche, The Artist's Model – signed twice, and signed twice again once with initials, inscribed and dated 1949 on the reverse – oil on board – 24 x 16½in.
(Christie's) $1,347   £770

DUNCAN GRANT – The Barn At Charleston – signed – oil on canvas – 17 x 21in.
(Christie's) $3,916   £2,200

FREDERICK M. GRANT – A Canal In Venice – signed – oil on canvas – 40¼ x 40in.
(Christie's) $2,860   £1,764

GORDON HOPE GRANT – Old Coaster – signed in pencil – lithograph – 9 x 11½in.
(Bruce D. Collins) $209   £118

AUGUSTE GRASS-MICH – Le Paddock – signed with initials and inscribed – mixed media – 21.5 x 35cm.
(Phillips) $319   £190

GRAVES

ABBOTT FULLER GRAVES – An Abundance Of Roses – signed – oil on canvas – 24 x 30in.
(Christie's) $31,900 £17,822

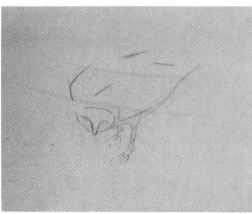

MORRIS GRAVES – Spirit Bird – signed and dated '53 – charcoal on brown paper laid down on board – unframed – 18 x 24in.
(Christie's) $2,420 £1,492

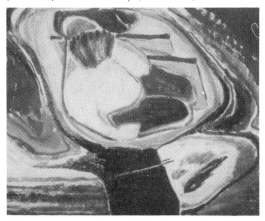

MORRIS GRAVES – Man Sleeping In Central Park – signed – gouache on board – 15¾ x 18¾in.
(Christie's) $3,850 £2,375

EDMUND WILLIAM GREACEN – Provincetown – inscribed on the reverse – oil on canvasboard – 8 x 10in.
(Christie's) $2,860 £1,752

DERRICK GREAVES – Reclining Nude – signed, inscribed and dated 1974 – acrylic on canvas – 48 x 72½in.
(Christie's) $1,561 £935

ANTHONY GREEN – The 16th Wedding Anniversary, Our Carpet – signed and dated '77, and signed again and inscribed and dated on the reverse – oil on board – 94 x 78in.
(Christie's) $5,143 £3,080

HENRY TOWNELEY GREEN – Childhood Days; and companion – signed and dated 1866 – watercolour and bodycolour – 15 x 12cm.
(Phillips) $2,655   £1,500 Pair

KATE GREENAWAY – A Spring Dance – signed with initials – watercolour over pencil – 23 x 31cm.
(Phillips) $1,770   £1,000

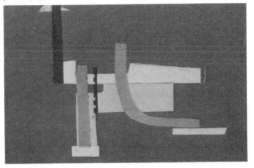

GERTRUDE GREENE – Collage–Gray Abstract – signed and dated '37 – paper collage – 8 x 12in.
(Christie's) $2,200   £1,347

R. GREEN – 'Sea Swallows, Some Beautiful British Terns' – signed and dated 1935, and inscribed on the reverse – watercolour – 16 x 10in.
(Messrs. G. A. Key) $600   £330

LOUIS FREDERICK GRELL – Indian By Firelight – signed – oil on canvas – 24 x 20¼in.
(Christie's) $1,650   £1,017

WALTER GRIFFIN – Spring Fields – signed and dated 1892 – oil on canvas – 28¼ x 43¼in.
(Christie's) **$14,300** **£8,821**

JOHN ATKINSON GRIMSHAW – Glasgow Lights – signed and dated '92 – oil on canvas – 30.5 x 46cm.
(Sotheby's) **$18,920** **£11,000**

WALTER GRIFFIN – Norway, 1909 – signed – pastel on board – 5¾ x 7½in.
(Robt. W. Skinner Inc.) **$1,000** **£558**

JOHN ATKINSON GRIMSHAW – Liverpool Lights – signed – on canvas – 11½ x 15½in.
(Phillips) **$7,568** **£4,300**

JOHN ATKINSON GRIMSHAW – Late October – signed and dated 1886, and also signed, dated and inscribed on the reverse – on canvas – 30 x 25in.
(Phillips) **$28,800** **£18,000**

JOHN ATKINSON GRIMSHAW – The Moonlight Walk – signed – on board – 17 x 13in.
(Phillips) **$8,800** **£5,000**

JUAN GRIS – Femme dans un Fauteuil – signed
and dated '25 – oil on canvas – 21¼ x 18in.
(Christie's)   **$230,230   £126,500**

JUAN GRIS – Nature Morte avec Bouteille –
signed and dated 1910 – pastel and pencil on paper
– 15¾ x 11¾in.
(Christie's)   **$61,600   £38,500**

JUAN GRIS – Scene galante – signed and dated
'09 – brush and indian ink with pencil
heightened with gouache on paper – 14½ x 11¼in.
(Christie's)   **$10,010   £5,500**

JUAN GRIS – La Flatterie – signed – watercolour,
charcoal and pencil on tracing paper – 15¼ x
10¾in.
(Christie's)   **$28,160   £17,600**

GROMAIRE

MARCEL GROMAIRE – Nature morte au Pichet
– signed – oil on canvas – 80 x 60cm.
(Phillips) **$3,024** **£1,800**

WILLIAM GROPPER – Attorney And Client –
brush and sepia ink on paper – 25¾ x 20in.
(Christie's) **$1,540** **£943**

A DE GROOTE – A Winter River Landscape With
Figures Skating By A Cottage – signed – on panel
– 9¼ x 14in.
(Christie's) **$2,516** **£1,430**

A DE GROOTE – A Winter River Landscape With
Skaters By A Bridge – signed – on panel – 6¾ x
8¼in.
(Christie's) **$2,323** **£1,320**

GEORGE GROSZ – Das Paar – signed –
watercolour on paper – 22½ x 18in.
(Christie's) **$60,060** **£33,000**

GEORGE GROSZ – Zwei Tanzende Neger (The Christmas Brothers) – signed – chalk, pencil, pen and black ink on paper – 11¾ x 7½in.
(Christie's) **$11,440** **£7,150**

GEORGE GROSZ – Schneeraumende Manner – signed – watercolour and pen and black ink on paper – 18 x 24in.
(Christie's) **$7,920** **£4,950**

GIOVANNI GRUBACS – The Doge's Palace And The Grand Canal – signed – oil on panel – 15 x 25cm.
(Phillips) **$4,140** **£2,300**

GEORGE GROSZ – Haus un den Dunen – signed and dated 1940 – oil on canvas laid down on board – 16 x 20in.
(Christie's) **$5,005** **£2,750**

CHARLES PAUL GRUPPE – Autumn Reflections – signed – oil on canvas – 14 x 16in.
(Robt. W. Skinner Inc.) **$650** **£393**

GRUPPE

EMILE ALBERT GRUPPE – Monhegan Island –
signed – oil on canvas – 20 x 30in.
(Bruce D. Collins)   **$4,400**   **£2,485**

EMILE ALBERT GRUPPE – Waterville, Vermont/
Autumn – signed and inscribed – oil on canvas –
30 x 36in.
(Robt. W. Skinner Inc.)   **$5,000**   **£2,793**

EDUARD VON GRUTZNER – Monastic Produce
– signed and dated '88 – on panel – 15¼ x 11¾in.
(Christie's)   **$26,730**   **£16,500**

ARMAND GUILLAUMIN – Vallee de la Sedelle
– signed – oil on canvas – 32 x 45¾in.
(Christie's)   **$119,680**   **£74,800**

ARMAND GUILLAUMIN – Paysage a
Pontgibaud – signed – oil on canvas – 25½ x
31¼in.
(Christie's)   **$49,280**   **£30,800**

ARMAND GUILLAUMIN – Paturages des
Granges a Crozant – signed, inscribed and dated
1897 – oil on canvas – 24 x 29in.
(Christie's)   **$123,200**   **£77,000**

ARMAND GUILLAUMIN – Paturage des
Granges, Fin de Mars, le Soir – signed, inscribed
and dated – oil on canvas – 29 x 39½in.
(Christie's)   **$52,800   £33,000**

SIR HERBERT JAMES GUNN – Pauline – signed
– oil on canvas – 36 x 28in.
(Christie's)   **$10,103   £6,050**

OCTAVE DENIS VIDORI GUILLONNET –
Enfant et Tortue – signed – oil on canvas – 20½
x 25¼in.
(Christie's)   **$10,010   £5,500**

JOHN GULLY – On Lake Wakitipu Going
Towards Kingston-Morning – signed and dated
1877, and inscribed on the reverse – watercolour
over pencil – 28 x 37.5cm.
(Sotheby's)   **$9,361   £5,060**

SIR HERBERT JAMES GUNN – Portrait Of The
Artist's Wife, Half Length – signed – oil on canvas
– 29½ x 23½in.
(Christie's)   **$5,511   £3,300**

HAAROT

A. HAAROT – The Peaceful Hearth – signed –
oil on panel – 23 x 19cm.
(Phillips) $1,080   £600

LOUIS HAGHE – The Sebeel, Or Holy Well Of
Cairo – signed and dated 1850 – pencil and
watercolour heightened with white – 37 x 29¼in.
(Christie's) $3,850   £2,200

ARTHUR HACKER – Portrait Of Mrs. Frederic
Pomeroy – signed and dated 1913, and also signed,
inscribed and dated on the reverse – oil on canvas
– unframed – 76 x 63.5cm.
(Phillips) $5,012   £2,800

A. VAN HADDENHAM – Daffodils And Other
Flowers In A Basket – signed – 34 x 40in.
(Christie's) $9,982   £6,050

JOSHUA ANDERSON HAGUE – Still Life Of
Apple Blossom In A Spherical Glass Vase – signed
– on canvas – 15 x 10in.
(Phillips) $880   £500

JOSHUA ANDERSON HAGUE – Still Life Of
Orchids In A Cylindrical Glass Vase – signed – on
canvas – 15½ x 20in.
(Phillips) $5,632   £3,200

THE EARL HAIG – The Rocky Road – signed –
oil on canvas – 20 x 20in.
(Christie's) $577   £330

JOHANN GEORG HAINZ (HEINSIUS) – A Still
Life With A Delft Bowl Containing Grapes, A
Nautilus Shell, Peaches And Oranges Rest On A
Table Covered With A Red Cloth – on canvas –
38¼ x 34in.
(Phillips) $23,660   £13,000

THE EARL HAIG – The Gate – signed – oil on
canvas – 21 x 16½in.
(Christie's) $616   £352

LILIAN WESTCOTT HALE – Portrait Of
Harriet Blake – signed – charcoal on paper – 24
x 18in.
(Christie's) $3,850   £2,358

HALE

PHILIP LESLIE HALE – Mother And Child – oil on canvas – 22¼ x 48¼in.
(Christie's) $132,000   £73,748

PHILIP LESLIE HALE – Golden Sunlight – oil on canvas – 30 x 25in.
(Christie's) $44,000   £24,582

ALICE HALICKA – Hommage au Douanier Rousseau – signed and inscribed – collage of feathers, paper, stuffing and other media on canvas – 21½ x 17¾in.
(Christie's) $2,802   £1,540

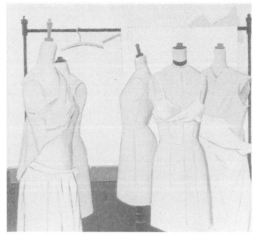

CLIFFORD HALL – The Mannequins – signed and dated '60 – oil on board – 23½ x 28½in.
(Christie's) $1,501   £858

J. V. HALL – Recollections Of Rio De Janeiro – signed on label attached to reverse, and again on another label attached to backing paper – oil on board – 16.5 x 36.5cm.
(Sotheby's) $2,035   £1,100

THEOPHILE HAMEL – Portrait Of Jacques Cartier – signed and dated 1848 – oil on canvas – 17¾ x 13¾in.
(Sotheby's) $44,770   £24,200

JOHN McCLURE HAMILTON – The New Coat – signed and dated 1880, and signed and inscribed on an old label on the reverse – on panel – 19½ x 34¼in.
(Christie's)   **$4,356**   **£2,640**

THEOPHILE HAMEL – Three Indian Chiefs And Peter McLeod Presenting A Petition To Lord Elgin – indistinctly signed and dated 1848 – oil on canvas – 17¼ x 13½in.
(Sotheby's)   **$111,925**   **£60,500**

CAPTAIN AUGUSTUS TERRICK HAMILTON – Quebec From Point Levi – signed – watercolour over traces of pencil heightened with gum arabic and scratching out – 10¼ x 14¼in.
(Sotheby's)   **$2,442**   **£1,320**

VILHELM HAMMERSHOI – Solskin i dagligstuen, no. 1 – signed – 23 x 21in.
(Christie's)   **$133,650**   **£82,500**

JAMES HAMILTON – Dragging In The Nets – signed and dated 1871 – oil on canvas – 22 x 36in.
(Christie's)   **$9,900**   **£6,107**

ARTHUR HENRY KNIGHTON HAMMOND – Tea Time, The Artist's Family – signed – watercolour, bodycolour and pencil – 21¼ x 30¼in.
(Christie's)   **$770**   **£440**

HAMMOND

ARTHUR J. HAMMOND – 'Three Gloucester Sisters' – signed, and inscribed on reverse – oil on board – 12 x 16in.; oil sketch on reverse – signed. *(Robt. W. Skinner Inc.)* **$1,300**   **£787**

ARTHUR J. HAMMOND – Gloucester Harbour Scene – signed – oil on canvas – 13¾ x 17¾in. *(Robt. W. Skinner Inc.)* **$550**   **£307**

WILLIAM LEE HANKEY – The Fish Market, Dieppe – signed – oil on canvas – unframed – 61 x 51cm. *(Phillips)*   **$9,840**   **£6,000**

GEORGE HARCOURT – At The Harpsichord: My Children – signed and dated 1907 – 110½ x 76½in. *(Christie's)*   **$49,896**   **£30,800**

GEORGE HARCOURT – The Royal Family: King George VI, Queen Elizabeth And Their Two Daughters, Princess Margaret And Princess Elizabeth – signed – oil on canvas – 119 x 76in. *(Christie's)*   **$3,426**   **£1,925**

HEYWOOD HARDY – A Call At The Manor –
signed, and also signed and inscribed on the reverse
– on canvas – 9¾ x 7½in.
(Phillips)   **$1,760**   **£1,100**

M DOROTHY HARDY – Thicker And Faster
Come Grief And Disaster; and All But The Good
Ones Are Weeded At Last – signed and inscribed
– pen and ink and watercolour on pale green paper
– 26 x 45cm.
(Sotheby's)   **$2,502**   **£1,430 Pair**

THOMAS BUSH HARDY – Dutch Pincks
Assisting A Wreck – signed and dated 1879 –
watercolour – 17½ x 28in.
(Barbers Fine Art
*   Auctioneers)*   **$2,275**   **£1,300**

WALTER MANLY HARDY – The Duck Pond –
signed and dated 1905 – watercolour – 5 x 9in.
(Bruce D. Collins)   **$110**   **£62**

WILLIAM MICHAEL HARNETT – Still Life
With Stein, Pipe And Paper – signed with initials
in monogram and dated 1888 – oil on panel – 8 x
10¼in.
(Christie's)   **$264,000** **£147,496**

WILLIAM MICHAEL HARNETT – Still Life,
Pipe And Mug – signed with initials in monogram
and dated 1878 – oil on canvas – 12¼ x 9¼in.
(Christie's)   **$57,200**   **£35,046**

WILLIAM ST. JOHN HARPER – Mid-Summer,
East Hampton, New York – signed and dated
1893 – oil on canvas – 30 x 44in.
(Christie's)   **$52,800**   **£32,350**

LAWREN STEWART HARRIS – Mountains
East Of Maligne Lake – signed, signed again and
inscribed on the reverse – oil on board –
unframed – 10¾ x 12¾in.
(Christie's)   **$12,100**   **£7,413**

JOHN CYRIL HARRISON – Kingfisher –
watercolour – 9 x 13in.
*(Prudential Fine Art
   Auctioneers)*   **$2,220**   **£1,200**

JOHN CYRIL HARRISON – Teal Alighting Onto
A Lake – signed – pencil and watercolour
heightened with white – 18¼ x 12¾in.
(Christie's)   **$3,657**   **£2,090**

JOHN CYRIL HARRISON – Male Montagu's
Harrier Fending Off A Sparrowhawk – watercolour
– 17.5 x 12.5in.
*(Prudential Fine Art
   Auctioneers)*   **$2,127**   **£1,150**

JOHN CYRIL HARRISON – Pheasant Flushed
From A Copse – watercolour – 12.5 x 18in.
(Prudential Fine Art
Auctioneers) **$3,700** **£2,000**

MARSDEN HARTLEY – Peonies – pastel on
paper – 23 x 18in.
(Christie's) **$15,400** **£9,435**

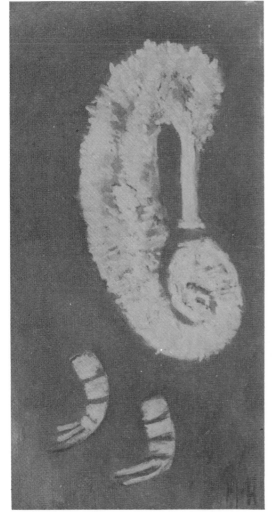

MARSDEN HARTLEY – Seahorse And Shrimp –
signed with initials – oil on masonite – 16¼ x 8in.
(Christie's) **$6,600** **£4,043**

MARSDEN HARTLEY – Mountains At Garmisch
– signed with initials – oil on board – 29¾ x 21in.
(Christie's) **$93,500** **£57,287**

MARSDEN HARTLEY – Bird Of Paradise –
signed – oil on canvas – 19½ x 24in.
(Christie's)   **$39,600**   **£24,262**

ARCHIBALD STANDISH HARTRICK – The
Prodigal Son – signed, and also signed, inscribed
and dated 1899 on the reverse – oil on canvas –
71 x 91cm.
(Phillips)   **$1,344**   **£820**

MARSDEN HARTLEY – Trees By The Lake –
oil on board – 9¾ x 14in.
(Christie's)   **$19,800**   **£11,062**

MARSDEN HARTLEY – Red Still Life With Fish
– signed with initials, and signed and inscribed on
the reverse – oil on canvasboard – 13¾ x 18in.
(Christie's)   **$28,600**   **£15,978**

HANS HARTUNG – T.1962 H 50 – signed and
dated '62 – oil on canvas – 162 x 100cm.
(Sotheby's)   **$94,864**   **£53,900**

HANS HARTUNG – T. 1963 E 41 – signed and
dated '63, and inscribed on the reverse – oil on
canvas – 39¼ x 63¾in.
(Christie's)   **$80,080**   **£44,000**

GEORGE HARVEY – Black Boy Blowing
Bubbles – signed and dated '87 – watercolour and
pencil on paper laid down on paper – 16¾ x
11¼in.
(Christie's)   **$6,050**   **£3,732**

HAROLD HARVEY – Sketching On The Quay –
signed – black chalk and watercolour – 24 x
16cm.
(Phillips)   **$1,312**   **£800**

HAROLD HARVEY – Moored Fishing Boats In
Newlyn Harbour – signed and dated '07 – oil on
canvas-board – 11½ x 9¼in.
(Christie's)   **$11,022**   **£6,600**

HAROLD HARVEY – By The Wayside – signed
and dated '37 – oil on canvas – 20 x 16in.
(Christie's)   **$5,143**   **£3,080**

HASSAM

FREDERICK CHILDE HASSAM – The Toll Bridge, New Hampshire Near Exeter – signed and dated 1906 – oil on canvas – 20¼ x 30¼in. *(Christie's)* $308,000   £188,711

FREDERICK CHILDE HASSAM – Confirmation Day – signed and dated 1881 – oil on canvas – 15 x 18¼in. *(Christie's)* $330,000   £202,191

FREDERICK CHILDE HASSAM – The Bather – signed and dated 1919, and signed again, also signed with monogrammed initials and dated again twice on the reverse – oil on panel – 9½ x 6¼in. *(Christie's)* $33,000   £20,219

FREDERICK CHILDE HASSAM – A Familiar Tune – signed – watercolour on board – 15 x 21¼in. *(Christie's)* $55,000 £30,728

GEORGE M. HATHAWAY – The Steamship
Forest City – signed – oil on board – 6 x 10½in.
(Bruce D. Collins) **$2,420** **£1,367**

GEORGE M. HATHAWAY – Path Along
Casco Bay – oil on canvas – 8 x 10in.
(Bruce D. Collins) **$577** **£325**

MARIE OCTAVIA NIELSON HAUGE – Playing
With Baby – signed – 37 x 31½in.
(Christie's) **$4,259** **£2,420**

HELEN HOWARD HATTON – Saying His Prayers
– oil on canvas – unframed – 91 x 71cm.
(Phillips) **$6,265** **£3,500**

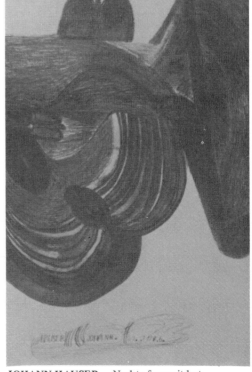

JOHANN HAUSER – Nackte frau mit hut –
signed and dated 1986 – pencil and coloured
crayon on paper – 40¼ x 28¾in.
(Christie's) **$21,384** **£13,200**

HAUSMANN

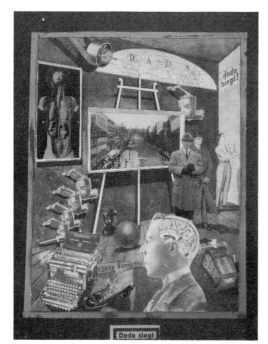

RAOUL HAUSMANN – Dada siegt – signed and dated 1920, and inscribed on the reverse – collage mounted on black paper – 23¾ x 16¾in.
(Christie's)   **$480,480**   **£264,000**

EDWIN HAYES – Yachts Off A Rocky Headline In Rough Seas – signed – oil on canvas – 20 x 29½in.
(Worsfolds)   **$1,428**   **£850**

GEORGE ARTHUR HAYS – Afternoon Shade – signed – mixed media – 12 x 16in.
(Bruce D. Collins)   **$467**   **£263**

LEWIS WELDEN HAWKINS – 'The Dead Favourite' – signed – oil on canvas – 22 x 15¼in.
(Robt. W. Skinner Inc.)   **$3,750**   **£2,094**

ALFRED HAYWARD – Harbour Scene, Unloading On The Quay – signed and dated '09 – oil on canvas laid down on board – 14¾ x 17¾in.
(Christie's)   **$866**   **£495**

ALFRED HAYWARD — The Cottage Garden —
signed and dated '07 — oil on panel — 6½ x 8½in.
(Christie's) $770 £440

ERICH HECKEL — Madchen — recto — signed and
dated '09 — black crayon on paper; Madchen —
verso — brush and indian ink on paper — 16¼ x
13½in.
(Christie's) $17,017 £9,350

ARTHUR HAYWARD — Morning, Pedn Oliver,
St. Ives — signed, and also signed and inscribed on
the reverse — oil on panel — 25 x 34cm.
(Phillips) $5,248 £3,200

ARTHUR HAYWARD — Morning Light, St. Ives —
signed, and also signed and inscribed on the
reverse — oil on panel — 25 x 34cm.
(Phillips) $5,904 £3,600

ERICH HECKEL — Gebirgstal — signed, dated '26
and inscribed — watercolour and charcoal on buff
paper — 23¼ x 18in.
(Christie's) $24,640 £15,400

251

HECKEL

ERICH HECKEL – Pfingstrose und Tulpen – signed and dated '19 – watercolour and pencil on paper – 20 x 13½in.
(Christie's) $26,026 £14,300

RALPH HEDLEY – Separating Wheat From The Chaff – signed and dated 1898 – oil on canvas – 43 x 33in.
(Christie's) $7,832 £4,400

RALPH HEDLEY – The Village Sweet Shop – signed and dated '97 – 28 x 34in.
(Christie's) $21,384 £13,200

JEAN HELION – Composition – signed and dated '35 – watercolour, pen and ink on paper – 8¼ x 11¾in.
(Christie's)   **$13,613**   **£7,480**

DIRCK HELMBRECKER – Travelling Actors – on canvas – 23¾ x 28½in.
(Phillips)   **$12,740**   **£7,000**

FRANCIS HELPS – Still Life With A Vase Of Anemones – signed and dated '48 – oil on canvas – 51 x 40.5 cm.
(Phillips)   **$445**   **£270**

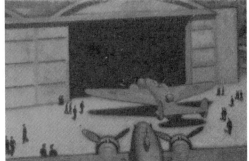

PAUL CESAR HELLEU – Daisy, Princess Of Pless In The Artist's Studio – signed – 46½ x 28¾in.
(Christie's)   **$605,880**   **£374,000**

KEITH HENDERSON – Two Bombers Outside Their Hangars – signed – oil on canvas – 18 x 22¼in.
(Christie's)   **$1,837**   **£1,100**

HENRI

FLORENCE HENRI – Composition – signed and dated 1926 – gouache and pencil on paper – 13½ x 11in.
(Christie's)   **$1,692**   **£1,045**

ROBERT HENRI – St. Nozaire, France – signed, inscribed and dated 14 July 1890 – oil on canvas – unframed – 15¾ x 10¼in.
(Christie's)   **$15,400**   **£9,435**

ROBERT HENRI – Ballet Girls, Philadelphia – signed – oil on canvas – 12¼ x 9¼in.
(Christie's)   **$55,000**   **£30,728**

ROBERT HENRI – Luxembourg Gardens, Stormy Sky – signed and inscribed on the reverse, and inscribed on a label affixed to the reverse – oil on panel – 6¼ x 5in.
(Christie's)   **$7,700**   **£4,301**

ROBERT HENRI – Atlantic City – signed and
dated '91 – oil on canvas – unframed – 10¼ x
18¼in.
(Christie's)   **$14,300   £8,761**

ROBERT HENRI – Seated Spanish Lady – signed
– watercolour and charcoal on paper – 8½ x 10in.
(Christie's)   **$3,080   £1,900**

ROBERT HENRI – At Joinville – signed and
signed again twice, and dated Oct. '96 and
inscribed – oil on canvas – unframed.
(Christie's)   **$462,000   £283,067**

ROBERT HENRI – A Parisian Park – signed,
signed and dated Dec '96 – oil on canvas –
unframed – 25½ x 31¾in.
(Christie's)   **$30,800   £18,871**

ROBERT HENRI – Early Morning, Venice –
signed and dated '91 – oil on canvas – unframed
– 10¾ x 15¾in.
(Christie's)   **$55,000   £33,698**

ROBERT HENRI – Coastal Scene At Sunset –
inscribed on the reverse – oil on canvas – 9 x 12in.
(Christie's)   **$9,900   £6,107**

HENRI

ROBERT HENRI – Study Of A Woman – bears
signature and initials – pencil on paper – 11 x
8½in.
(Christie's) $2,860 £1,764

ROBERT HENRI – Portrait Of A Man, After
Rembrandt; and An Old Beggar, Bretagne – the
first signed, dated '89 and inscribed – the second
signed, and signed again and inscribed – oil on
canvas – unframed – 32 x 25½in. and 32 x 23¾in.
(Christie's) $4,400 £2,714 Two

ROBERT HENRI – Lighting A Lantern; and By
The Hearth – signed – oil on canvas
– 32 x 25¾in. and 25½ x 31¾in.
(Christie's) $4,620 £2,850 Two

ROBERT HENRI – Newsgirl–Madrid, Spain –
inscribed – oil on canvas – 24¼ x 20¼in.
(Christie's) $38,500 £21,509

ROBERT HENRI – Nora – signed on the reverse,
and inscribed – oil on canvas – 24 x 20in.
(Christie's)   **$27,500   £15,364**

ARMAND HENRION – Moods Of A Pierrot –
signed – oil on panel – 21.5 x 16cm.
(Phillips)   **$864   £480** Two

ROBERT HENRI – Pat Roberts – signed, dated
1910 and inscribed, and signed and dated again,
and inscribed on the reverse – oil on canvas –
23¾ x 20in.
(Christie's)   **$20,900   £11,676**

ARMAND HENRION – A Coaxing Pierrot –
signed – oil on panel – 22cm. diam.
(Phillips)   **$864   £480**

HENRY

EDWARD LAMSON HENRY – What Luck –
signed and dated 1910 – oil on board – 12¼ x
18¼in.
(Christie's) $28,600   £17,523

EDWARD LAMSON HENRY – Bear Hill –
signed and dated 1908 – oil on canvas – 22¼ x
26¼in.
(Christie's) $33,000   £20,219

AUGUSTE HERBIN – Bouquet de Fleurs au Bord
de la Fenetre – signed – oil on canvas – 28½ x
23¼in.
(Christie's) $10,692   £6,600

AUGUSTE HERBIN – Olivier a Cassis – signed –
oil on canvas – 21¾ x 17in.
(Christie's) $18,018   £9,900

GEORGE EDWARDS HERING – Figures Resting
On A Terrace In A Mediterranean Coastal
Landscape – signed – on canvas – 15½ x 26in.
(Phillips) $1,232   £700

F. VAN HERLE – A Wooded River Winter
Landscape With Skaters – signed and dated 1858
– 9¾ x 14in.
(Christie's) $2,359   £1,430

GERTRUDE HERMES — Snoozing Cat — signed
and dated 1957 — black chalk — 25.5 x 36cm.
(Phillips) **$330** **£200**

JOSEF HERMAN — Man And Woman — signed and
inscribed on the reverse — oil on canvas — 20 x
24in.
(Christie's) **$2,887** **£1,650**

DANIEL HERNANDEZ — In The Studio — signed
and dated 1886 — oil on panel — 15¾ x 13in.
(Robt. W. Skinner Inc.) **$8,500** **£4,748**

JOSEF HERMAN — Still Life With Flowers In A
Vase — oil on canvas — 54 x 38cm.
(Phillips) **$1,650** **£1,000**

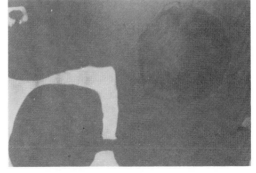

PATRICK HERON — Pink Enclosing Brown With
Violet Disc — signed, inscribed and dated 1968 on
the reverse — gouache — 22¾ x 31¼in.
(Christie's) **$2,937** **£1,650**

HERVE

JULES HERVE – Les Tuileries – signed – oil on canvas – 74 x 92cm.
(Phillips)   **$8,736**   **£5,200**

JULES-ALFRED HERVE-MATHE – The Racecar – signed and inscribed – watercolour on paper – 12 x 18¼in.
(Robt. W. Skinner Inc.)   **$3,300**   **£1,843**

JULES HERVE – Enfants et Pigeons dans le Jardin – signed, also signed on the reverse – oil on canvas – 13 x 16in.
(Christie's)   **$3,003**   **£1,650**

HERMAN HERZOG – Mountain Scene – signed – oil on canvas – 24¼ x 33in.
(Christie's)   **$6,050**   **£3,706**

JULES HERVE – Notre Dame un Jour de Pluie – signed – oil on canvas – 38 x 46cm.
(Phillips)   **$2,436**   **£1,450**

HERMAN HERZOG – Woodland Pool – signed – oil on canvas – 30 x 40¼in.
(Christie's)   **$66,000**   **£40,438**

HERMAN HERZOG – Nature's Majesty – signed
and dated 1872 – oil on canvas – 32½ x 46½in.
(Christie's) $60,500 £37,068

OTTO JOHANN HEINRICH HEYDEN – On The
Banks Of The Nile Near Cairo – signed – oil on
canvas – 72 x 123cm.
(Phillips) $32,400 £18,000

HERMAN HERZOG – Woodland Fishing – signed
– oil on canvas – 24¼ x 22in.
(Christie's) $18,700 £10,447

ARTHUR HEYER – A Dangerous Opponent –
signed – 23¼ x 31in.
(Christie's) $10,067 £5,720

ARTHUR HEYER – The Intruder – signed and
dated 1929 – 21¾ x 26¾in.
(Christie's) $4,719 £2,860

ALDRO THOMPSON HIBBARD – Vermont
Winter – signed – oil on canvasboard – 16 x
19¾in.
(Christie's) $2,860 £1,764

HERMAN HERZOG – View Of The Cascades –
signed and dated 1871 – oil on canvas – 24 x
18¾in.
(Christie's) $33,000 £18,437

HICKS

GEORGE ELGAR HICKS – The Orphans (In Procession) – signed and dated 1870 – oil on canvas – 51 x 76cm. *(Sotheby's)*   **$4,919 £2,860**

GEORGE ELGAR HICKS – Found – signed and dated 1874 – 24 x 20in.
(Christie's)   **$19,602   £12,100**

ADRIAN HILL – The Outpost – signed – oil on board – 21 x 27¼in.
(Christie's)   **$1,155   £660**

JOHN WILLIAM HILL – Plums And Apple – signed and dated 1874 – oil on board – 9¾ x 7¾in.
(Christie's)   **$4,400   £2,695**

THOMAS HILL – The Mountain Pass – signed and dated 1900 – oil on canvas – 30¼ x 40¼in.
(Christie's)   **$24,200   £14,827**

TRISTRAM HILLIER – The Lake At Guijo de Coria – signed with initials and dated '75, and inscribed and dated again – oil on canvas – 13¾ x 20in.
(Christie's)   **$7,715   £4,620**

WILLIAM HENRY HILLIARD – Reflections – signed – oil on canvas – 14 x 24in.
(Bruce D. Collins)   **$825   £466**

TRISTRAM HILLIER – Coastal Landscape – oil on board – 14½ x 17½in.
(Christie's)   **$1,860   £1,045**

WILLIAM HENRY HILLIARD – September In The North Country – signed – oil on canvas – 15 x 12in.
(Bruce D. Collins)   **$1,045   £590**

ROBERT ALEXANDER HILLINGFORD – Surrounded! General Desnouettes Captured By British Cavalry – signed, and also inscribed on a label on the stretcher – on canvas – 20 x 30in.
(Phillips)   **$3,840   £2,400**

HILLS

ROBERT HILLS – Cattle In Water – watercolour
over pencil – 23 x 24.5cm.
(Sotheby's) $654   £374

ROBERT HILLS – Stag At Bay – signed –
watercolour – 22 x 18cm.
(Phillips) $708   £400

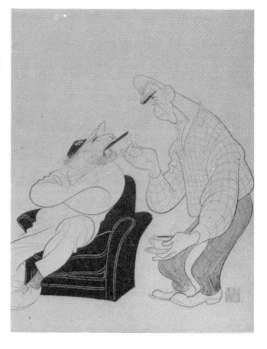

AL HIRSCHFELD – The Odd Couple – signed –
pen and black ink on board – 25¼ x 18¾in.
(Christie's) $3,300   £2,035

JOSEPH HIRSCH – Reflecting Policeman –
signed – oil on canvas – 18¼ x 14¼in.
(Christie's) $4,400   £2,458

GEORGE HITCHCOCK – The Godmother –
signed – oil on canvas – 43¼ x 35¼in.
(Christie's) $19,800   £11,062

IVON HITCHENS – Trees Overhanging Water – signed and dated 1975 – oil on canvas – 51 x 103cm.
(Phillips) **$9,845** **£5,500**

GEORGE HITCHCOCK – A Dream Of Christmas – signed – oil on canvas – 35¼ x 24¼in.
(Christie's) **$17,600** **£10,783**

IVON HITCHENS – Nude, Variation No. 6 – signed – oil on canvas – 84 x 56cm.
(Phillips) **$12,172** **£6,800**

IVON HITCHENS – Early Daffodils In Spring Woodland – signed and dated 1975, and inscribed on a label on the stretcher – oil on canvas – 42 x 89cm.
(Phillips) **$10,740** **£6,000**

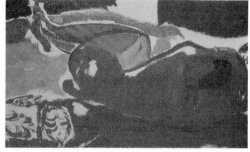

GEORGE HITCHCOCK – The Stork's Nest – signed – oil on canvas – 22¼ x 17¼in.
(Christie's) **$24,200** **£14,827**

IVON HITCHENS – August Nude No. 4 – signed, and also signed and inscribed on a label on the stretcher – oil on canvas – 61 x 74cm.
(Phillips) **$5,370** **£3,000**

HOARE

WILLIAM HOARE of Bath – Half Length Portrait
Of A Woman – pastel – 59 x 44cm.
(Phillips) $6,372   £3,600

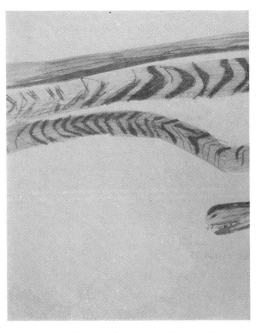

DAVID HOCKNEY – 3 Snakes – signed with the
initials and dated '62 – coloured pencil on paper –
35.5 x 30.5cm.
(Sotheby's) $10,648   £6,050

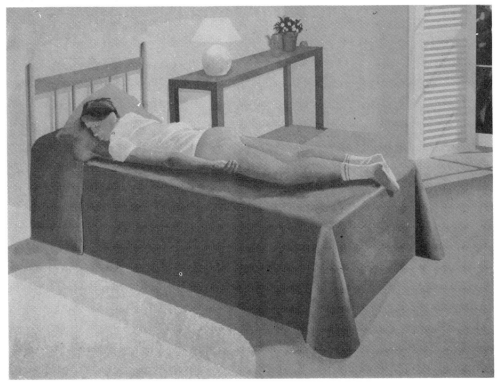

DAVID HOCKNEY – The Room, Tarzana – acrylic and pencil on canvas – 95 x 95in. *(Christie's)*
$520,520 £286,000

JESSIE HODGE – Festival Of Spring – signed, and signed again and inscribed on label on the reverse – tempera on canvas – 36 x 28in.
(Christie's)   **$1,732**   £990

ELIOT HODGKIN – Flint And Feathers – signed and dated '51, and signed and inscribed on a label on the reverse – tempera on paper – 8¾ x 11½in.
(Christie's)   **$2,755**   £1,650

FRANCES HODGKINS – Motor Transport – signed and dated 1941 – watercolour and bodycolour – 15¾ x 21¼in.
(Christie's)   **$29,392**   £17,600

WILLIAM MERRIT HODGES – 'Adoration' – signed – oil on canvas – 36¼ x 32¼in.
(Christie's)   **$2,502**   £1,430

FRANCES HODGKINS – Evening – signed with incised signature twice – oil on canvas – 21 x 25in.
(Christie's)   **$107,690**   £60,500

HODGKINS

FRANCES HODGKINS – Mother And Children – signed – pencil, charcoal and white heightening – 37.5 x 41.5cm.
(Phillips) $6,802   £3,800

DAVID HODGSON – Tinkers By A Camp Fire In A Wooded Landscape – oil – 18 x 24in.
(Messrs. G. A. Key) $1,911   £1,050

KARL HOFER – Drei Badende – signed and dated '44, twice – oil on canvas – 32 x 20¼in.
(Christie's) $76,076   £41,800

KARL HOFER – Zwei Badende am Luganer See – signed with initials and dated '34 – oil on board – 33¾ x 48in. *(Christie's)* $61,600   £38,500

CHARLES HOFFBAUER – 'Lantern Parade, Chinatown, San Francisco, Study' – signed – tempera on paper – 7 x 7½in.
(Robt. W. Skinner Inc.)   **$300**   **£167**

GILBERT HOLIDAY – Show Jumping – signed – coloured crayon and pencil – 14 x 10in.
(Christie's)   **$866**   **£495**

CLAUDE-JEAN-BAPTISTE HOIN – Portrait Of J-B. Brizard – signed and dated 1783 – pastel on paper laid down on canvas – 21¾ x 17¾in.
(Phillips)   **$9,100**   **£5,000**

FRANK HOLL – Deserted – signed and dated 1874 – 36¼ x 53½in.
(Christie's)   **$14,256**   **£8,800**

ABEL HOLD – Still Life Of Dead Grouse In An Extensive Moorland Landscape – signed and dated 1883 – on canvas – 24½ x 29½in.
(Phillips)   **$1,584**   **£900**

JAMES HOLLAND – Merchant Ship, Venice – monogrammed and dated 1864 – watercolour – 12 x 20in.
(Bruce D. Collins)   **$715**   **£403**

HOLLAND

JAMES HOLLAND – Piazza San Marco – signed with monogram and dated 1855 – on panel – 12 x 17¾in.
(Phillips)   **$3,520**   **£2,000**

EDWIN FREDERICK HOLT – The Pets Of A Bygone Age – signed, inscribed and dated 1878, and signed, inscribed and dated on the reverse – oil on canvas – 51 x 61cm.
(Sotheby's)   **$9,838**   **£5,720**

CARL HOLSOE – Children In An Interior – signed – 21 x 23½in.
(Christie's)   **$44,550**   **£27,500**

HANS HOLSOE – An Interior – signed – 21½ x 25½in.
(Christie's)   **$2,904**   **£1,760**

CARL HOLTY – Geometric Abstraction, 1936 – oil on masonite – 17¾ x 11¾in.
(Christie's)   **$4,950 £2,765**

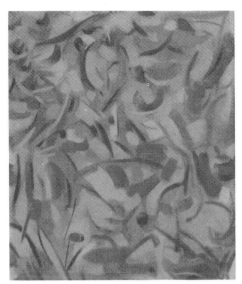

CARL HOLTY – Halfshadow – signed, and signed again, dated 1948 and inscribed on the reverse – oil on masonite – 14 x 18in.
(Christie's) **$1,870** **£1,153**

ROWLAND HOLYOAKE – The Toast Of The Tavern – signed – 21½ x 30in.
(Christie's) **$3,267** **£1,980**

WINSLOW HOMER – Young Girl In Woods – signed and dated 1880 – watercolour and pencil on paper laid down on board – 8¾ x 11¼in.
(Christie's) **$99,000** **£55,311**

CARL ROBERT HOLTY – Odalisque – signed, dated 1937 and inscribed on the reverse – oil on masonite – 35¾ x 24in.
(Christie's) **$7,700** **£4,301**

BERNARD DE HOOG – A Father's Love – signed – 20 x 17¼in.
(Christie's) **$7,744** **£4,400**

HORMANN

THEODOR VON HORMANN – Dorfmotiv aus Lofer im Salzkammergut – signed and inscribed, and signed and inscribed on the reverse – on panel – unframed – 14¾ x 21½in.
(Christie's)   **$33,858**   **£20,900**

PAUL HORNINGER – Flusslandschaft – signed and dated 1910 – oil on canvas – 45¼ x 58¼in.
(Christie's)   **$26,026**   **£14,300**

JOHN CALCOTT HORSLEY – The Love Letter – signed and dated 1868 – on canvas – 23 x 18in.
(Phillips)   **$7,680**   **£4,800**

WALTER CHARLES HORSLEY – Striking A Bargain – signed, and signed on the reverse – oil on canvas – 91.5 x 71cm.
(Sotheby's)   **$18,920**   **£11,000**

ALBERT HORSTMEIER – Hampton Beach – signed – oil on canvas – 17 x 23in.
(Christie's)   **$5,500**   **£3,392**

ELMYR DE HORY – Interior With Balcony, After Matisse – signed – oil on canvas – 46 x 61cm.
(Phillips)   **$840**   **£500**

GEORGE HOWARD, 9th Earl of Carlisle – Portrait Of Sir Edward Coley Burne-Jones – pencil – 33.5 x 24cm.
(Sotheby's)   **$3,465**   **£1,980**

JOHN HOYLAND – 29.12.65 – oil on canvas – 61 x 112in.
(Christie's)   **$6,265**   **£3,520**

KARL HUBBUCH – Strassenszene – signed – pen and black ink on paper – 14¾ x 14¾in.
(Christie's)   **$2,112**   **£1,320**

SAMUEL HOWELL – Seated Portrait Study Of A Young Lady Wearing A Blue Dress–A Member Of The Cozens–Hardy Family – inscribed and dated 1851 on the reverse – oil on canvas – 44 x 34in.
*(Prudential Fine Art
    Auctioneers)*   **$756**   **£450**

KARL HUBBUCH – Lustmord – oil on canvas – 27¼ x 30¾in.
(Christie's)   **$7,607**   **£4,180**

HUBBUCH

KARL HUBBUCH – Blumenstilleben – signed –
watercolour on paper – 2¾ x 16¾in.
(Christie's)   **$5,280**   **£3,300**

EDWARD ROBERT HUGHES – Bell And Dorothy
– signed, inscribed and dated 1889, and also
inscribed on an old label on reverse – watercolour
– 91 x 74cm.
(Phillips)   **$14,514**   **£8,200**

LEON CHARLES HUBER – A Kitten – signed –
on panel – 12 x 9½in.
(Christie's)   **$1,742**   **£990**

TALBOT HUGHES – Self Portrait – signed,
inscribed and dated 1892 – oil on board – 40.5 x
31.5cm.
(Phillips)   **$660**   **£400**

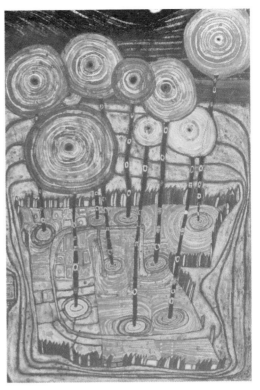

FRIEDENSREICH HUNDERTWASSER – Jardin
Publique-Park – signed and dated '77, and signed
and dated on the reverse – watercolour, egg
tempera, oil and foil on primed paper mounted on
linen – 73 x 53.1cm.
(Sotheby's)   **$57,024   £29,700**

JOHN FREDERICK HULK – A Dutch Street
Scene; and A Dutch Canal Scene – both signed –
39 x 29in.
(Christie's)   **$24,948   £15,400 Pair**

FRIEDRICH HUNDERTWASSER – Three Nose
Rivers – signed and dated 1961 on the reverse –
watercolour, tempera, CH3 and oil on rice-paper
mounted on canvas – 18¼ x 20¾in.
(Christie's)   **$44,550   £27,500**

CHARLES HUNT – A Game Of Draughts – signed – oil on canvas – 71 x 91.5cm.
(Sotheby's) **$8,514 £4,950**

EDGAR HUNT – Goats, Geese, Pigeons And A Duck – signed and dated 1907 – oil on
canvas – 51 x 76cm. *(Sotheby's)* **$22,704 £13,200**

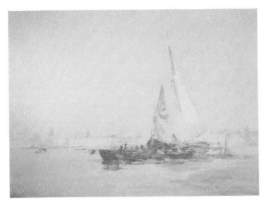

EDWARD AUBREY HUNT – Venice –
signed – watercolour – 20½ x 28½in.
(Bruce D. Collins) **$1,540** **£870**

ROBERT GEMMELL HUTCHINSON – 'Granny's
Pet' – signed – oil on canvas – 13 x 10in.
(Robt. W. Skinner Inc.) **$2,500** **£1,396**

MAX HUNZIKER – Two Figures Òn A Bed –
signed with initials – oil on paper laid down – 37
x 46cm.
(Phillips) **$672** **£400**

PETER HURD – Twilight Glow – signed –
watercolour, gouache and pen and black ink on
paper – 23¾ x 29in.
(Christie's) **$8,800** **£5,428**

JAN VAN HUYSUM, Follower of – A Still Life
Of Flowers In A Basket Upon A Marble Ledge –
oil on canvas – 41 x 31cm.
(Sotheby's) **$22,836** **£13,200**

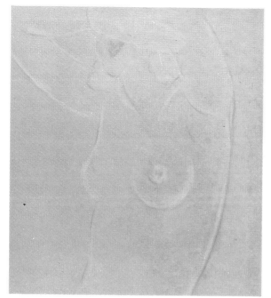

LOUIS ICART — Femme nue aux Bras leves — signed — coloured chalks and charcoal on buff paper — 21 x 16in.
(Christie's) $891   £550

RUDOLPH IHLEE — Landscape With Tree-Lined Road And Bridge — signed and dated 1925 — oil on canvas — 24 x 29½in.
(Christie's) $3,916   £2,200

RUDOLPH IHLEE — View From The Bedroom Window — signed and dated 1925 — oil on canvas — 25 x 30in.
(Christie's) $5,511   £3,300

JAMES DICKSON INNES — Mountainous Lake Landscape — signed and dated 1912 — watercolour, pen and ink — 10 x 14in.
(Christie's) $3,720   £2,090

GEORGE INNESS — Golden Sunset — signed — oil on canvas — 18¼ x 12in.
(Christie's) $26,400   £16,175

GEORGE INNESS — The Bathers — signed and dated 1888 — oil on canvas — 30¼ x 45¼in.
(Christie's) $66,000   £40,438

GEORGE INNESS — Sunset At Etretat, Normandy — signed — oil on canvas — 20¼ x 30¼in.
(Christie's) $49,500   £27,655

GUGLIELMO INNOCENTI – The Peaceful Hearth
– signed, inscribed and dated 1869 – oil on panel
– 34 x 39cm.
(Phillips)   **$1,440**   **£800**

ITALIAN SCHOOL, early 19th century – A View
Of Florence And The Arno – oil on canvas – 41 x
64cm.
(Phillips)   **$8,640**   **£4,800**

ITALIAN SCHOOL, 19th century – A Street
Scene With Figures At A Pasta Shop – on board –
9¾ x 14½in.
(Christie's)   **$1,633**   **£990**

GILBERT JACKSON – Portrait Of John, Baron
Belasyse (1614-1689) – signed and dated 1636 –
oil on canvas – 188 x 129.5cm.
(Sotheby's)   **$302,720**   **£176,000**

LEE JACKSON – The Green Laundry Wagon –
signed – oil on board – 16 x 20in.
(Christie's)   **$1,540**   **£950**

SAMUEL PHILLIPS JACKSON – Unloading The
Catch At Penzance – signed and dated 1862 –
watercolour heightened with bodycolour – 21¼ x
22in.
(Christie's)   **$9,240**   **£5,280**

JACOBIDES

GEORGES JACOBIDES – The Flower Seller –
signed – 18½ x 14½in.
(Christie's)   **$24,948**   **£15,400**

A. JACOBSEN – A Lake In A Forest – signed –
22¾ x 36½in.
(Christie's)   **$1,645**   **£935**

ANTONIO JACOBSEN – The Ceres At Sea –
signed and dated 1881 – oil on canvas – 29 x
48¾in.
(Sotheby's)   **$22,385**   **£12,100**

CHARLES EMILE JACQUE – A Swineherd At
The Edge Of A Forest – signed – on panel – 35¾
x 52¼in.
(Christie's)   **$6,897**   **£4,180**

ROSA JAMESON – The Intruder – signed – on
canvas – 11½ x 25½in.
(Phillips)   **$2,288**   **£1,300**

MERODEC JANNEAU – Sur le Zinc – indistinctly
signed – oil on paper laid on board – 27 x 21in.
(Christie's)   **$712**   **£440**

GEORGES JEANNIN – A Basket Of Peaches And
Raspberries – signed – 21¼ x 25¾in.
(Christie's) **$3,267** **£1,980**

JOHAN LAURENTS JENSEN – A Basket Of
Roses, Lilies And Pansies By A Rose Bush – signed
and dated 1855 – 26¼ x 33¾in.
(Christie's) **$81,972** **£50,600**

BLANCHE JENKINS – Hush – oil on canvas – 76
x 63.5cm.
(Sotheby's) **$5,297** **£3,080**

SOYA JENSEN – Piccadilly Circus, London –
signed with initials – 18¾ x 17¾in.
(Christie's) **$1,996** **£1,210**

HUMPHREY JENNINGS – Sketch For The Reaper
– signed and inscribed on the reverse – oil on
canvas – 14½ x 18½in.
(Christie's) **$1,653** **£990**

HOLGAR HVITFELD JERICHAU – Marina
Grande, Capri – signed and inscribed, and
inscribed on the reverse – 16½ x 25¼in.
(Christie's) **$5,445** **£3,300**

JERICHAU

HOLGAR HVITFELD JERICHAU – A
Washerwoman, Capri – signed and inscribed – 39¼
x 24¼in.
(Christie's)   **$3,267   £1,980**

FLORIS JESPERS – La Toilette – signed twice
– oil and gold leaf on glass – 26¼ x 20½in.
(Christie's)   **$24,640   £15,400**

CHARLES JERVAS – Portrait Of A Lady, Said To
Be Lady Mary Wortley Montagu – oil on canvas –
125 x 102cm.
(Sotheby's)   **$9,081   £5,280**

AUGUSTUS JOHN – The Woman In The Tent –
oil on canvas – 21 x 17in.
(Christie's)   **$8,811   £4,950**

AUGUSTUS JOHN − Portrait Of Robin, The
Artist's Son, Bust Length In A Brown Shirt − oil
on panel − 15½ x 12½in.
(Christie's) **$54,824** **£30,800**

AUGUSTUS JOHN − Portrait Of A Gentleman −
signed and dated 1955 − red and black chalk
heightened with white on grey paper − 16¾ x
11¼in.
(Christie's) **$1,193** **£682**

AUGUSTUS JOHN − Studies Of A Baby's Head −
signed and dated '48 − red chalk − 20 x 21cm.
(Phillips) **$660** **£400**

AUGUSTUS JOHN − Portrait Of Charles McCray,
Bust Length − signed and inscribed on the reverse
− pencil − 14 x 10in.
(Christie's) **$6,980** **£4,180**

JOHN

AUGUSTUS JOHN – Portrait Of A Gentleman, Bust Length – signed – red, brown and black chalk heightened with white – 17 x 12in.
(Christie's) **$962** **£550**

DAVID JOHNSON – Study Of A Cedar – signed with initials and dated July 4 – oil on canvas – 20 x 14in.
(Christie's) **$28,600** **£17,523**

HJALMAR JOHNSEN – Midtsommer – signed and dated 1891, and inscribed on the reverse – 31½ x 27in.
(Christie's) **$3,993** **£2,420**

DAVID JOHNSON – Self Portrait In Colonial Dress – signed with monogrammed initials and dated '74 – oil on board laid down on panel – 12¼ x 9¼in.
(Christie's) **$7,150** **£4,380**

DAVID JOHNSON – Path Along The River –
signed with initials and dated '62 – oil on canvas
– 10¼ x 8¼in.
(Christie's) $7,150   £4,380

FRANK TENNEY JOHNSON – A Brush With
The Posse – signed – oil on canvas – 16¼ x 12in.
(Christie's)   **$12,100**   **£6,760**

MARTIN GWILT JOLLEY – Hilda, 'The General',
Lodgings In Pimlico – signed and inscribed on the
reverse – gouache – 23¾ x 9¼in.
(Christie's)   **$9,398**   **£5,280**

JONCIERE

J. DE JONCIERE – Interieur du Chateau – signed and dated '44 – oil on panel – 51 x 42.5 cm.
(Phillips) **$1,344** **£800**

HUGH BOLTON JONES – Spring – signed – oil on canvas – 35¾ x 30¼ in.
(Christie's) **$9,350** **£5,223**

DAVID JONES – Still Life: Hierarchy – signed and dated '32 – watercolour, brush, black ink and pencil – 29¼ x 21½ in.
(Christie's) **$7,048** **£3,960**

VAN JONES – The Yellow Shirt – signed – oil on board – 28 x 20¼ in.
(Christie's) **$7,832** **£4,400**

TINUS DE JONGH – Cape Farmstead; and A Dutch House, The Cape – signed – oil on canvas – 23 x 29cm.
(Sotheby's)   **$3,256**   **£1,760 Two**

JOHAN BARTHOLD JONGKIND – Paysage hollandais – signed and dated 1862 – oil on canvas – 13½ x 22¼in.
(Christie's)   **$70,840**   **£44,000**

ASGER JORN – L'Amere sans amertume – signed, and also signed, inscribed and dated '70 on the reverse – oil on canvas – 51¼ x 38¼in.
(Christie's)   **$196,020**   **£121,000**

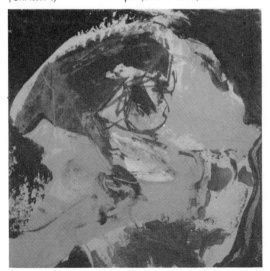

ASGER JORN – Untitled – signed and dated '68 – oil on cardboard – 11¼ x 10¾in.
(Christie's)   **$23,166**   **£14,300**

ASGER JORN – Universellement buvable, a tenir au frais – signed and dated '64 – poster decollage mounted on board – 19½ x 15¼in.
(Christie's)   **$13,365**   **£8,250**

JORN

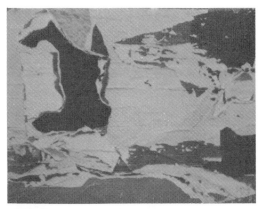

ASGER JORN – Untitled – signed and dated
1968 – poster decollage mounted on board – 23 x
30¾in.
(Christie's)   **$12,474**   **£7,700**

ASGER JORN – Curious Country – signed and
dated '66, and inscribed on the reverse – oil on
paper – 12¾ x 15¾in.
(Christie's)   **$17,820**   **£11,000**

ASGER JORN – Quo Vadis – signed, and signed
and dated '69 on the reverse – acrylic and oil on
canvas – 54 x 65cm.
(Sotheby's)   **$44,528**   **£25,300**

NELLIE JOSHUA – The Dragonfly – signed – on
canvas – 18 x 12in.
(Phillips)   **$6,080**   **£3,800**

NICO JUNGMANN – 'Love Wants No Words For
His Explaining . . .' – signed with monogram, and
signed again with monogram and inscribed on the
reverse – tempera on panel – 11½ x 8¼in.
(Christie's)   **$2,153**   **£1,210**

BELA KADAR – Les Amoureux a la Fenetre –
signed twice – gouache on paper – 18¾ x 12½in.
(Christie's) **$3,920** **£2,420**

BELA KADAR – Portrait Of A Young Woman –
signed – gouache on paper – 52 x 36cm.
(Phillips) **$2,184** **£1,300**

BELA KADAR – Le Village – signed –
watercolour and pencil on paper – 6½ x 9½in.
(Christie's) **$1,960** **£1,210**

BELA KADAR – Gossiping – signed – oil on
board – 14½ x 19in.
(Christie's) **$3,920** **£2,420**

WOLF KAHN – Bridal Path, Vermont – signed –
oil on canvas – 36 x 54in.
(Christie's) **$12,100** **£6,760**

WOLF KAHN – River – signed – oil on canvas –
44 x 64in.
(Christie's) **$15,400** **£8,603**

J

KANDINSKY

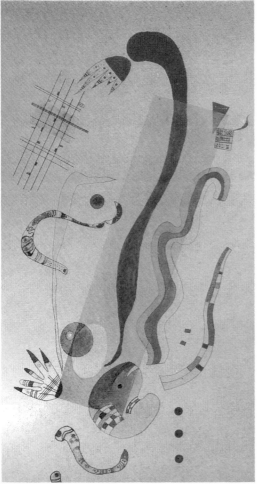

WASSILY KANDINSKY – In Einander – signed with monogram and dated '28, and inscribed and dated again – watercolour, pen and black ink on paper – 19 x 12½in.
(Christie's) $220,000   £137,500

WASSILY KANDINSKY – Rampante – signed with the monogram and dated '34 – watercolour and indian ink – 53 x 30cm.
(Sotheby's)   **$147,070   £77,000**

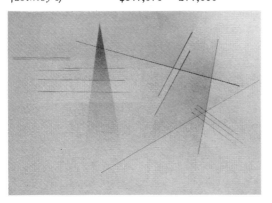

WASSILY KANDINSKY – Leichte Lasten – signed with monogram and dated '31 – watercolour on paper – 12¼ x 19in.
(Christie's)   **$70,070   £38,500**

STANISLAWA DE KARLOWSKA – A Devon Farm – signed – oil on canvas – 48 x 56cm.
(Phillips)   **$7,160   £4,000**

STANISLAWA DE KARLOWSKA – Looking
Towards The Farm, c. 1916 – signed – oil on
canvas – 56 x 48cm.
(Phillips)   **$6,888**   **£4,200**

LAJOS KASSAK – Composition With A Guitar –
signed with initials and dated '54 – gouache on
paper – unframed – 9½ x 7½in.
(Christie's)   **$1,158**   **£715**

HUGO KAUFFMANN – Postillion im Wirtshaus – signed and dated '87 – on panel – 19½
x 24in. *(Christie's)*   **$71,280 £44,000**

KAUFFMANN

JOSEPH MALACHY KAVANAGH – Landscape –
signed and dated '03 – oil on panel – 6¼ x 10¼in.
(Christie's) **$3,524** **£1,980**

HUGO WILHELM KAUFFMANN – The Innkeeper
– signed – oil on panel – 25.5 x 21cm.
(Phillips) **$9,000** **£5,000**

KARL KAUFMANN – A Venetian Backwater –
signed and dated 1897 – 19¾ x 32¼in.
(Christie's) **$3,484** **£1,980**

GOTTFRIED KELLER – Marguerite And Martha
– signed and dated 1862 – oil on panel – 19 x
17cm.
(Phillips) **$1,116** **£620**

MAX KAUS – Landschaft – signed, and signed
and inscribed on the reverse – oil on canvas – 80
x 100.5cm.
(Phillips) **$3,696** **£2,200**

SIR GERALD KELLY – Kennington Oval – oil on
panel – 5¾ x 6¾in.
(Christie's) **$1,347** **£770**

SIR GERALD KELLY – The White Dress – signed and dated '10 – oil on canvas – 102 x 128cm. *(Phillips)* **$11,635 £6,500**

ROBERT KEMM – A Halt By A Spring, Granada – signed – on canvas – 36¼ x 29in. *(Phillips)* **$7,200 £4,500**

CECIL KENNEDY – Christmas Roses – signed – oil on canvas – 31 x 26cm. *(Phillips)* **$3,580 £2,000**

KERN

HERMANN KERN – The Fortune Teller; and The Travelling Musician – signed – 20¾ x 17in. *(Christie's)* **$7,744 £4,400 Pair**

JAMES E. KESSELL – 'A Corner Of Coventry City Football Ground: Coventry vs. Bournemouth, March 14th 1953' – signed – oil on board – 26½ x 34¼in.
(Anderson & Garland)   **$1,826   £1,100**

ANSELM KIEFER – How To Paint – oil on canvas – 19¾ x 23¾in.
(Christie's)   **$24,948   £15,400**

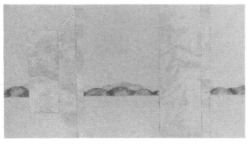

ANSELM KIEFER – Untitled – signed and dated '68 – tempera, paper collage and pencil on paper – 16¾ x 22¾in.
(Christie's)   **$12,012   £6,600**

ANTON EDVARD KIELDRUP – Salzburg – signed with initials, inscribed and dated '58 – 11¾ x 16in.
(Christie's)   **$5,420   £3,080**

CONRAD KIESEL – A Spanish Lady – signed – on panel – 17½ x 13¼in.
(Christie's)   **$1,936**   **£1,100**

GEORGE GOODWIN KILBURNE – Alone – signed and dated '77 – watercolour – 18 x 13cm.
(Sotheby's)   **$3,465**   **£1,980**

GEORGE GOODWIN KILBURNE – A Lullaby – signed – watercolour – 18.5 x 25.5cm.
(Sotheby's)   **$4,812**   **£2,750**

MARY EVELINA KINDON – A Busy Street – signed – oil on canvas – 21¼ x 17¼in.
(Christie's)   **$5,511**   **£3,300**

ALBERT F. KING – Pears, Apples, Grapes And Canteloupe – signed and dated '94 – oil on canvas laid down on board – 18 x 27¾in.
(Christie's)   **$4,950**   **£3,053**

KING

CHARLES BIRD KING – Blowing Bubbles –
signed on the reverse – oil on panel – 17½ x
13½in.
(Christie's) **$9,900** **£6,065**

ALAN KINGSBURY – Still Life On A Kitchen
Table – signed, and signed again and dated '87 on
the reverse – oil on board – 13¾ x 10in.
(Christie's) **$1,155** **£660**

PAUL KING – Silver Sails – signed, and signed
again and inscribed on the reverse – oil on
masonite – 25¼ x 30¼in.
(Christie's) **$6,050** **£3,732**

DONG KINGMAN – Bethesda Fountain, Central
Park – signed – watercolour on paper – 15¼ x
22½in.
(Christie's) **$440** **£269**

ERNST LUDWIG KIRCHNER – Bergabhang
mit gelben Baumen – oil on canvas – 25½ x
21¾in.
(Christie's) **$150,150** **£82,500**

ERNST LUDWIG KIRCHNER – Stilleben mit
Krug und Afrikanischer Schale – signed – oil on
canvas – 47½ x 36 in.
(Christie's) $584,430 £363,000

PER KIRKEBY – Untitled (Maria mit kind) – oil
on canvas – 81¼ x 50¾ in.
(Christie's) $18,418 £10,120

RAPHAEL KIRCHNER – La Toilette – signed
and inscribed – watercolour and pencil on buff
paper – 25 x 19½ in.
(Christie's) $2,673 £1,650

MOISE KISLING – Portrait de Femme – signed
– oil on canvas – 22 x 15 in.
(Christie's) $35,200 £22,000

KISLING

YVES KLEIN – Ant 25 – signed and dated 1960, and inscribed on the reverse – pigment on paper mounted on canvas – 42¾ x 29¾in.
(Christie's) **$133,650** **£82,500**

MOISE KISLING – Vase de Fleurs – signed – oil on canvas – 39½ x 29in.
(Christie's) **$100,100** **£55,000**

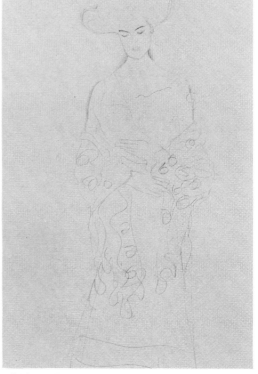

PAUL KLEE – Dorfkirche (Blauer Zwiebelturm) – signed and dated 1917 – watercolour on paper – 9 x 5¾in.
(Christie's) **$116,116** **£63,800**

GUSTAV KLIMT – Stehende Frau Mit Schal – pencil – 55.5 x 37cm.
(Sotheby's) **$39,919** **£20,900**

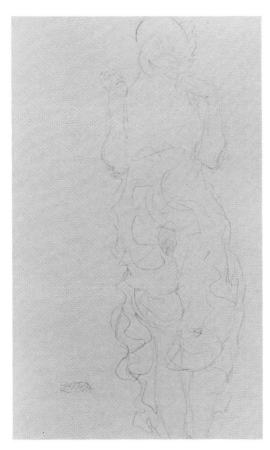

GUSTAV KLIMT – Stehender Akt Mit Erhobenen
Armen – signed – pencil – 56.5 x 37cm.
(Sotheby's) **$23,111** **£12,100**

KARL KNATHS – Lilacs And Candlestick –
signed, and dated 1962 and inscribed – oil
on canvas – 40 x 40¼in.
(Christie's) **$2,860** **£1,764**

OTTO KARL KNATHS – Haney's Rose – signed,
and signed again, dated 1954 and inscribed – oil
on canvas – 24¼ x 30¼in.
(Christie's) **$3,520** **£1,966**

CONSTANTINE KLUGE – Scene de Rue a Paris –
signed – oil on canvas – 54 x 65cm.
(Phillips) **$2,688** **£1,600**

OTTO KARL KNATHS – Painter's Cap – signed,
and signed again, dated 1954 and inscribed – 24¼
x 30¼in.
(Christie's) **$4,620** **£2,581**

DAME LAURA KNIGHT – Portrait Study Of A Young Woman – signed – oil on canvas – 19 x 14½in.
(Worsfolds) $1,344 £800

DAME LAURA KNIGHT – Hans – signed – black chalk – 35.5 x 25cm.
(Phillips) $1,980 £1,200

DAME LAURA KNIGHT – Harold Knight And Edith Bartlett – signed and inscribed – black chalk, coloured crayon and wax crayons – 26 x 36cm. *(Phillips)* $1,815 £1,100

DAME LAURA KNIGHT – Coventry Cathedral –
black and red chalk – 17½ x 22in.
(Christie's) $770   £440

DAME LAURA KNIGHT – The Looking Glass –
signed – pencil and watercolour heightened with
white – 22 x 15in.
(Christie's) $17,622   £9,900

DAME LAURA KNIGHT – Last Up – signed and
dated 1956 – watercolour and charcoal – 22 x
17½in.
(Christie's) $7,440   £4,180

DAME LAURA KNIGHT – Goliath – signed and
inscribed – black chalk – 35.5 x 25cm.
(Phillips) $3,465   £2,100

KNIGHT

DAME LAURA KNIGHT – Reclining Nude – black chalk, pastel and wash on buff paper – 39 x 75cm.
(Phillips) **$4,833** **£2,700**

DAME LAURA KNIGHT – Togare And Paris – signed, inscribed and dated 1930, and also signed and inscribed – black chalk – 34 x 25cm.
(Phillips) **$1,023** **£620**

DAME LAURA KNIGHT – Girl Standing – signed and dated 1890 – oil on canvas board – 44 x 27cm.
(Phillips) **$2,685** **£1,500**

DAME LAURA KNIGHT – Studio Reflections – signed – oil on canvas – 40 x 50in.
(Christie's) **$9,185** **£5,500**

DAME LAURA KNIGHT – Girl With A Mandolin – signed and dated 1890 – oil on canvas board – 44 x 26cm.
(Phillips) **$3,580** **£2,000**

DAME LAURA KNIGHT – Polishing The Horse's Harness – signed – black chalk – 35 x 25cm.
(Phillips) **$1,023** **£620**

DAME LAURA KNIGHT – The Fitting – recto –
signed – watercolour over black chalk heightened
with gouache – 74 x 61cm.; The White Dress –
verso – a sketch – oil on board.
(Phillips)   **$10,740   £6,000**

DAME LAURA KNIGHT – Hail Smiling Morn –
signed and dated 1957 – oil on canvas – 76 x
94cm.
(Phillips)   **$2,952   £1,800**

DAME LAURA KNIGHT – The Bather – signed
– oil on canvas – 10½ x 14½in.
(Christie's)   **$8,223   £4,620**

DAME LAURA KNIGHT – The Contortionist –
signed – black chalk, wax crayons and coloured
crayon – 36.5 x 27cm.
(Phillips)   **$891   £540**

DAME LAURA KNIGHT – The Finishing Horse –
signed – coloured chalks – 48.5 x 62cm.
(Phillips)   **$4,833   £2,700**

KNIGHT

DANIEL RIDGWAY KNIGHT – Girl In A Landscape – signed and inscribed – oil on canvas – 22¼ x 18¼in.
(Christie's) $24,200   £14,928

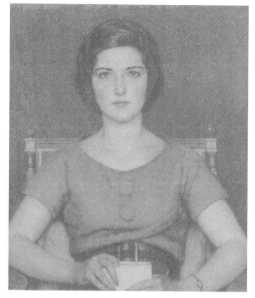

HAROLD KNIGHT – Angela – signed – oil on canvas – 76.5 x 63.5cm.
(Phillips) $3,608   £2,200

JOHN BUXTON KNIGHT – Evening In The Woods – signed – oil on canvas – 18¼ x 25½in.
(Christie's) $866   £495

DANIEL RIDGWAY KNIGHT – Dutch Girl By A Pond – signed and inscribed – oil on panel – 15 x 10¾in.
(Christie's) $4,400   £2,458

LOUIS ASTON KNIGHT – The Golden Hour – signed and inscribed, inscribed on the reverse – oil on canvas – 25½ x 31¾in.
(Christie's) $12,100   £7,413

FREDERICK J. KNOWLES – The Fringe Of The Forest – signed and dated 1916 – watercolour – 19½ x 29in.
(Prudential Fine Art Auctioneers) $990 £600

HENRIETTE RONNER KNIP – Coquins! – signed and dated 1892 – 50 x 40in.
(Christie's) $74,844 £46,200

FREDERICK J. KNOWLES – Prestbury – signed – watercolour – 9½ x 14½in.
(Prudential Fine Art Auctioneers) $1,320 £800

FREDERICK J. KNOWLES – Across The Heath – signed – watercolour – 19 x 29½in.
(Prudential Fine Art Auctioneers) $1,980 £1,200

GEORGE SHERIDAN KNOWLES – On The River – signed and dated 1903 – oil on canvas – 70 x 97cm. *(Sotheby's)* $9,460 £5,500

KNOWLTON

HENDRIK PIETER KOEKKOEK – A Wooded
River Landscape With Foresters Round A Camp
Fire – signed – 40 x 36in.
(Christie's) **$4,259** **£2,420**

HELEN M. KNOWLTON – 'White And Gold' –
signed and dated 1906 – oil on canvas – 24 x
18in.
(Robt. W. Skinner Inc.) **$600** **£363**

PETRA KOCH – Flowers In A Vase – signed with
initials and dated 1837 – 39 x 30in.
(Christie's) **$15,147** **£9,350**

WILLIAM HENRY DETHLEF KOERNER –
Summer Days – signed and dated 1916 – oil on
canvas – 36 x 26in.
(Christie's) **$7,150** **£4,410**

WILLIAM HENRY DETHLEF KOERNER – Herding Across The River – signed and dated 1923 – oil on canvas – 24 x 36in. *(Christie's)*   **$11,000 £6,145**

ALEXANDER KOESTER – Ducks On A Bank – signed – 21¼ x 32¼in. *(Christie's)*   **$53,460   £33,000**

ALEXANDER KOESTER – Enten im reflixlicht am seeufer – signed – 28½ x 46in. *(Christie's)*   **$89,100   £55,000**

OSKAR KOKOSCHKA – Tulpen Und Irisse – signed and dated '72 – watercolour – 64.8 x 50.2cm. *(Sotheby's)*   **$67,232   £35,200**

307

OSKAR KOKOSCHKA – Portrait Of A Girl – oil on canvas – 18 x 12in.
(Christie's)   **$18,018**   **£9,900**

JOHANN KONIG – The Flagellation – signed, and inscribed and dated 1600 on the reverse – on copper – 18¾ x 12¾in.
(Phillips)   **$43,680**   **£24,000**

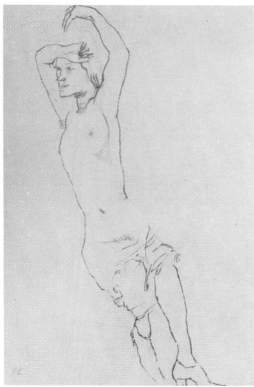

OSKAR KOKOSCHKA – Halbliegender Akt – signed with the initials – charcoal on buff-coloured paper – 45.1 x 31.6cm.
(Sotheby's)   **$14,707**   **£7,700**

LEON KOSSOFF – Fidelma No. 2 – charcoal and coloured chalk on joined paper – 45¾ x 31½in.
(Christie's)   **$7,607**   **£4,180**

JACOB KRAMER – The Jew; Meditation –
signed – oil on canvas – 40 x 30in.
(Christie's) **$31,328 £17,600**

W. V. KRAUCZ – A Beggar In Istanbul – signed
and dated 1906 – oil on board – 52.5 x 40.5 cm.
(Sotheby's) **$1,729 £935**

OTOLIA KRASZEWSKA – A Young Beauty – signed – 26 x 35½in. *(Christie's)* **$11,583 £7,150**

KRIEGHOFF

CORNELIUS KRIEGHOFF – Man With Red Hat
And Pipe – signed – oil on canvas – 13 x 11in.
(Christie's) **$39,600** **£24,262**

LEON KROLL – Nude In A Blue Interior –
signed and dated 1919 – oil on canvas – 47½ x
36in.
(Christie's) **$28,600** **£17,523**

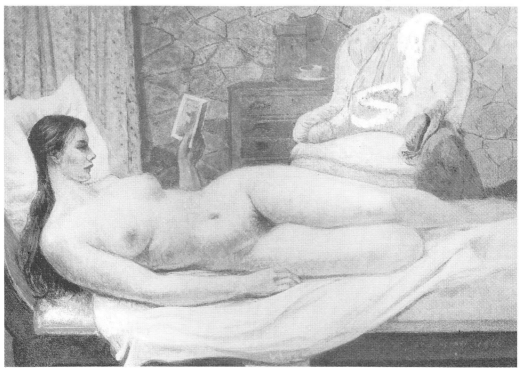

LEON KROLL – Interior With Nude (Isabel) – signed and dated 1966 – oil on canvas –
16¼ x 24¼in. *(Christie's)* **$6,600 £3,687**

LOUIS KRONBERG – Mademoiselle Regina – signed, and signed again, dated 1913 and inscribed – pastel on paper – 36¼ x 25½in.
(Christie's) **$1,980 £1,221**

WALT KUHN – Girl In Pierrot's Hat – signed and dated 1940 – oil on canvas – 40¼ x 30¼in.
(Christie's) **$143,000 £87,616**

ERIC KUBIERSCHKY – A Bavarian Village – signed and dated 1896 – on panel – 7½ x 11in.
(Christie's) **$9,801 £6,050**

IVAN KUDRIASHEV – Abstract Composition – signed in cyrillic – gouache and watercolour on paper – 8¾ x 14¼in.
(Christie's) **$9,209 £5,060**

OVE KUNERT – After The Ball – signed and dated 1916 – 42¾ x 34in.
(Christie's) **$1,548 £880**

LABORNE

EMILE LABORNE – A View Of The Cathedral
And Market Of Troyes – signed, inscribed and
dated 1876 – oil on canvas – 55 x 38cm.
(Phillips)   **$5,040   £2,800**

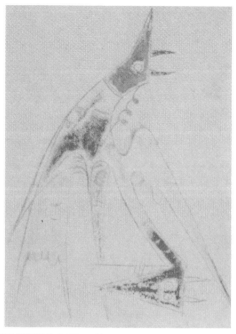

WILFREDO LAM – Oiseaux – watercolour and
pencil on canvas – 15½ x 12in.
(Christie's)   **$2,138   £1,320**

JOHN LAFARGE – Female Figure – signed and
dated 1882 – watercolour and pencil on board –
13 x 9¾in.
(Christie's)   **$8,800   £4,916**

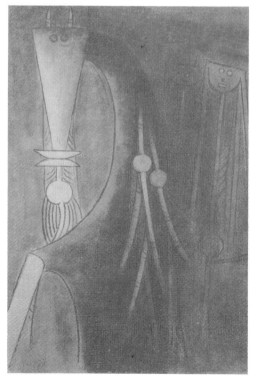

WIFREDO LAM – La Capigiatura Gialla – signed
and dated 1965 – oil on canvas – 70 x 50cm.
(Sotheby's)   **$42,592   £24,200**

WIFREDO LAM – Seated Figure – signed and dated '37, and signed on the reverse – watercolour and gouache on paper – 37 x 30cm.
(Sotheby's)   **$13,552**   **£7,700**

PERCY LANCASTER – A Vegetable Market In A Breton Town – signed with monogram – pencil and watercolour heightened with white – 6¼ x 9¼in.
(Christie's)   **$1,443**   **£825**

GEORGE COCHRAN LAMBDIN – Pink And Yellow Roses – signed and dated 1882 – oil on canvas – 24 x 17¾in.
(Christie's)   **$9,350**   **£5,223**

EGISTO LANCEROTTO – Portrait Of An Italian Lady – signed and inscribed – 59 x 23¾in.
(Christie's)   **$7,744**   **£4,400**

LANCEROTTO

EGISTO LANCEROTTO – An Italian Fisherwoman
– signed – 59 x 29¾in.
(Christie's)   **$9,680**   **£5,500**

WALTER LANGLEY – Distant Thoughts –
signed – watercolour – 15 x 13in.
(Christie's)   **$5,143**   **£3,080**

OLAF VIGGO PETER LANGER – Winter In
Sollerod – signed and dated 1929 – 36¾ x 47¼in.
(Christie's)   **$774**   **£440**

WALTER LANGLEY – The Lesson – signed with
monogram – watercolour – 24 x 16.5cm.
(Phillips)   **$1,320**   **£800**

ANDRE LANSKOY – Untitled – signed –
gouache on paper – 25¾ x 18¾in.
(Christie's)   **$5,346   £3,300**

ANDRE LANSKOY – Untitled – oil on canvas –
39¼ x 25¾in.
(Christie's)   **$26,730   £16,500**

CHARLES LAPICQUE – Le Tennis – signed and dated '65, and signed and dated again and
inscribed on the reverse – oil on canvas – 38¼ x 51¼in. *(Christie's)*   **$35,200 £22,000**

315

LAPRADE

GEORGE LARA – Rural Landscapes With Numerous Figures And Building – oil – 8½ x 11½in.
(Chancellors)　　　　　$5,376　　£3,200 Pair

PIERRE LAPRADE – Nature Morte – signed – oil on canvas – 100 x 81cm.
(Phillips)　　　　$10,080　　£6,000

MIKAEL LARIONOV – Still Life With Cards – watercolour and gouache – 20.5 x 28cm.
(Phillips)　　　　$873　　£520

GEORGE LARA – Bringing Home The Harvest; and A Rest Along The Way – signed – oil on board – 23 x 30.5cm.
(Sotheby's)　　　　$14,757　　£8,580 Pair

MIKAEL LARIONOV – Two Figures Under A Tree – watercolour – 32.5 x 24cm.
(Phillips)　　　　$1,041　　£620

GASPARD LATOIX – Papoose – signed, dated '95 and inscribed – oil on canvas – 12 x 10in.
(Christie's) $2,860 £1,752

WILLIAM LARKIN, Studio of – Portrait Of A Man, Bust Length, Wearing A Lace Embroidered Doublet And Lace Ruff – oil on panel – 22¾ x 17½in.
(Phillips) $4,810 £2,600

LOUIS SIMON LASSALLE – Waiting His Turn – signed – on panel – 17½ x 14in.
(Christie's) $3,872 £2,200

GASTON LATOUCHE – The Telephone Call – signed – on panel – unframed – 30½ x 22in.
(Christie's) $12,474 £7,700

LAURENCE

SYDNEY LAURENCE – Alaska Fireweed –
signed – oil on masonite – 10 x 8in.
(Christie's)   **$5,000   £3,084**

MARIE LAURENCIN – Femme au Chapeau Rose
– signed – oil on canvas – 18¼ x 15in.
(Christie's)   **$132,000   £82,500**

SYDNEY LAURENCE – Mount McKinley –
signed – oil on canvas – 20¼ x 16¼in.
(Christie's)   **$33,000   £18,437**

MARIE LAURENCIN – La Liseuse – signed –
oil on canvas – 36 x 28¼in.
(Christie's)   **$425,040   £264,000**

MARIE LAURENCIN – Bouquet de Fleurs –
signed – oil on canvas in original mirrored frame –
25½ x 21½in.
(Christie's) **$88,000 £55,000**

SIR JOHN LAVERY – Posthumous Portrait Of
Jane Lavery – signed, inscribed and dated 1935,
and signed again, inscribed and dated on the
reverse – oil on canvas-board – 20 x 14in.
(Christie's) **$11,940 £7,150**

SIR JOHN LAVERY – Portrait Of Miss Elizabeth
Asquith, Small Half-Length – signed and dated
1914-5, and signed again, inscribed and dated on
the reverse – oil on canvasboard – 14 x 9¾in.
(Christie's) **$8,811 £4,950**

SIR JOHN LAVERY – Portrait Of A Turk, Bust
Length – signed and dated 1880 – oil on canvas –
18 x 12in.
(Christie's) **$4,408 £2,640**

LAVERY

SIR JOHN LAVERY – A Moorish Courtyard –
signed – oil on canvas – 51 x 61cm.
(Phillips) $25,060 £14,000

SIR JOHN LAVERY – The Wharf – signed, and
signed again, inscribed and dated 1916 on the
reverse – oil on canvas-board – 24¼ x 29½in.
(Christie's) $119,405 £71,500

SIR JOHN LAVERY – The Terrace, Cap d'Ail –
signed, and also signed, inscribed and dated 1921
on the reverse – oil on canvas – 64 x 76cm.; verso
– Study For The Amazon – charcoal – circa
1910.
(Phillips) $213,200 £130,000

SIR JOHN LAVERY – Bathing Studies – signed, and signed again, inscribed and dated
1930 on the reverse – oil on canvas-board – 19¾ x 25¾in. *(Christie's)* $8,817 £5,280

SIR JOHN LAVERY – He Won't Bite – signed, inscribed and dated 1886 – oil on canvas – 51 x 61cm.
(Phillips)   **$6,560**   **£4,000**

SIR JOHN LAVERY – Portrait Of A Girl In Nurse's Uniform, Possibly The Artist's Sister Jane – signed and dated 1880 – oil on canvas – 18 x 12in.
(Christie's)   **$3,306**   **£1,980**

SIR JOHN LAVERY – Portrait Of Lady Beauchamp, Half Length Wearing A White Dress – signed, and signed again, inscribed and dated 1935 on the reverse – oil on canvas – 31½ x 23¾in.
(Christie's)   **$3,306**   **£1,980**

SIR JOHN LAVERY – Portrait Of Viscountess Castlerosse In Eighteenth Century Riding Habit – signed, and also signed, inscribed and dated 1936 – oil on canvas – 61 x 36cm.
(Phillips)   **$20,500**   **£12,500**

JACOB LAWRENCE – Harlem Diner – signed and
dated 1938 – gouache on paper laid down on
board – 12¾ x 19¼in.
(Christie's) $13,200 £7,374

JAMES KERR LAWSON – The Arch Of Titus –
oil on canvas – 66¼ x 46½in.
(Christie's) $15,614 £9,350

CECIL LAWSON – The Country Fair – signed,
and signed again and inscribed on the reverse – oil
on canvas – 19¼ x 29in.
(Christie's) $6,265 £3,520

ERNEST LAWSON – Winter Stream – signed
indistinctly – oil on canvas – 30¼ x 40¼in.
(Christie's) $132,000 £73,748

ERNEST LAWSON – Evening By A River –
signed – oil on canvas – 14 x 20in.
(Christie's) $18,700 £11,457

JAMES KERR LAWSON – The Piazzetta
Looking South Towards San Giorgio Maggiore –
oil on canvas – 66¼ x 46¼in.
(Christie's) $20,207 £12,100

BENJAMIN WILLIAMS LEADER – Figures By A Cottage In A Wooded Landscape – signed and dated 1899 – on canvas – 15½ x 23½in.
(Phillips)   **$5,632   £3,200**

BENJAMIN WILLIAMS LEADER – Figures Resting On A Riverbank In A Mountainous Wooded Landscape – signed – on board – 10½ x 16½in.
(Phillips)   **$2,816   £1,600**

BENJAMIN WILLIAMS LEADER – Near Harlech, Caernarvonshire Coast – signed and dated 1887 – on canvas – 26 x 42in.
(Phillips)   **$9,920   £6,200**

HENRI LEBASQUE – La Partie de Campagne – signed – oil on canvas – 9¼ x 13in.
(Christie's)   **$31,680   £19,800**

HENRI LEBASQUE – Femme au Bouquet de Fleurs – oil on board – 22 x 18¾in.
(Christie's)   **$16,016   £8,800**

HENRI LEBASQUE – Le Jardin – signed – oil on canvas – 21¾ x 18¼in.
(Christie's)   **$76,076   £41,800**

LEBASQUE

İHENRI LEBASQUE – La Marne a Lagny – signed
– oil on canvas – 21¼ x 28¾in.
(Christie's) $66,880   £41,800

HENRI LEBASQUE – La Femme en Robe
blanche – signed – oil on canvas – 16¾ x 24in.
(Christie's) $73,920   £46,200

HENRI LEBASQUE – Nu allonge contre un Lit – oil on canvas – 25 x 31¼in. *(Christie's)*
$61,600 £38,500

HENRI LEBASQUE – Le Jardin sur la Baie a
Morgat – signed – oil on canvas – 19¾ x 24in.
(Christie's)   **$100,100**   **£55,000**

PAUL EMILE LECOMTE – A French Fishing
Port – signed – 13 x 16in.
(Christie's)   **$3,484**   **£1,980**

HENRI LEBASQUE – En Barque – signed – oil
on panel – 8 x 7in.
(Christie's)   **$45,760**   **£28,600**

FERDINAND LEEKE – Parsifal In Quest Of The
Holy Grail – signed and dated 1912 – 53 x 40½in.
(Christie's)   **$7,260**   **£4,400**

CHARLES LEBON – Paysage Eneige – signed –
oil on canvas – 50.5 x 60.5cm.
(Phillips)   **$840**   **£500**

JEFF LOUIS VAN LEEMPUTTEN – Chickens On
The Bank Of A River – signed and dated 1893 –
on panel – 9½ x 14in.
(Christie's)   **$1,361**   **£825**

LEGER

FERNAND LEGER – Deux Figures – signed and
dated '30, and signed and dated again and inscribed
on the reverse – oil on canvas – 18¼ x 13¼in.
(Christie's) $59,840   £37,400

FERNAND LEGOUT-GERARD – Port Breton –
signed – oil on panel – 40 x 32cm.
(Phillips) $5,880   £3,500

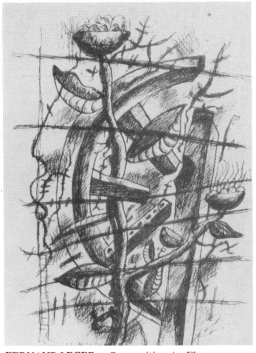

FERNAND LEGER – Composition Au Fleur –
signed with the initials and dated 1945 – pen and
brush and brown ink – 27.5 x 17.8cm.
(Sotheby's) $18,909   £9,900

RUDOLF LEHMANN – 'La Lavandaja' – signed,
inscribed and dated 1864 – oil on canvas – 155 x
107cm.
(Phillips) $15,300   £8,500

CHARLES LEICKERT – A River Scene, Figures Embarking In A Small Boat By A Windmill – signed with initials – oil on panel – 11 x 8.5cm.
(Phillips) **$936** **£520**

FREDERIC, LORD LEIGHTON – Figure Studies For 'At The Fountain' – inscribed – black and white chalk on brown paper – 11¼ x 12¾in.
(Christie's) **$1,828** **£1,045**

ADOLPHE LELEUX – 'Discussions At A Local Level' – signed and dated 1857 – oil on canvas – 43 x 72cm.
(Phillips) **$7,200** **£4,000**

FRANZ VON LENBACH – A Young Girl – signed and dated 1900 – on board – 16¼in. diam.
(Christie's) **$23,166** **£14,300**

STANISLAS LEPINE – Riviere: La Baignade – signed – oil on canvas – 15 x 21¾in.
(Christie's) **$24,640** **£15,400**

STANISLAS LEPINE – Le Canal au Clair de Lune – signed – oil on canvas – 18 x 21¼in.
(Christie's) **$19,019** **£10,450**

LEPINE

STANISLAS LEPINE – Vue de Paris et la Construction de la Tour Eiffel – oil on canvas – 15¼ x 21¾in.
(Christie's) $32,032   £17,600

RICHARD HAYLEY LEVER – High Bridge, St. Austell, Cornwall, England – signed and dated 1911 – oil on canvas – 18¼ x 24¼in.
(Christie's) $5,500   £3,392

PAUL LEROY – Maternity – signed and dated 1899 – unframed – 25½ x 21¼in.
(Christie's) $10,335   £6,380

RICHARD HAYLEY LEVER – The Jetty, Nantucket, Massachusetts – signed – oil on canvas – 20¼ x 24in.
(Christie's) $10,450   £6,446

GEORGE DUNLOP LESLIE – Lucy, Daughter Of C. Andrew Esq – signed and dated 1880 – oil on canvas – 91.5 x 71cm.
(Sotheby's) $11,352   £6,600

RICHARD HAYLEY LEVER – A Harbour In Brittany – signed – oil on canvas – 19¾ x 24in.
(Christie's) $18,700   £11,457

JACK LEVINE – The Spanish Prison – signed –
oil on canvas – 28 x 32in.
(Christie's) $41,800   £23,353

JACK LEVINE – The Gangster Wedding – signed
– oil on canvas – 16 x 14in.
(Christie's) $30,800   £17,207

JACK LEVINE – Pinafore-Pentagon-Strange Love
– signed – oil on canvas – 32 x 26¼in.
(Christie's) $16,500   £9,218

EDMUND DARCH LEWIS – Pennsylvania
Landscape – signed and dated 1860 – oil on
canvas – 26 x 38¼in.
(Christie's) $18,700   £10,447

JOHN FREDERICK LEWIS – The Squirrel Inn,
Winkfield, Berkshire – inscribed on a letter
attached to the reverse – oil on panel – 13.5 x
20.5cm.
(Sotheby's) $29,326   £17,050

ANDRE LHOTE – Tete de Marin – signed – oil
on canvas – 17¾ x 13in.
(Christie's) $18,018   £9,900

MAX LIEBERMANN – Der Lotse – signed – oil on board – 14¼ x 11¾in.
(Christie's)   **$11,011**   **£6,050**

JONAS LIE – Ladies In The Park – signed – oil on canvas – 26½ x 20¼in.
(Christie's)   **$37,400**   **£22,914**

MAX LIEBERMANN – Selbstbildnis als Maler – signed and dated 1922 – oil on canvas – 29½ x 33½in.
(Christie's)   **$64,064**   **£35,200**

ROGER LIMOUSE – Nature morte a la Table – signed – oil on canvas – 60 x 73cm.
(Phillips)   **$2,688**   **£1,600**

HERMANN KARL HEINRICH LINDENSCHMIDT
– Idle Gossip – signed – 21½ x 27½in.
(Christie's) **$4,259** **£2,420**

JEAN ETIENNE LIOTARD – A Tea Tray With
Imari And Polychrome Chinese Export Porcelain
– oil on canvas – 53.5 x 63cm.
(Sotheby's) **$57,090** **£33,000**

EDWARD D'ARCY LISTER – Unloading Ships –
signed on the reverse – oil on canvas – 30 x 25in.
(Christie's) **$734** **£440**

SIR JAMES DROMGOLE LINTON – Cecilia From
'As You Like It' – signed with initials, and signed
and inscribed on a label on the backboard –
watercolour heightened with bodycolour – 121 x
58.5 cm.
(Sotheby's) **$2,502** **£1,430**

DOROTHY M. LITZINGER – On The Lake – oil
on canvas – 42 x 40in.
(Robt. W. Skinner Inc.) **$500** **£303**

LLOYD

KATHERINE LLOYD – The Farmyard – signed
– oil on canvas – 28 x 36in.
(Christie's) **$2,204** **£1,320**

GUSTAVE LOISEAU – Gelee Blanche;
Environs de Pontoise – signed and dated 1906 –
oil on canvas – 23¾ x 36¼in.
(Christie's) **$70,400** **£44,000**

GIOVANNI LOMI – Piazza del Villagio – signed
– oil on panel – 39.5 x 49.5cm.
(Phillips) **$840** **£500**

GEORGE EDWARD LODGE – Tree Sparrow –
signed – watercolour and bodycolour – 22.5 x
14.5cm.
(Phillips) **$1,858** **£1,050**

AUGUST LOHR – 'Ixtaccihuatl' – signed,
inscribed and dated 1897 – watercolour on paper
– 10 x 16¾in.
(Robt. W. Skinner Inc.) **$375** **£227**

RAOUL DE LONGPRE – Roses And Lilacs –
signed – watercolour and gouache on board – 28¼
x 20¾in.
(Christie's) **$4,400** **£2,714**

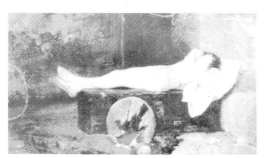

ANTONIO LONZA – The Sleeping Circus Boy –
signed – on panel – 9½ x 14½in.
(Christie's)   **$1,270**   **£770**

RUPERT SCOTT LOVEJOY – 'The Broken Fence'
– signed – oil on board – 14 x 16in.
(Robt. W. Skinner Inc.)   **$1,000**   **£558**

BASILE DE LOOSE – The Rivals – signed and
dated 1840 – on panel – 29 x 23½in.
(Christie's)   **$10,692**   **£6,600**

FRANK W. LOVEN – Village In Winter – signed
and dated '28 – oil on canvas – 25¼ x 30¼in.
(Christie's)   **$2,860**   **£1,764**

RICARDO LOPEZ-CABRERA – The Apple-
Picker – signed and inscribed – 19¾ x 21¾in.
(Christie's)   **$3,872**   **£2,200**

LAURENCE STEPHEN LOWRY – Figure On A
Seat – signed and dated 1960 – oil on canvas –
20 x 24in.
(Christie's)   **$12,859**   **£7,700**

LOWRY

LAURENCE STEPHEN LOWRY – Industrial Scene – signed and dated 1936 – pencil – 10 x 15¼in.
(Christie's)   **$9,398   £5,280**

LAURENCE STEPHEN LOWRY – Figures In A Street – signed and dated 1957 – pencil – 13 x 10¼in.
(Christie's)   **$2,937   £1,650**

LAURENCE STEPHEN LOWRY – Two Brothers – signed and dated 1962 – oil on panel – 9½ x 5¼in.
(Christie's)   **$11,022   £6,600**

LAURENCE STEPHEN LOWRY – A Country Road – signed and dated 1963, and inscribed on the reverse – oil on board – 14½ x 19½in.
(Christie's)   **$19,580   £11,000**

LAURENCE STEPHEN LOWRY – Blythe Ferry
– signed – felt tip pen and pencil – 9½ x 13¼in.
(Christie's) **$3,132** **£1,760**

LAURENCE STEPHEN LOWRY – A Street –
signed and dated 1962, signed, and again inscribed
and dated on the reverse – oil on panel – 11 x
8¾in.
(Christie's) **$23,881** **£14,300**

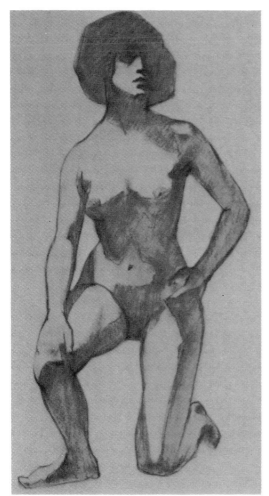

LAURENCE STEPHEN LOWRY – Nude Study –
signed – pencil – 22 x 15in.
(Christie's) **$2,755** **£1,650**

LAURENCE STEPHEN LOWRY – Boy With A
Stomach Ache – signed and dated 1966 – oil on
board – 40 x 30cm.
(Phillips) **$7,380** **£4,500**

LUBIANES

MAXIMILIEN LUCE – La Seine a Rolleboise –
signed – oil on board – 15¼ x 17¼in.
(Christie's) **$14,256** **£8,800**

J. L. LUBIANES – The Gardens Of A Palatial Villa
– signed and dated 1873 – 63 x 39.5in.
(Christie's) **$1,089** **£660**

MAXIMILIEN LUCE – Le Verger de Pissarro a
Eragny – signed and dated '95 – oil on canvas –
31½ x 39in.
(Christie's) **$619,850** **£385,000**

DESIRE LUCA – Personnages dans la Rue –
signed and dated 1924, and inscribed on the
reverse – oil on canvas – 65 x 54cm.
(Phillips) **$2,016** **£1,200**

MAXIMILIEN LUCE – Scene du Rue – oil on
canvas – 13 x 16¼in.
(Christie's) **$15,015** **£8,250**

MAXIMILIEN LUCE – Le Pont Notre Dame –
signed – oil on canvas – 15¼ x 24¼in.
(Christie's) **$12,432** **£7,770**

MAXIMILIEN LUCE – Les Chantiers de Paris,
Boulevard de la Madeleine – signed – oil on canvas
– 25¾ x 21¼in.
(Christie's) **$14,960** **£9,350**

MAXIMILIEN LUCE – Femme nue assise –
signed and dated '88 – blue crayon on paper –
11¼ x 7¼in.
(Christie's) **$1,871** **£1,155**

MAXIMILIEN LUCE – Paysage aux Pommiers –
signed – oil on board – 10 x 15½in.
(Christie's) **$29,920** **£18,700**

MAXIMILIEN LUCE – Femme revelant ses Bas –
recto – signed – coloured crayons on paper; Le
Baiser – verso – brown crayon on paper – 12 x
9½in.
(Christie's) **$3,029** **£1,870**

MAXIMILIEN LUCE – Le Port – signed – soft
pencil on paper – 13¾ x 19¾in.
(Christie's) **$1,901** **£1,045**

GEORGE BENJAMIN LUKS – The Ledge, Cape
Elizabeth, Maine – signed – oil on canvas – 16¼ x
20¼in.
(Christie's) **$15,400** **£8,603**

WILLIAM LUKER – Burnham Marshes – signed
with monogram, inscribed and dated 1890 – on
board – 9¾ x 17in.
(Phillips) **$1,040** **£650**

GEORGE BENJAMIN LUKS – Foggy Night, New
York – signed – oil on canvas – 30¼ x 25in.
(Christie's) **$28,600** **£15,978**

GEORGE BENJAMIN LUKS – Street Urchin –
signed – oil on canvas – 20 x 16in.
(Christie's) **$19,800** **£12,131**

THOMAS LUNY – A Sloop, Cutter And Other
Vessels On The Teignmouth Estuary, Devon –
signed and dated 1832 – oil on panel – 9 x 12in.
(Phillips) **$4,810** **£2,600**

MARKUS LUPERTZ – Brown Stake – signed on
the reverse – acrylic on canvas – 27¾ x 19¾in.
(Christie's)   **$10,692**   **£6,600**

MARKUS LUPERTZ – Der Mann im Mond –
signed with initials and inscribed on the reverse –
oil on canvas – 39¼ x 31½in.
(Christie's)   **$32,076**   **£19,800**

MARKUS LUPERTZ – Uber Orpheus – signed
with initials – black chalk, coloured crayon and
gouache on paper – 27 x 19½in.
(Christie's)   **$3,207**   **£1,980**

NEVIL OLIVER LUPTON – Figures Resting By A
Brook, While Sheep Graze In An Extensive Wooded
Landscape – signed and dated 1857-8 – on canvas
– 16 x 23½in.
(Phillips)   **$4,048**   **£2,300**

JEAN LURCAT – Paysage; Poissons, Compotier –
signed, and signed again, dated 1953 and inscribed
– oil on canvas – 28¾ x 36¼in.
(Christie's)   **$79,200**   **£49,500**

MICHAEL LYNE – The Duke Of Beaufort's Hunt,
Near Tetbury – signed, dated 1946 and inscribed
on the reverse – watercolour and gouache – 14 x
20in.
(Christie's)   **$3,674**   **£2,200**

McAULIFFE

JAMES J. McAULIFFE – Sailing Vessels – signed – oil on canvas – 20 x 30in.
(Bruce D. Collins) $1,320   £745

ROBERT WALKER MacBETH – The Trysting Place – signed with initials, watercolour heightened with white and gum arabic – 10¼ x 14¼in.
(Christie's) $770   £440

CHARLES McCALL – The Great Hall, Dutton Homestall – signed and dated 1948 – oil on canvas – 36 x 28in.
(Christie's) $1,762   £990

HENRY McCARTER – View Through The Trees – signed and dated '33 – pastel on paper – 20 x 26in.
(Christie's) $1,540   £950

JERVIS McENTEE – Maples In Autumn – inscribed on the reverse – oil on canvas – 10¼ x 13¾in.
(Christie's) $4,180   £2,578

JERVIS McENTEE – Quakerbridge Road Looking North – signed with monogrammed initials and dated 1867 – oil on canvas laid down on cardboard – 16¼ x 27¾in.
(Christie's) $8,800   £4,916

JERVIS McENTEE – Roman Aqueduct – signed with conjoined initials and dated '75 – oil on canvas – 6 x 12in.
(Christie's) $7,700   £4,717

AMBROSE McEVOY — Portrait Of The Hon.
Lois Stuart II, Half Length, Wearing An Orange
Dress — oil on canvas — 30 x 25in.
(Christie's) **$22,044 £13,200**

AUGUST MACKE — Winklige Formen — pastel
and watercolour on paper — 3¾ x 6¼in.
(Christie's) **$13,013 £7,150**

CAMPBELL MACKIE — Sams, Breaghy, Co.
Donegal — oil on canvas — 24 x 28in.
(Christie's) **$5,143 £3,080**

HENRY LEE McFEE — Farm Scene — signed —
oil on canvas — 20 x 24¼in.
(Christie's) **$1,980 £1,213**

JAMES MACKAY — A Young Girl Feeding Ducks
— signed — watercolour — 16 x 22cm.
(Phillips) **$3,363 £1,900**

JOHN WATSON McLEA — Awaiting The Next
Move — signed, inscribed and dated 1846 — on
canvas — 30 x 24½in.
(Phillips) **$1,440 £900**

MACLET

ELISEE MACLET – La Rue de Eaux a Poissy –
signed – oil on canvas – 61 x 38.5cm.
(Phillips) $6,720 £4,000

CONROY MADDOX – The Source – signed and
dated '71 – oil on canvas – 24 x 18in.
(Christie's) $616 £352

ELISEE MACLET – La Quaie – signed – oil on
canvas – 46 x 55cm.
(Phillips) $4,116 £2,450

RAIMUNDO DE MADRAZO Y GARRETA – An
Elegant Beauty – signed – 36½ x 24¾in.
(Christie's) $53,460 £33,000

JAMES CHARLES MAGGS – A Coach And Four
Outside The Hand And Shears, Smithfield –
signed – 14½ x 26in.
(Christie's)   **$9,075   £5,500**

JAMES CHARLES MAGGS – Gloucester Coffee
House, Piccadilly – signed – 14½ x 26in.
(Christie's)   **$12,705   £7,700**

RENE MAGRITTE – L'Aube a Cayenne –
signed, signed and inscribed – oil on canvas –
38¼ x 29in.
(Christie's)   **$194,810   £121,000**

ALBERTO MAGNELLI – Paesaggio no. V., or
Trois Maisons – signed and dated 1914, and
inscribed on the reverse – oil on canvas – 27½ x
21¾in.
(Christie's)   **$96,096   £52,800**

RENE MAGRITTE – Corps humain – signed –
brush and black ink on paper – 14¾ x 9½in.
(Christie's)   **$19,360   £12,100**

MAGRITTE

RENE MAGRITTE – Raminagrobis – signed – gouache – 43 x 61cm. *(Sotheby's)*
$126,060 £66,000

RENE MAGRITTE – Sans Titre – signed – oil on canvas – 21 x 28¾in. *(Christie's)*
$160,160 £88,000

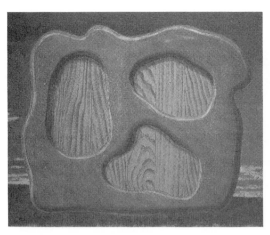

RENE MAGRITTE – La Demon de la Perversite; or L'Ombre monumentale – signed and inscribed on the reverse – oil on board – 10¾ x 13¾in. *(Christie's)* $51,040   £31,900

RENE MAGRITTE – Le Chateau au Ciel – signed – watercolour on paper – 5¼ x 6¾in. *(Christie's)* $17,600   £11,000

RENE MAGRITTE – Le Chant d'Amour – signed, inscribed with title on the reverse – oil on canvas – 18 x 21in. *(Christie's)* $460,460 £286,000

MAIGNAN

ALBERT PIERRE RENE MAIGNAN – Portrait de ma niece Alberte Duparc – signed, and inscribed and dated 1877 on the reverse – 27¼ x 17¼in.
(Christie's)   **$13,068**   **£7,920**

LEO MALAMPRE – Girl Seated On A Terrace Overlooking A Village – signed and dated 1898 – on canvas – 17 x 13in.
(Phillips)   **$6,720**   **£4,200**

PAUL MAITLAND – Street Scene, Early Evening – signed – oil on canvas – 18 x 14in.
(Christie's)   **$3,720**   **£2,090**

HENRI MANGUIN – 'La Breste', Maison Rouge, Environs de Marseille – signed – oil on canvas – 28¾ x 23¾in.
(Christie's)   **$105,600**   **£66,000**

HENRI MANGUIN – Jeanne en Chemise – signed
– oil on canvas – 20 x 24in.
(Christie's)   **$105,600**   **£66,000**

EDWARD MIDDLETON MANIGAULT –
Gazebo In Central Park – signed – oil on
canvas – 20 x 20in.
(Christie's)   **$16,500**   **£10,109**

HENRI MANGUIN – Le Golfe de St. Tropez –
signed – oil on canvas laid down on board – 12¾
x 17¾in.
(Christie's)   **$35,200**   **£22,000**

CATHLEEN MANN – Santa Maria della Salute,
Venice – signed and dated – oil on canvas – 20¼
x 24¼in.
(Christie's)   **$1,155**   **£660**

HENRI MANGUIN – Saint-Tropez vu du Jardin
de l'Hotel Latitude – signed – oil on canvas –
13 x 16in.
(Christie's)   **$20,020**   **£11,000**

CATHLEEN MANN – The Piazzetta With The
Church Of San Giorgio Maggiore, Venice – signed
and dated 1952 – oil on canvas – 20 x 24in.
(Christie's)   **$1,194**   **£715**

JAMES BOLIVAR MANSON – Mixed Flowers In A Vase – signed – oil on canvas – 18 x 12in.
(Christie's) $4,592   £2,750

JAMES BOLIVAR MANSON – Brittany – signed – oil on canvas – 17½ x 21in.
(Christie's) $1,377   £825

JAMES BOLIVAR MANSON – 'Too-Too' – signed and dated 1912 – oil on panel – 9½ x 14in.
(Christie's) $1,837   £1,100

G. F. MAPORTILLO – A Mexican River Landscape – signed and dated 1888 – oil on canvas – 50 x 66cm.
(Sotheby's) $1,526   £825

GIANNINO MARCHIG – La Fille des Marins – signed and dated 1935 – oil on canvas – 39¼ x 32in.
(Christie's) $10,692   £6,600

GIANNINO MARCHIG – San Gimignano – signed and dated 1917 – pencil on buff paper – unframed – 9¼ x 10¾in.
(Christie's) $1,514   £935

GIANNINO MARCHIG – Nu Couche – signed with monogram and dated MCXXXI – 34½ x 70in.
(Christie's) $24,024   £13,200

ODON MARFFY – Girl From Nyerges – signed –
oil on board – 34¾ x 24in.
(Christie's)   **$3,920**   **£2,420**

WILLIAM HENRY MARGETSON – Teatime –
signed and dated 1926 – oil on canvas
– 81 x 61cm.
(Phillips)   **$20,585**   **£11,500**

WILLIAM HENRY MARGETSON – Picnic By The
River – signed and dated 1921 – oil on canvas –
unframed – 107 x 86cm.
(Phillips)   **$20,585**   **£11,500**

WILLIAM HENRY MARGETSON – In The
Garden – oil on canvas – unframed – 81 x 65cm.
(Phillips)   **$6,265**   **£3,500**

MARINI

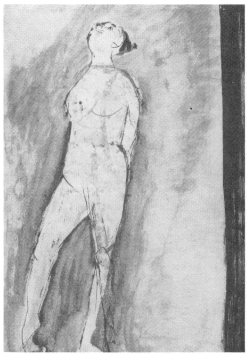

MARINO MARINI – Danzatrice – signed and
dated 1952 – gouache on paper – 24 x 16½in.
(Christie's)   **$28,160   £17,600**

MARINO MARINI – Trio policromo – signed
and dated 1954 – oil on canvas – 59 x 57¼in.
(Christie's)   **$283,360   £176,000**

MARINO MARINI – Cavallo rosso – signed with
initials – oil on canvas – 78¾ x 55in.
(Christie's)   **$354,200   £220,000**

MARINO MARINI – Portrait Of Prince Angelo
Lanza di Trabia – pencil on paper – 14 x 9½in.
(Christie's)   **$2,640   £1,650**

MARINO MARINI – Cavallo e Cavalier – signed
and dated 1950 – thinned oil, brush and black ink
on paper laid on canvas – 15½ x 11¾in.
(Christie's)   **$32,032   £17,600**

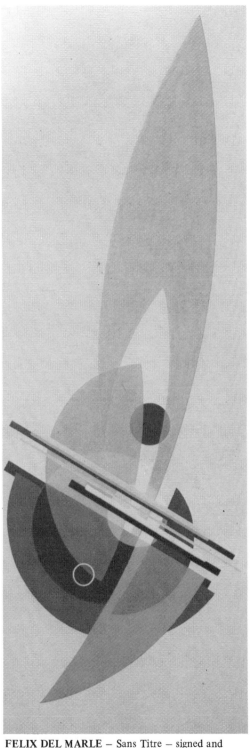

HENRY STACY MARKS – Storks – signed with
initials – pencil and watercolour – 29 x 20¼in.
(Christie's)   **$3,850   £2,200**

FELIX DEL MARLE – Sans Titre – signed and
dated '47 on the reverse – oil on panel – 61 x
22¾in.
(Christie's)   **$26,026   £14,300**

MARQUET

ALBERT MARQUET – Alger, Fleurs et Fruits –
signed – oil on panel – 13½ x 16¾in.
(Christie's)   **$46,046   £25,300**

ALBERT MARQUET – La Baie d'Alger – signed
– oil on canvas – 25½ x 32in.
(Christie's)   **$220,220   £121,000**

ALBERT MARQUET – Le Port – signed – oil on
canvas – 13¼ x 18¼in.
(Christie's)   **$70,070   £38,500**

THEODORE MARSDEN, Attributed to – Snipe
Shooting – oil on canvas – 17½ x 25in.
(Bruce D. Collins)   **$2,090   £1,180**

REGINALD MARSH – Chatham Square, Under
The El – signed and dated 1952 – tempera on
masonite – 19 x 24in.
(Christie's)   **$20,900   £11,676**

REGINALD MARSH – The Pennsylvania Railroad
– signed, dated 1927 and inscribed – watercolour
and pencil on paper – 13¾ x 19¾in.
(Christie's)   **$7,150   £3,994**

HENRI MARTIN – Vue de la Bastide-du-Vert,
Lot – signed – oil on canvas – 22½ x 39½in.
(Christie's) **$109,120** **£68,200**

REGINALD MARSH – On The Boardwalk – a
double-sided painting – recto – signed; verso –
signed and dated '51 – oil on board – 13½ x 9¾in.
(Christie's) **$5,500** **£3,392**

HENRI MARTIN – Le Loing a Moret – signed –
oil on canvas – 30¾ x 37¼in.
(Christie's) **$180,180** **£99,000**

REGINALD MARSH – Boardwalk Beauties –
signed – watercolour and brush and black ink on
paper – 21¼ x 14in.
(Christie's) **$8,800** **£5,428**

HENRI MARTIN – Portrait d'Homme barbu –
signed – oil on paper laid on canvas – 12¼ x 10in.
(Christie's) **$8,008** **£4,400**

MASON

ALICE TRUMBULL MASON – Forms Withdrawn
– signed, dated 1947 and inscribed on the reverse
– oil and casein on masonite – 33½ x 46¼in.
(Christie's)   **$22,000**   **£12,291**

FORTUNINO MATANIA – Going Swimming –
signed – 24 x 20in.
(Christie's)   **$2,904**   **£1,650**

ALEXANDRE CHARLES MASSON – Spring –
signed – 39½ x 22in.
(Christie's)   **$4,537**   **£2,750**

CAMILLE MATISSE – Vase de Chrysanthemes –
signed and inscribed – oil on canvas – 64 x 52cm.
(Phillips)   **$1,344**   **£800**

HENRI MATISSE – Bouquet De Fleurs – signed
and dated '44 – pen and ink – 52.5 x 40cm.
(Sotheby's) **$105,050 £55,000**

HENRI MATISSE – Nu rose – signed and dated
'36 – oil on canvas – 24¼ x 15¼in.
(Christie's) **$1,682,450 £1,045,000**

HENRI MATISSE – Jeune Fille debout – signed
and inscribed – pencil on paper – 12¼ x 9¼in.
(Christie's) **$35,200 £22,000**

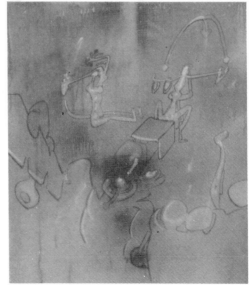

MATTA – Untitled – signed – oil on canvas – 30
x 25¼in.
(Christie's) **$10,692 £6,600**

MATTA – Untitled – signed on the reverse – oil on canvas – 65 x 72cm.
(Sotheby's) **$19,360 £11,000**

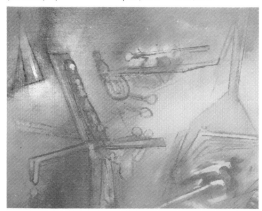

MATTA – Sans Titre – signed, and signed and dated '57 on the reverse – oil on canvas – 59 x 72cm.
(Sotheby's) **$27,456 £14,300**

ALFRED HENRY MAURER – Standing Nude – signed – gouache on gessoed board – 21¾ x 18in.
(Christie's) **$12,100 £7,413**

MAXIME MAUFRA – Barques de Peche sur la Greve – signed – oil on canvas – 17½ x 22in.
(Christie's) **$26,400 £16,500**

ANTON RUDOLF MAUVE – A Girl Cleaning A Copper Pan – signed with monogram – 36¼ x 26¼in.
(Christie's) **$7,356 £4,180**

PAUL MAZE – Sailing Boats In The Harbour, La Rochelle – signed twice – pastel – 16½ x 25in.
(Christie's) $2,741   £1,540

PAUL MAZE – Still Life With Vase Of Flowers And A Book – signed – brush and indian ink and watercolour – 55.5 x 65.5cm.
(Phillips) $1,320   £800

LAWRENCE MAZZANOVICH – Early Spring – oil on canvas – 30¼ x 30¼in.
(Christie's) $4,950   £2,765

ARTHUR JOSEPH MEADOWS – Bringing In The Fishing Boats, Off Dover Harbour – signed and dated 1875 – oil – 13½ x 23½in.
(Prudential Fine Art Auctioneers) $3,630   £2,200

ARTHUR JOSEPH MEADOWS – Figures Unloading Their Catch Before A Town In An Extensive Continental Lake Landscape – signed – on canvas – 16 x 24in.
(Phillips) $4,160   £2,600

JAMES MEADOWS, Snr. – Fishing Boat Off The Coast – signed and dated 1859 – oil on canvas – 23 x 41in.
(Phillips) $2,464   £1,400

LEWIS HENRY MEAKIN – Blue Shadows – signed – oil on canvas – 19¼ x 24in.
(Christie's) $9,900   £5,531

MEEGAN

WALTER MEEGAN – Cleopatra's Needle, Thames Embankment, By Moonlight – signed – on canvas – 16 x 24½in.
(Phillips) **$1,040** **£650**

JULIUS GARI MELCHERS – Hippodrome – signed – oil on canvas – 18 x 22in.
(Christie's) **$22,000** **£12,291**

XAVIER MELLERY – L'Ame des Choses; La Lecture sous la Lampe – signed with initials – soft pencil, grey wash, pen and ink on paper – 7¾ x 10in.
(Christie's) **$23,023** **£12,650**

CAMPBELL MELLON – Shottisham Village, Norfolk – signed, and indistinctly inscribed on the reverse – oil on board – 9 x 12in.
(Christie's) **$2,117** **£1,210**

ANDREW MELROSE – Mount Shasta, California – signed and dated '85 – oil on canvas – 29¼ x 47¾in.
(Christie's) **$15,400** **£9,435**

ANNA ELKAN MELTZER – Filing Her Nails – signed and dated '42 – oil on canvas – 43 x 35in.
(Christie's) **$1,650** **£1,017**

ARTHUR MELVILLE – The Verandah – signed
– watercolour – 34 x 52cm.
(Phillips) $5,310   £3,000

MARIE AUGUSTE EMILE RENE MENARD – A
Coastal Landscape With Cattle Resting – signed –
19¾ x 28¾in.
(Christie's) $907   £550

BERNARD MENINSKY – The Bathers – signed –
gouache and pencil – 15 x 22in.
(Christie's) $5,775   £3,300

ANNA ELKAN MELTZER – Duet – signed and
dated 1942 – oil on canvas – 69¾ x 38in.
(Christie's) $2,860   £1,764

ARTHUR MELTZER – Sleighing Weather –
signed and dated '30 – oil on canvas – 25 x 30¼in.
(Christie's) $7,700   £4,750

ARTHUR W. METCALF – A Fair Wind – signed –
watercolour – 10 x 16½in.
(Bruce D. Collins) $495   £279

WILLARD LEROY METCALF – Fiesole Gardens
– signed – oil on canvas – 29¼ x 26¼in.
(Christie's)   **$121,000   £74,136**

MICHELANGELO MEUCCI – Finches In Nests –
signed – on panel – 8½ x 7in.
(Christie's)   **$1,542   £935 Pair**

LORD METHUEN – Meconopsis Betonicifolia –
signed – oil on canvas – 28¾ x 20¼in.
(Christie's)   **$1,443   £825**

HERMANN MEYERHEIM – A Town On A River
With Figures – signed – 13¾ x 19in.
(Christie's)   **$5,808   £3,300**

JOHN MIDDLETON – Figure And Cattle Fording
A Stream Beside A Thatched Barn – signed and
indistinctly dated, and also bears a false signature
– oil on canvas – 10 x 18in.
(Phillips)   **$4,810   £2,600**

ABRAHAM MIGNON – A Still Life Of Assorted Flowers In A Glass Vase, Standing On A Stone Ledge – bears signature and date 1731 – on canvas – 24 x 18¾in.
(Phillips) $109,200 £60,000

JOHN MILES, of Northleach – A Prize Hog, The Property Of Mr. C. Gillett Beside A Sty – inscribed – oil on canvas – 45 x 56cm.
(Sotheby's) $28,380 £16,500

THOMAS ROSE MILES – Striving Hard To Reach The Wreck – signed, and also signed and inscribed on the reverse – on canvas – 22 x 34in.
(Phillips) $1,040 £650

SIR JOHN EVERETT MILLAIS – Study Of A Baby – signed with monogram and dated 1854 – pencil and watercolour – 5½ x 4½in.
(Christie's) $3,850 £2,200

LADY LUFTON AND THE DUKE OF OMNIUM.

SIR JOHN EVERETT MILLAIS – Lady Lufton And The Duke Of Omnium: An Illustration To Framley Parsonage – signed with monogram, inscribed and dated 1861 – pencil and watercolour – 9¾ x 6¾in.
(Christie's) $12,512 £7,150

MILLAIS

FRED MILLARD – Children Before A Cottage, Newlyn, One Carrying Water The Other Scrubbing The Steps – signed – oil on panel – 25 x 17½cm. *(W. H. Lane & Son)* **$2,310** **£1,400**

SIR JOHN EVERETT MILLAIS – Mrs. Gresham And Miss Dunstable: An Illustration To Framley Parsonage – signed with monogram, inscribed and dated 1861 – watercolour – 9¾ x 6¾in. *(Christie's)* **$12,512** **£7,150**

RAOUL MILLAIS – Horses In A Field – signed – oil on canvas – 20 x 24in. *(Christie's)* **$5,143** **£3,080**

WILLIE WATT MILNE – River Scene With Punt And Figures Picnicking On The River Bank Under Trees – signed – oil on canvas – 39 x 32in. – painted with same scene on reverse and complete with original charcoal sketch. *(Prudential Fine Art Auctioneers)* **$8,910** **£5,500**

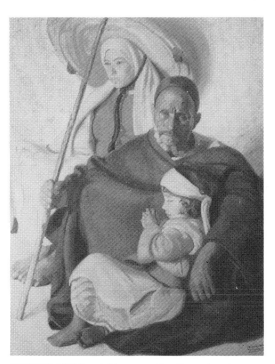

MINGORANCE – A Moroccan Family – signed
and dated 1933 – 50 x 39in.
(Christie's)   **$5,808   £3,520**

JOHN MINTON – Beach With Still Life On A
Table – signed – oil on canvas – 40 x 25in.
(Christie's)   **$7,048   £3,960**

R. T. MINSHULL – A Girl With Her Pet Rabbit –
signed – water colour – 23 x 17cm.
(Sotheby's)   **$1,155   £660**

JOAN MIRO – Composition – signed with initial
– oil on paper laid on canvas – 39¼ x 27½in.
(Christie's)   **$105,600   £66,000**

MIRO

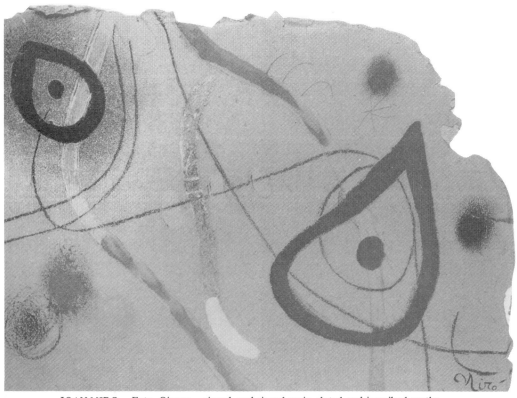

JOAN MIRO – Fete, Oiseau – signed, and signed again, dated and inscribed on the reverse – oil, black chalk and pencil on board – 14¼ x 20¼in. *(Christie's)*
$44,044 £24,200

JOAN MIRO – Deux Personnages; Etude pour 'L'Enfance d'Ubu' – signed – brush and black ink and coloured crayons on paper – 12¾ x 19¾in. *(Christie's)* $34,034 £18,700

JOAN MIRO – Personnages – signed and dated '34 on the reverse – black crayon and pastel on buff-coloured paper – 27 x 21cm.
(Sotheby's) $37,818 £19,800

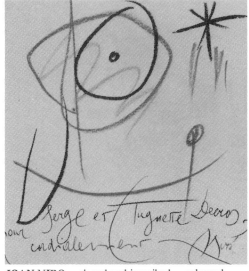

JOAN MIRO – signed and inscribed – coloured chalks on paper – 10½ x 10½in.
(Christie's) $4,804 £2,640

LOUIS CHARLES MOELLER – Your Move – signed – oil on canvas – 18 x 24in.
(Christie's) **$38,500 £21,509**

LOUIS CHARLES MOELLER – Chess Game – signed – oil on canvas – 18 x 24in.
(Christie's) **$6,875 £4,241**

MOELLER

LOUIS CHARLES MOELLER — A Good Joke — signed — oil on canvas — 18¼ x 24in.
(Christie's) **$9,900 £6,065**

JOHN HENRY MOLE — Breaking Up Of A Wreck On The Black Middens, Tynemouth — signed and dated, and also signed, inscribed and dated 1839 on a label on the reverse — on board — 10 x 14in.
(Phillips) **$800 £500**

JOHN HENRY MOLE — A Young Girl Seated By A Spring — signed and dated 1854 — watercolour heightened with white — 13¾ x 10¼in.
(Christie's) **$1,925 £1,100**

JOHN HENRY MOLE — Lobster Fishing, Salcombe — signed and dated 1872 — watercolour — 49 x 84cm.
(Phillips) **$5,664 £3,200**

THORVALD CHRISTIAN BENJAMIN MOLLER
– Fishing Boats And Other Shipping Off Shore –
signed and dated 1900 – 37¼ x 49in.
(Christie's)   **$2,170   £1,320**

PEDER MONSTED – The Ravello Coastline –
signed and dated 1926 – 15¾ x 24in.
(Christie's)   **$9,438   £5,720**

LORENZO MONACO – The Prophet Isaiah –
inscribed – tempera on panel – 19.5cm. diam.
(Sotheby's)   **$475,750   £275,000**

PIERRE EUGENE MONTEZIN – La Potiche
chinoise – signed – oil on panel – 21¾ x 18¼in.
(Christie's)   **$10,692   £6,600**

JOHN AUSTIN SANDS MONKS – Barn Interior
With Sheep – signed – oil on board – 6¾ x 8¾in.
(Robt. W. Skinner Inc.)   **$950   £575**

PIERRE EUGENE MONTEZIN – Le Bateau plat
– signed – oil on canvas – 23½ x 28¾in.
(Christie's)   **$38,038   £20,900**

EDWARD MORAN – Homeward Bound –
signed – oil on canvas – 15½ x 19½in.
(Christie's) $7,150 £4,380

HENRY MOORE – Seated Nude – signed and
dated '54 – pen and ink and wash and charcoal –
49 x 36cm.
(Sotheby's) **$21,010** **£11,000**

THOMAS MORAN – The Slave Hunt – signed –
oil on board – 7 x 9¼in.
(Christie's) **$6,600** **£4,071**

FRANCIS LUIS MORA – Mercedes – signed and
dated 1909 – oil on canvas – 30¼ x 25¼in.
(Christie's) **$15,400** **£9,435**

THOMAS MORAN – Rising Of The Moon –
signed with conjoined initials and dated 1906, and
signed and dated again and inscribed on the
reverse – oil on canvas – 30 x 40¼in.
(Christie's) **$52,800** **£29,499**

PAUL CHARLES CHOCARNE MOREAU – Le petit boulanger – signed – 15 x 21½in.
(Christie's) **$8,131 £4,620**

HENRI MORET – La Cote de Moelan – signed
and dated '96 – oil on canvas – 29 x 23¼in.
(Christie's) **$49,280 £30,800**

FREDERICK MORGAN – Playtime – signed –
oil on canvas – 76 x 48cm.
(Sotheby's) **$24,596 £14,300**

MORLEY

ROBERT MORLEY – The Playful Interlude –
signed – on canvas – 36 x 27¾in.
(Phillips) **$7,360** **£4,600**

WILLIAM W. MORRIS – The Church Lane –
signed and dated 1852 – on canvas – 44 x 35¾in.
(Phillips) **$3,840** **£2,400**

ANTONIO MORO – Portrait Of A Nobleman In
Armour – oil on canvas – 54 x 39.5cm.
(Sotheby's) **$38,060** **£22,000**

W. S. MORRISH – Near Rushford, Chagford –
signed, dated 1885 and inscribed on the reverse –
oil on panel – 17¾ x 11¾in.
(Christie's) **$2,388** **£1,430**

TOM MOSTYN – Bideford, North Devon – signed
– oil on canvas – 22 x 30in.
(Christie's) $10,103   £6,050

HENRY SIDDONS MOWBRAY – 'Fleur De
Luce' – signed – oil on canvas – 22 x 32in.
(Christie's) $33,000   £20,219

ROBERT EDWARD MORRISON – Joyce And
Monica, Daughters Of Jno. E. Shaw Esq, J. P. –
signed and dated 1905, and signed and inscribed on
a label on the stretcher – oil on canvas – 132 x
104cm.
(Sotheby's)   **$17,974**   **£10,450**

OSWALD MOSER – A Man In A Fur Coat –
signed and inscribed on a label on the backboard –
on board – 36 x 36in.
(Phillips)   **$1,520**   **£950**

**ANNA MARY ROBERTSON ('GRANDMA')
MOSES** – Pennsylvania – signed – oil and glitter
on canvasboard – 8 x 10in.
(Christie's)   **$7,150**   **£4,410**

ALPHONSE MUCHA – Spring – signed and dated
'99 – 33½ x 21½in.
(Christie's) $48,114   £29,700

MUELLER

ALEXANDER MUELLER – Eastern Souvenir – signed and dated '98 – oil on canvas – 29¼ x 10¼in.
(Christie's)   **$8,250**   **£5,054**

OTTO MUELLER – Waldstuck mit Stein und Gebusch – signed with initials, also signed on reverse – 43½ x 30¼in.
(Christie's)   **$100,100**   **£55,000**

DAVID MUIRHEAD – The Glade – signed – oil on canvas – 14 x 20in.
(Christie's)   **$1,347**   **£770**

FREDERICK JOHN MULHAUPT – Children At A Rocky Coast – signed – oil on canvas – 8¼ x 10in.
(Christie's)   **$7,700**   **£4,717**

CLAUDE MUNCASTER – Fishing Boats At Lisbon – signed – oil on canvas – 56 x 76.5cm.
(Phillips)   **$1,320**   **£800**

ALFRED J. MUNNING – 'Study Of Hyperion, Newmarket' – watercolour – 20 x 36½cm.
(W. H. Lane & Son)   **$5,115**   **£3,100**

SIR ALFRED MUNNINGS – The Ford; Two Greys And A Chestnut Drinking – signed and dated 1911 – oil on canvas – 20 x 24in.
(Christie's)   **$82,665**   **£49,500**

SIR ALFRED MUNNINGS – A Sow And Her Piglets – oil on canvas – 25 x 30in.
(Christie's)   **$137,775**   **£82,500**

SIR ALFRED MUNNINGS – Happy Wroxham – signed and dated 1903 – pencil and watercolour heightened with white – 24 x 34.5cm.
(Phillips)   **$15,215**   **£8,500**

SIR ALFRED J. MUNNINGS – Study Of Violet, Duchess Of Westminster, 2nd Wife Of The 2nd Duke, In Hunting Costume – signed – oil on panel – 13¼ x 9¾in.
(Christie's)   **$11,022**   **£6,600**

GABRIELE MUNTER – Dalien und Rosen – signed, and signed with monogram and dated – gouache, watercolour and pencil on paper – 20¾ x 16½in.
(Christie's)   **$26,026**   **£14,300**

MUNTHE

GERHARD PETER FRANTZ VILHELM
MUNTHE – A Settlement Beside A Fjord –
signed and dated 1913 – oil on canvas – 51 x
69cm.
(Phillips) **$1,980** **£1,100**

WALTER MURCH – Directions – gouache and
pencil on paper – 9¼ x 11¾in.
(Christie's) **$2,530** **£1,560**

WALTER MURCH – American Dream –
watercolour and pencil on paper – 3¼ x 3¼in.;
and Time And Tide – oil and pencil on paper –
9½ x 13½in.
(Christie's) **$2,640** **£1,617 Pair**

JOHN FRANCIS MURPHY – Autumn – signed
and dated '90 – oil on canvas – 18¼ x 30¼in.
(Christie's) **$6,600** **£4,071**

SCOTT MYLES – 'Butterflies' – on canvas – 18½
x 13in.
(Phillips) **$1,936** **£1,100**

CARLOS NADAL – Le Dejeuner – signed, and
inscribed, dated 1961 and signed again on the
reverse – oil on canvas – 23½ x 28½in.
(Christie's) **$9,801** **£6,050**

CARLOS NADAL – Concert a Paris – signed and dated '77, and inscribed, signed and dated on the reverse – oil on canvas – 23¾ x 28¾in.
(Christie's)   **$9,801**   **£6,050**

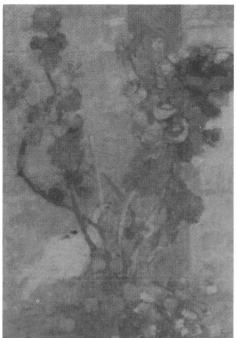

JOHN NAPPER – Duck And Geraniums – signed – oil on canvas – 44 x 34in.
(Christie's)   **$3,306**   **£1,980**

FRANK A. NANKIVELL – Laughing Boy – oil on canvas – 14¼ x 9½in.
(Christie's)   **$1,980**   **£1,221**

FILIPPO NAPOLETANO, Attributed to – Orpheus And Euridice – on canvas – 27 x 41½in.
(Phillips)   **$12,740**   **£7,000**

JOHN NASH – The Weir – signed – oil on canvas – 30 x 22in.
(Christie's)   **$6,429**   **£3,850**

NASH

JOHN NASH – The Moat, Grange Farm, Great Kimble – signed, inscribed and dated 1922 – watercolour, crayon and pencil – squared for transfer – 23 x 17in.
(Christie's)   **$1,653**   **£990**

JOHN NASH – Trees On The Edge Of A Wood – signed and dated 1918 – oil on canvas – 31½ x 24in.
(Christie's)   **$2,571**   **£1,540**

JOHN NASH – Boxted Mill Pool, Essex – signed – oil on canvas – 26 x 33¼in.
(Christie's)   **$10,769**   **£6,050**

PAUL NASH – Landscape Study – signed – pen and ink and pencil – 11¾ x 15¾in.
(Christie's)   **$962**   **£550**

HEINRICH NAUEN – Park In Dilborn – signed and dated '21 – oil on canvas – 27¾ x 27¾in.
(Christie's)   **$18,018**   **£9,900**

PHILIP NAVIASKY — A Mountain Lake — signed — oil on board — 19¼ x 23½in.
(Christie's) $577 £330

NEAPOLITAN SCHOOL, late 19th century — A Beach In The Bay Of Naples, Looking Towards Capri — signed indistinctly — oil on panel — 20 x 33cm.
(Phillips) $1,440 £800

PHILIP NAVIASKY — Seated Lady — signed — oil on panel — 29½ x 23½in.
(Christie's) $979 £550

AERT VAN DER NEER — A Village Landscape In Winter With Skaters — oil on canvas — 35.5 x 43cm.
(Sotheby's) $133,210 £77,000

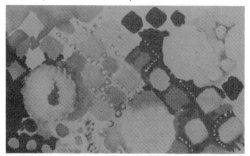

ERNST WILHELM NAY — Untitled — signed and dated '55 — gouache and watercolour on paper — 15¼ x 21½in.
(Christie's) $23,166 £14,300

HERMANIA SIGVARDINE NEERGAARD — Roses And Other Flowers In A Vase — signed and dated 1835 — 20 x 16in.
(Christie's) $11,583 £7,150

NEIMAN

E. J. NEIMAN – Extensive Yorkshire Landscape, With Bridge Crossing A River, Church And Cottages – oil on canvas – 24 x 41in.
(Prudential Fine Art Auctioneers)   **$3,696**   **£2,200**

ALFRED ARTHUR BRUNEL DE NEUVILLE – Kittens At Play – signed – 15 x 18in.
(Christie's)   **$7,260**   **£4,400**

CHRISTOPHER RICHARD WYNNE NEVINSON – Verey Lights – signed and dated 1918 – oil on canvas – 15½ x 19½in.
(Christie's)   **$31,328**   **£17,600**

CHRISTOPHER RICHARD WYNNE NEVINSON – Summer – signed and inscribed on a label on the stretcher – oil on canvas – 24 x 20in.
(Christie's)   **$15,664**   **£8,800**

CHRISTOPHER RICHARD WYNNE NEVINSON – Hampton Court – signed – oil on canvas – 61.5 x 46cm.
(Phillips)   **$33,115**   **£18,500**

BEN NICHOLSON – Painting (Version I) 1937 –
oil on board – 10¾ x 8¾in.
(Christie's) **$80,080** **£44,000**

NEWLYN SCHOOL – Full Length Nude Portrait
Of Phyllis (Pog) Iglesias, A Rear View Posing At
The Art Class With Students At Easels In The
Background – oil on canvas – 77 x 51cm.
(W. H. Lane & Son) **$1,650** **£1,000**

DALE NICHOLS – A Fisherman And His Dog –
signed and dated 1944 – oil on canvas – 30 x
22¼in.
(Christie's) **$5,500** **£3,369**

BEN NICHOLSON – Still-Life–St. Ives – signed
and dated 1930 – oil and pencil on canvas – 8¼ x
6¼in.
(Christie's) **$38,720** **£24,200**

NICHOLSON

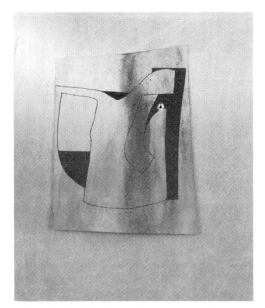

BEN NICHOLSON — Green And Black, April 1978 — signed, inscribed and dated '78 on the reverse — mixed media on paper — 12¾ x 11in.
(Christie's) **$9,609** **£5,280**

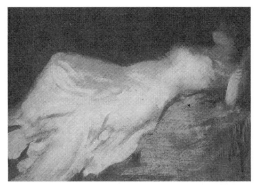

SIR WILLIAM NICHOLSON — Annie — inscribed and dated 1934 — oil on canvas — 15½ x 19½in.
(Christie's) **$19,580** **£11,000**

WINIFRED NICHOLSON — Sea Holly — recto; and Narcissi — verso — signed and dated 1970 — oil on board — 24¼ x 24¼in.
(Christie's) **$7,748** **£4,640**

G. W. NICHOLSON — An Arab Gateway — signed — oil on canvas — 32 x 23cm.
(Sotheby's) **$1,017** **£550**

REINHOLDT NIELSEN — Deer Watering In Dyrehaven — signed — 30½ x 36in.
(Christie's) **$1,452** **£880**

PAUL NIETSCHE – A View From Castlewellan – signed and dated '39 – oil on board – 27½ x 31½in.
(Christie's)   **$2,310**   **£1,320**

NOEL LAURA NISBET – The Dressing Of The Bride – signed – watercolour and pencil – 27 x 40in.
(Christie's)   **$5,005**   **£2,860**

BONSAI LOKI·NIKKO – View Of Mount Fujiyama – signed – watercolour over pencil – 61.5 x 97.5cm.
(Sotheby's)   **$915**   **£495**

THORVALD SIMEON NISS – Winter In Dyrehaven – signed and dated 1883 – 17¾ x 22¼in.
(Christie's)   **$1,839**   **£1,045**

HENRY NINHAM – South Porch Of St. Michael At Plea; and North Porch Of St. Peter Mancroft – watercolour – 9 x 6in.
(Messrs. G. A. Key)   **$637**   **£350 Pair**

JOHN NIXON – A Group Of Musicians – signed – pen and black ink and grey and brown wash – 18 x 13cm.
(Sotheby's)   **$539**   **£308**

NOELSMITH

T. NOELSMITH – Country Cottages – signed –
watercolour heightened with bodycolour – 35.5 x
25.5 cm.
(Sotheby's)   **$1,540**   **£880 Pair**

GIUSEPPE NOGARI – Portrait Of A Bearded
Man With Turban – on canvas – 20¾ x 17 in.
(Phillips)   **$9,100**   **£5,000**

GIUSEPPE NOGARI – Portrait Of A Young Man
With Fur Hat – on canvas – 20¾ x 17 in.
(Phillips)   **$9,100**   **£5,000**

EMIL NOLDE – Zwei Krieger – signed –
watercolour and pen and black ink on Japan
paper – 7¾ x 5¾ in.
(Christie's)   **$32,032**   **£17,600**

EMIL NOLDE – Weisse Paonien und blaue Bluten – signed – watercolour on Japan paper – 13¾ x 18¼in.
(Christie's) $100,100   £55,000

EMIL NOLDE – Blumengarten K (Weisse Lilien) – signed, signed and inscribed on the stretcher – oil on canvas – 28¾ x 34¾in.
(Christie's) $600,600   £330,000

BROR JULIUS OLSSON NORDFELDT – Man Under Portico – signed – oil on canvas – 32 x 29in.
(Christie's) $28,600   £17,523

BROR JULIUS OLSSON NORDFELDT – Eagle Dance – signed – oil on canvas – 29 x 36in. *(Christie's)*
$26,400 £16,175

NORDFELDT

BROR JULIUS OLSSON NORDFELDT – The Rooster – signed and dated '42 – oil on canvas – 32¼ x 40in.
(Christie's) $3,850   £2,358

BROR JULIUS OLSSON NORDFELDT – New Mexico Landscape – signed – oil on canvas – 26 x 32¼in.
(Christie's) $20,900   £11,676

BROR JULIUS OLSSON NORDFELDT – Indian Woman Pouring Grain – signed – oil on canvas – 29 x 35¾in. *(Christie's)* $16,500   £9,218

ELIZABETH NOURSE – 'Chapelle de St. Jean, Plougastel, Brittany' – signed – watercolour and gouache on paper – 19 x 24¾in.
(Robt. W. Skinner Inc.) **$3,100** **£1,731**

GEORGE LOFTUS NOYES – Summer Scene With Haystacks – signed – oil on canvas – 24 x 25in.
(Robt. W. Skinner Inc.) **$10,000** **£6,060**

GEORGE LOFTUS NOYES – The Valley In Autumn – signed – oil on board – 13¼ x 14¾in.
(Robt. W. Skinner Inc.) **$4,500** **£2,727**

STEFANO NOVO – The Vegetable Seller – signed and dated '89 – on panel – 18½ x 10in.
(Christie's) **$3,267** **£1,980**

GEORGE LOFTUS NOYES – 'Under du Palms At Biskra Algeria' – signed and dated 1892 – oil on canvas – 29½ x 24in.
(Robt. W. Skinner Inc.) **$5,000** **£2,793**

OCTAVIUS OAKLEY – The Fisherman And His Boy – watercolour over pencil heightened with bodycolour and scratching out – 44.5 x 31cm.
(Sotheby's)   **$1,058**   **£605**

RODERIC O'CONOR – Femme assise aux Fleurs – oil on canvas – 22 x 18in.
(Christie's)   **$22,044**   **£13,200**

RODERIC O'CONOR – A Breton Girl – signed and dated '31 – oil on card laid down on canvas – 13¾ x 12½in.
(Christie's)   **$6,657**   **£3,740**

RODERIC O'CONOR – La Femme au Gilet rouge – signed, and signed again and inscribed – oil on canvas – 36¼ x 25¾in.
(Christie's)   **$8,817**   **£5,280**

HUGO OEHMICHEN – Going Shopping – signed
– 25½ x 16¾in.
(Christie's) **$13,365** **£8,250**

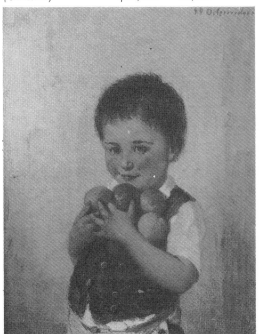

HUGO OEHMICHEN – Stolen Apples – signed –
on panel – 10¾ x 8¼in.
(Christie's) **$9,801** **£6,050**

JOHANNES ADAM SIMON OERTEL – Dash For
Safety – signed – oil on canvas – 18¼ x 30in.
(Christie's) **$20,900** **£11,676**

TOSCA OLINSKY – 'Young Girl' – signed – oil
on masonite – 15¾ x 11¾in.
(Robt. W. Skinner Inc.) **$250** **£151**

JULIUS OLSSON – Yacht Off A Cornish Headland
– signed, and inscribed on the reverse – oil on
canvas – 24 x 30in.
(Christie's) **$2,117** **£1,210**

O'NEILL

GEORGE BERNARD O'NEILL – The Young Virtuoso – signed and dated '96 – oil on
canvas – 51 x 61 cm. *(Sotheby's)* **$28,380 £16,500**

GEORGE BERNARD O'NEILL – Under The
Mistletoe – signed – oil on canvas – 46 x 35.5 cm.
(Sotheby's) **$12,865 £7,480**

JACQUES VAN OOST, The Elder – Portrait Of
Louis Bacchuys; and Portrait Of Marie Bacchuys –
on canvas – 30¼ x 22 in.
(Phillips) **$7,644 £4,200 Pair**

ERNST OPPLER – A Beach Scene, Haakenborg –
signed – on panel – 9¼ x 13in.
(Christie's) **$5,033** **£2,860**

SIR WILLIAM ORPEN – The Artist's Model,
Yvonne – signed and dated '17 – oil on canvas –
29¼ x 24¼in.
(Christie's) **$33,066** **£19,800**

SIR WILLIAM ORPEN – Portrait Of Lady Evelyn
Herbert, Half Length – signed and inscribed – oil
on canvas – 30 x 25in.
(Christie's) **$91,850** **£55,000**

ABEL ORRY – Ladies Reading In An Interior –
signed and dated 1872 – unframed – 39 x 51½in.
(Christie's) **$13,365** **£8,250**

FRANCOIS AUGUSTE ORTMANS – A Wooded
River Landscape With A Shepherd Driving Sheep
Across A Bridge – signed and dated 1850 – on
panel – 13¼ x 16¾in.
(Christie's) **$5,033** **£2,860**

ERWIN DOM O-SEN – Bergdorf (Im Tauerntal) –
signed – oil on canvas – 27½ x 27½in.
(Christie's) **$8,008** **£4,400**

ADRIAEN VAN OSTADE – A Man And A Woman
Drinking At A Table – signed – oil on panel –
36.5 x 23cm.
(Sotheby's) **$108,471 £62,700**

ADRIAEN VAN OSTADE, Follower of – A Man
Leaning Over The Door Of A House – indistinctly
signed – oil on panel – 30 x 22cm.
(Sotheby's) **$12,369 £7,150**

EDMUND HENRY OSTHAUS – On The Scent – signed – watercolour on paper laid down
on board – 18¾ x 27in. *(Christie's)* **$7,150 £3,994**

JEAN-BAPTISTE OUDRY – A Spaniel Chasing
Wild Ducks – signed and dated 1749 – oil on
canvas – 92.5 x 152cm.
(Sotheby's)   **$361,570   £209,000**

JEAN-BAPTISTE OUDRY – A Hound And A
Goldfinch – signed and dated 1746 – oil on
canvas – 82.5 x 103.5cm.
(Sotheby's)   **$266,420   £154,000**

M. OSUNA – Washerwomen; and A Horseman In
A Wooded Landscape – signed and dated 1913 –
16 x 12in.
(Christie's)   **$1,996   £1,210 Pair**

PIERRE OUTIN – The Dream – signed –
unframed – 26 x 36½in.
(Christie's)   **$9,801   £6,050**

JEAN-BAPTISTE OUDRY – An Allegory Of
Europe; and An Allegory Of Asia – signed and
dated 1722 – oil on canvas – 162 x 152cm.
(Sotheby's)   **$723,140   £418,000 Two**

ROBERT EMMETT OWEN – The Old Mill –
signed – oil on canvas – 36¼ x 46¼in.
(Christie's)   **$10,450   £5,838**

PACE

MICHELANGELO PACE, Called I1 Campidoglio – A Still Life Of Fruit And An Urn – oil on canvas – 85.5 x 65 cm.
(Sotheby's)   **$34,254**   **£19,800**

PAUL PAESCHKE – Stilleben, Lilien in einer Vase – signed – oil on board – 21¼ x 17¾in.
(Christie's)   **$12,012**   **£6,600**

JULES EUGENE PAGES – Trees Near Douarnenez – signed – oil on canvas – 21¼ x 25¾in.
(Christie's)   **$7,700**   **£4,717**

JULES EUGENE PAGES – Chezy-On-The-Marne Near Chateau Thierry – signed and inscribed – oil on canvas – 19¾ x 24in.
(Christie's)   **$9,900**   **£6,065**

MIMMO PALADINO – Velenoso – signed and dated 1982 on the reverse – oil on paper mounted on canvas – 27½ x 19¾in.
(Christie's)   **$12,474**   **£7,700**

WALTER LAUNT PALMER – Winter Sunset –
signed – oil on canvas – 14¼ x 20¼in.
(Christie's)   **$12,100**   **£6,760**

JOHN ANTHONY PARK – 'The Island Walk'–St.
Ives – signed – oil on board – 32 x 40cm.
(W. H. Lane & Son)   **$957**   **£580**

PROFESSOR EDUARDO PAOLOZZI – Study
For A Sculpture – signed and dated '49 – pen,
ink, brown and grey wash – 14½ x 17½in. •
(Christie's)   **$2,204**   **£1,320**

JOHN ANTHONY PARK – The Harbour, St.
Ives – signed – oil on board – 41 x 51cm.
(Phillips)   **$5,248**   **£3,200**

ROGER PARENT – Les Fleurs jaunes – signed
and dated 1916, also signed and dated on the
reverse – oil on canvas – 31¾ x 28¾in.
(Christie's)   **$3,203**   **£1,760**

JOHN ANTHONY PARK – A Street, St. Ives,
Cornwall – signed, and inscribed on the reverse –
oil on panel – 11 x 15¾in.
(Christie's)   **$1,540**   **£880**

PARRISH

BEATRICE PARSONS – 'The Little Fountain, Drakelowe' – signed and inscribed – watercolour heightened with white – 26 x 38cm.
(Phillips)   **$4,956**   **£2,800**

MAXFIELD PARRISH – April Showers – signed with initials and inscribed, and signed and dated 1908 – oil on paper laid down on paper – 22¼ x 16¼in.
(Christie's)   **$11,000**   **£6,785**

BEATRICE PARSONS – Cherry Blossom – signed – watercolour over pencil – 32 x 25cm.
(Phillips)   **$2,566**   **£1,450**

BEATRICE PARSONS – The Blue Of The Border, The Blue Of The Sea – signed – watercolour – 39.5 x 29cm.
(Phillips)   **$2,655**   **£1,500**

JULES PASCIN – Jeune Femme assise – oil and charcoal on canvas – 19 x 19in.
(Christie's)   **$40,040**   **£22,000**

F. G. PASMORE, Jnr. — 'Pause For Thought' — signed — on canvas — 11 x 9½in.
(Phillips)   **$1,372**   **£780**

BORIS PASTOUKHOFF — Les Toits — signed, inscribed and dated 1942 — oil on canvas — 55 x 46cm.
(Phillips)   **$2,016**   **£1,200**

BORIS PASTOUKHOFF — Portrait de Clark Gable — signed, inscribed and dated 1952 — oil on canvas — 81 x 59.5cm.
(Phillips)   **$4,368**   **£2,600**

BORIS PASTOUKHOFF — Portrait d'une Femme assise — signed, inscribed and dated 1937 — oil on canvas — 92 x 73cm.
(Phillips)   **$3,192**   **£1,900**

PASTOUKHOFF

BORIS PASTOUKHOFF – Jeune Femme allongee
– signed, inscribed and dated 1952 – oil on canvas
– 60 x 73cm.
(Phillips) $1,176 £700

KAROLY PATKO – Hungarian Landscape –
signed – oil on board – 31½ x 40in.
(Christie's) $13,899 £8,580

BORIS PASTOUKHOFF – Le Studio de l'Artiste
– signed and dated 1944 – oil on canvas – 46 x
55cm.
(Phillips) $840 £500

FRANK PATON – Hares On A Stubble Field –
signed and dated 1901 – watercolour heightened
with white – 19 x 25.5cm.
(Sotheby's) $1,636 £935

BORIS PASTOUKHOFF – Nature morte aux
Bouteilles – signed and dated 1961 – oil on canvas
– 81 x 99.5cm.
(Phillips) $1,092 £650

AMBROSE PATTERSON – La Bretonne – signed
and dated '09, and also signed and inscribed on the
reverse – oil on panel – 35 x 26.5cm.
(Phillips) $2,148 £1,200

ERNST PAUL – Waldlandschaft – signed – oil
on canvas – 29½ x 25¼in.
(Christie's) $7,007   £3,850

WILLIAM MacGREGOR PAXTON – Interior Of
The Paris Studio – oil on panel – 13¾ x 10in.
(Christie's) $16,500   £10,109

ETHEL PAXSON – 'Mary Wearing A Black Cape'
– signed and dated 1928 – oil on board – 22 x
18in.
(Robt. W. Skinner Inc.) $400   £242

MERVYN PEAKE – Clown And Acrobat –
charcoal, pen, black ink and pencil – 10 x 8in.
(Christie's) $1,443   £825

PEAKE

MERVYN PEAKE – Girl's Head – signed – chinese brush and grey wash – 10¼ x 8¾in.
(Christie's) **$1,093** **£625**

MERVYN PEAKE – Study Of A Girl – chinese brush, grey wash and pencil – 12 x 9½in.
(Christie's) **$962** **£550**

MERVYN PEAKE – La Creme de la Creme – watercolour, bodycolour, brush, black ink and pencil – 10 x 7in.
(Christie's) **$1,347** **£770**

MERVYN PEAKE – Nude – brown chalk – 14½ x 8in.
(Christie's) **$481** **£275**

MERVYN PEAKE – Creature With Thatch-Like Hair – black crayon and pencil – 10½ x 7¼in. *(Christie's)* **$2,502** **£1,430**

MERVYN PEAKE – Profile Of A Girl With Fair Hair – green crayon – 11 x 8in. *(Christie's)* **$1,443** **£825**

MERVYN PEAKE – Child Asleep – pencil – 10 x 13½in. *(Christie's)* **$1,886 £1,078**

PEAKE

MERVYN PEAKE – Study Of A Woman's Head – brush, black ink, grey wash, pencil, white and black chalk on blue paper – 11¾ x 9in.
(Christie's)   **$1,732**   **£990**

MERVYN PEAKE – Drawing, Edgware Road – signed – watercolour, bodycolour, pen, brush, black ink, grey wash and pencil, heightened with white – 10 x 6½in.
(Christie's)   **$1,347**   **£770**

MERVYN PEAKE – The Picture Book – black crayon – 9 x 8in.
(Christie's)   **$1,540**   **£880**

MERVYN PEAKE – Girl's Head – pencil – 9¼ x 7¾in.
(Christie's)   **$1,771**   **£1,012**

REMBRANDT PEALE – George Washington –
signed – oil on canvas – 36¼ x 29¼in.
(Christie's) **$55,000 £33,698**

REMBRANDT PEALE – Niagara Falls Viewed
From The American Side – oil on canvas – 18¼ x
24 in.
(Christie's) **$19,800 £12,131**

TITIAN RAMSAY PEALE – American Bison
Bull – watercolour on paper – 6 x 8¼in.
(Christie's) **$35,200 £21,567**

CHARLES SPRAGUE PEARCE – The Path To
The River – signed and inscribed – oil on canvas
– 29 x 23¾in.
(Christie's) **$35,200 £19,666**

MARGUERITE S. PEARSON – Daffodils And
Narcissus – signed – oil on board – 24 x 20in.
(Bruce D. Collins) **$1,100 £621**

PEARSON

MARGUERITE S. PEARSON – Young Woman With Beaded Necklace – signed – oil on canvas – 40 x 36in.
(Bruce D. Collins) **$9,350** **£5,282**

MAX PECHSTEIN – Familie Monderosso – signed on the reverse – coloured crayons, brush and black ink on paper – 23¼ x 17¼in.
(Christie's) **$8,800** **£5,500**

MAX PECHSTEIN – Fischer am Quai – signed, dated '08 and inscribed – watercolour on brown card – 13¾ x 17in.
(Christie's) **$36,036** **£19,800**

MAX PECHSTEIN – Apfel II – signed with initials and dated 1928, also signed and inscribed on the reverse – oil on panel – 12½ x 16¼in.
(Christie's) **$17,017** **£9,350**

MAX PECHSTEIN – Kurenkahre, Nidden – signed and dated 1920 – watercolour on paper – 20¾ x 28¼in.
(Christie's) **$32,032** **£17,600**

F. AUGUSTINE PECKHAM – Portrait Of A Gentleman – signed – oil on canvas – 20 x 16in.
(Bruce D. Collins) $55   £31

CARL HENNING PEDERSEN – Red Familie – signed and dated 1978-9 on the reverse – 82 x 61.7cm.
(Sotheby's) $14,784   £7,700

CARL HENNING PEDERSEN – On The Black Sea – signed with initials and dated 1978 – watercolour on paper – 21¾ x 30¼in.
(Christie's) $5,346   £3,300

P. PEDERZOLI – Refreshment For The Evening – signed – oil on canvas – 56 x 40cm.
(Phillips) $1,530   £850

JAMES PEEL – 'The Furze Gatherers, Ellerby, Yorks' – signed with monogram – on canvas – 19½ x 29½in.
(Phillips) $4,224   £2,400

PEETERS

CLARA PEETERS – A Still Life Of Fish,
Vegetables And Kitchen Utensils – signed – oil on
panel – 35.5 x 51cm.
(Sotheby's) $49,478   £28,600

A. R. PENCK – Portrait Of Jutta (Woman Holding
Skull) – oil on fabric – 59¼ x 59¼in.
(Christie's) $8,008   £4,400

WILLIAM C. PENN – Delphiniums In A Vase –
signed – oil on canvas – unframed – 27¼ x 21½in.
(Christie's) $3,306   £1,980

WILLIAM C. PENN – Chrysanthemums In A Jug
By A Window – signed – oil on canvas –
unframed – 30 x 25¼in.
(Christie's) $3,306   £1,980

WILLIAM CHARLES PENN – Summertime –
with signature and date – oil on panel – 12½ x
9½in.
(Christie's) $1,409   £792

SIDNEY RICHARD PERCY — Evening—A Drover
Watering Cattle At A River, A Stone Bridge And
Hills Beyond — signed and dated 1873 — on canvas
— 24 x 38in.
(Phillips)   **$17,600   £11,000**

GRANVILLE PERKINS — Japanese Footbridge
— signed — watercolour — 13½ x 17½in.
(Bruce D. Collins)   **$3,850   £2,175**

JANE PETERSON — Pansies — signed — oil on
canvas — 24 x 18in.
(Christie's)   **$3,850   £2,375**

SOPHUS PETERSEN — Grapes On A Vine —
signed and dated 1884, and signed on an old label
on the reverse — 15 x 15½in.
(Christie's)   **$4,356   £2,640**

JANE PETERSON — Spring Still Life — signed —
oil on canvas — 22¼ x 18¼in.
(Christie's)   **$4,620   £2,581**

PETERSON

JANE PETERSON – Brittany Village – signed –
oil on canvas – 24 x 30¼in.
(Christie's)   **$11,000   £6,145**

EUGENE PETITJEAN – Le Port des Pecheurs –
signed – oil on board – 14½ x 23¼in.
(Christie's)   **$4,455   £2,750**

JANE PETERSON – 'Zinnias And Purple Vase' –
signed – oil on canvas – 18 x 24in.
(Robt. W. Skinner Inc.)   **$4,000   £2,424**

EDMOND PETITJEAN – A Village On The Banks
Of A River – signed – 18¾ x 26¼in.
(Christie's)   **$16,929   £10,450**

EDMOND PETITJEAN – Lavandieres au Bord de
la Riviere – signed – oil on canvas – 25¾ x 32in.
(Christie's)   **$14,256   £8,800**

JANE PETERSON – Vase Of Zinnias And
Marigolds – signed – oil on canvas – 23¾ x 23¾in.
(Robt. W. Skinner Inc.)   **$4,000   £2,234**

HIPPOLYTE PETITJEAN – Les Vagues –
watercolour – 19.5 x 35cm.
(Sotheby's)   **$15,967   £8,360**

HIPPOLYTE PETITJEAN — Paysage — oil on canvasboard — 10½ x 16in.
(Christie's) $4,004   £2,200

HIPPOLYTE PETITJEAN — La Ferme — signed — oil on canvas laid down — 33 x 41cm.
(Phillips) $3,360   £2,000

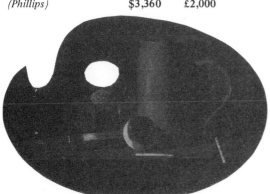

JOHN FREDERICK PETO — The Artist's Table — oil on panel — 6¼ x 9¼in.
(Christie's) $18,700   £10,447

MAXIMILIAN PFEILER — A Still Life Of Flowers Trailing Across A Glass Bowl Standing Beside A Pewter Plate With Fruit, In A Landscape — on canvas — 26¾ x 34¾in.
(Phillips) $13,650   £7,500

ROBERT PHILIPP — Summertime — signed — oil on canvas — 30 x 25in.
(Christie's) $20,900   £12,893

PAUL DOMINIQUE PHILIPPOTEAUX — At The Water's Edge — signed and dated 1896 — 28¼ x 21in.
(Christie's) $21,384   £13,200

PHILLIPS

WALTER JOSEPH PHILLIPS – River Landscape
– signed and dated '92 – watercolour – 11½ x
9in.
(Sotheby's) $814   £440

GLYN PHILPOT – Study Of A Negro – signed
with initials – oil on canvas – 28¼ x 23in.
(Christie's) $31,328   £17,600

GLYN PHILPOT – The Black Madonna – oil on
canvas – 55¼ x 43½in.
(Christie's) $70,488   £39,600

GLYN PHILPOT – Portrait Of Martyn Coleman –
signed with initials – oil on canvas – 109 x 74cm.
(Phillips) $60,680   £37,000

FRANCIS PICABIA – L'Eglise de Montigny –
Soleil de Septembre – signed and dated 1905, and
signed again on the reverse, and inscribed and
dated – oil on canvas – 36¼ x 29in.
(Christie's) $80,080 £44,000

FRANCIS PICABIA – Oliviers au Bord de
l'Etang de Berre – signed, dated 1907 and
inscribed – oil on canvas – 10½ x 13¾in.
(Christie's) $21,120 £13,200

FRANCIS PICABIA – Machaon – signed and
inscribed – watercolour, pen and ink on paper in a
red box frame with butterflies – 15 x 17¾in.
(Christie's) $44,000 £27,500

FRANCIS PICABIA – Craccae – signed – oil on
canvas – 45¾ x 35in.
(Christie's) $132,000 £82,500

FRANCIS PICABIA – Bord de Riviere – signed
and dated 1908 – oil on canvas – 21½ x 25¾in.
(Christie's) $59,840 £37,400

PICASSO

PABLO PICASSO – Tete d'Homme – dated on the reverse 31.7.71 – oil on canvas – 39¼ x 31¾in.
(Christie's) **$495,880   £308,000**

PABLO PICASSO – L'Escritoire – signed on the reverse – oil on canvas – 14¾ x 17¾in.
(Christie's) **$850,080   £528,000**

PABLO PICASSO – Tete d'Homme II – dated '64 – oil on canvas – 36¼ x 25½in.
(Christie's) **$400,400   £220,000**

PABLO PICASSO – Courses de Taureaux – with signature – pen and ink and coloured crayons on paper – 5¼ x 3½in.
(Christie's) **$31,680   £19,800**

PABLO PICASSO – Buste de Femme a l'Oiseau –
dated 1971 – oil on canvas – 39¼ x 31¾in.
(Christie's) **$280,280   £154,000**

PABLO PICASSO – Dejeuner sur l'Herbe – signed,
dated on the reverse '60 – oil on canvas – 23¾ x
28¾in.
(Christie's) **$500,500   £275,000**

PABLO PICASSO – 'Oedipe' – signed and dated
'26 – pen and brush and indian ink and wash – 38
x 29cm.
(Sotheby's) **$52,525   £27,500**

PABLO PICASSO – Femme En Costume Catalan
– charcoal – 14.7 x 9.8cm.
(Sotheby's) **$19,959   £10,450**

PICASSO —

PABLO PICASSO, After — Nature morte —
inscribed — hand-woven wool tapestry — 53½ x
60½in.
(Christie's) $8,910 £5,500

PABLO PICASSO — La Femme au Viole —
signed and dated '29 — oil on canvas — 15¾ x
10¼in.
(Christie's) $850,080 £528,000

PABLO PICASSO — La Nourrice et le Troupier —
signed — pastel and charcoal on paper — 18¼ x
15¼in.
(Christie's) $109,120 £68,200

M. S. PICKETT — Portrait Of Tennyson's 'Maude'
— signed and dated 1894 — watercolour — 27½ x
18½in.
*(Prudential Fine Art
Auctioneers)* $1,036 £640

WALDO PIERCE – Bouquet – conjoined initials
– oil on canvas – 24 x 20in.
(Bruce D. Collins) **$2,970** **£1,677**

FILIPPO DE PISIS – Ritratto di un Uomo –
signed – oil on panel – 49 x 34cm.; verso –•
Portrait Of A Girl.
(Phillips) **$8,400** **£5,000**

JOHN PIPER – The Bishops Palace, Saint David's
Cathedral, Pembrokeshire – signed – watercolour,
gouache, brown, black ink and soft pencil – 24 x
31¼in.
(Christie's) **$6,613** **£3,960**

OTTO PIPPEL – Unter den Linden, Berlin –
signed and dated 1920 – oil on canvas – 37 x
38¾in.
(Christie's) **$38,038** **£20,900**

CAMILLE PISSARRO – Laveuse – signed,
dated 1875 and inscribed – oil on canvas – 21¼
x 17¾in.
(Christie's) **$247,940** **£154,000**

PISSARRO

CAMILLE PISSARRO – Etude de Soleil couchant, Pontoise – signed and dated '77 – oil on canvas – 15¼ x 22in.
(Christie's) **$170,170 £93,500**

CAMILLE PISSARRO – Village dans la Vallee – pencil on paper – 8¼ x 10½in.
(Christie's) **$19,360 £12,100**

CAMILLE PISSARRO – Figure assise (Lucien) – oil on canvas – 25½ x 21¼in.
(Christie's) **$123,970 £77,000**

CAMILLE PISSARRO – L'Apres-Midi, Soleil, Avant-Port de Dieppe – signed and dated 1902 – oil on canvas – 26 x 32in.
(Christie's) **$920,920 £506,000**

CAMILLE PISSARRO – Portail de l'Eglise Saint-Jacques a Dieppe – signed and dated 1901 – oil on canvas – 30¼ x 26in.
(Christie's) **$800,800 £440,000**

CAMILLE PISSARRO – Le Pont Neuf et le
Statue de Henri IV – signed and dated 1901 –
oil on canvas – 18¼ x 21¼in.
(Christie's)   **$495,880   £308,000**

LUCIEN PISSARRO – The Stour At Stratford
Saint Mary – signed with monogram and dated
1934 – oil on canvas – 18½ x 21¾in.
(Christie's)   **$47,762   £28,600**

LUCIEN PISSARRO – Brookleton Dale,
Youlgrave, Derbyshire – oil on canvas – 10 x 8in.
(Christie's)   **$6,265   £3,520**

PISSARRO

LUCIEN PISSARRO – The Thames, Richmond –
signed with monogram, dated 1935 and inscribed
– oil on canvas – 55 x 65 cm.
(Phillips)   **$80,550   £45,000**

LUCIEN PISSARRO – Youlgrave, Derbyshire –
oil on canvasboard – 13¾ x 10in.
(Christie's)   **$9,398   £5,280**

LUCIEN PISSARRO – La Frette, The Seine –
signed with monogram and dated 1924 – pencil,
crayon and watercolour – 6¼ x 8in.
(Christie's)   **$4,425   £2,640**

LUCIEN PISSARRO – Village sur la Cote, An Old
Street Bormes les Mimosa – signed with monogram
and dated 1927, signed, and again inscribed and
dated on the reverse – oil on canvas – 18 x 15in.
(Christie's)   **$22,044   £13,200**

LUCIEN PISSARRO – The Glen, Kew Gardens –
signed with monogram, inscribed and dated 1920
– pen and ink, crayon and watercolour – 6¾ x
9½in.
(Christie's)   **$4,776   £2,860**

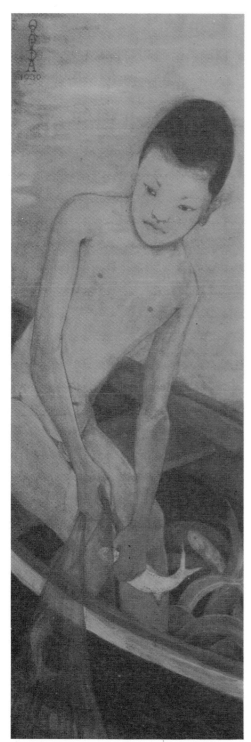

MICHELANGELO PISTOLETTO – Infirmiere et
Jeune Fille – signed and inscribed on the reverse –
oil on polished steel – 90½ x 47¼in.
(Christie's)   **$21,384**   **£13,200**

OROVIDA PISSARRO – The Young Fisherman
– signed and dated 1930 – tempera on linen –
121.5 x 36.5cm.
(Phillips)   **$6,802**   **£3,800**

ROLAND VIVIAN PITCHFORTH – Extensive
Landscape – signed – pastel – 19½ x 28½in.
(Christie's)   **$924**   **£528**

N

PLANSON

ANDRE PLANSON – Vue de l'Atelier, La Ferte-
sur-Marne – signed and dated '68 – oil on board –
23¾ x 28¾in.
(Christie's)   **$8,019**   **£4,950**

OGDEN MINTON PLEISSNER – Mountain
Landscape – signed – oil on canvas – 24¼ x
30¼in.
(Christie's)   **$8,800**   **£4,916**

OGDEN MINTON PLEISSNER – Church In The
Algarve – signed – watercolour and pencil on
paper – 19¾ x 28½in.
(Christie's)   **$14,300**   **£8,761**

W. PLUMMER – River Scene – signed –
watercolour – 9½ x 20in.
(Bruce D. Collins)   **$77**   **£43**

OGDEN MINTON PLEISSNER – St. Anne des Montes, Gaspe – signed – water colour on
paper – 16 x 22¾in. *(Christie's)*   **$13,200 £7,374**

WILLIAM PLUMMER – Leaping Trout – signed –
oil on board – 20 x 16in.
(Bruce D. Collins)   **$357**   **£201**

SERGE POLIAKOFF – Composition bleu et verte
– signed – gouache on paper – 24¾ x 18¾in.
(Christie's)   **$21,021**   **£11,550**

SERGE POLIAKOFF – Composition Abstraite
aux traits – signed – oil on canvas – 36¼ x 28¾in.
(Christie's)   **$40,040**   **£22,000**

SERGE POLIAKOFF – Jaune et noir sur fond
rouge fonce – signed – oil on canvas – 51¾ x
38¼in.
(Christie's)   **$160,380**   **£99,000**

POLIAKOFF

ALFRED POLLENTINE – A View Of The Grand Canal, Venice – signed – on canvas – 30 x 50in.
(Phillips) **$3,840** **£2,400**

SERGE POLIAKOFF – Composition – signed – oil on board – 130 x 96.5cm.
(Sotheby's) **$65,472** **£34,100**

ALFRED POLLENTINE – The Ducal Palace, Venice – signed, and also signed and inscribed on the reverse – on canvas – 20 x 30in.
(Phillips) **$1,280** **£800**

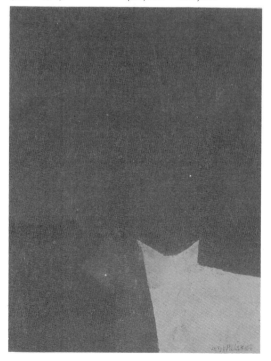

SERGE POLIAKOFF – Composition – signed – oil on canvas – 81 x 66cm.
(Sotheby's) **$81,312** **£46,200**

PAUL FALCONER POOLE, Attributed to – A Young Country Lass – bears indistinct monogram and dated 1832 – on canvas – 11¼ x 8½in.
(Phillips) **$640** **£400**

FAIRFIELD PORTER – Trees In Bloom – signed and dated '68, and signed again, dated and inscribed on the reverse – oil on canvas – 20 x 18in.
(Christie's)   **$13,200   £7,374**

FAIRFIELD PORTER – Girl And Geranium – signed and dated '63, and signed again and inscribed on the reverse – oil on canvas – 45 x 30in.
(Christie's)   **$66,000   £36,874**

FAIRFIELD PORTER – Horsechestnut Tree – signed and dated '68, and signed again, dated and inscribed on the reverse – oil on masonite – 18 x 14in.
(Christie's)   **$28,600   £15,978**

FAIRFIELD PORTER – Horsechestnut – signed and dated '63 – oil on canvas – 24¼ x 22in.
(Christie's)   **$28,600   £15,978**

PORTER

FREDERICK PORTER – Study Of A Seated
Lady – signed – oil on canvas – 24¼ x 21in.
(Christie's)   **$2,545   £1,430**

EDWARD PORTIELJE – Happy Tidings – signed
– oil on panel – 46 x 37cm.
(Phillips)   **$5,760   £3,200**

EDWARD PORTIELJE – Portrait Of A Young
Girl, Bust Length, Wearing A Bonnet – signed
twice – oil on panel – 24 x 19cm.
(Phillips)   **$1,620   £900**

LASLETT JOHN POTT – Awaiting An Answer –
signed and dated '94 – on canvas – 44¼ x 34in.
(Phillips)   **$7,680   £4,800**

EDWARD HENRY POTTHAST – Beach Scene –
signed – coloured pencil and watercolour on paper
– 4¾ x 5¾in.
(Christie's)   **$9,900   £6,065**

EDWARD HENRY POTTHAST – Long Beach –
signed, signed and inscribed on an old label
attached to the reverse – oil on board – 11¾ x
16in.
(Christie's)   **$71,500   £43,808**

JOHN POWELL – Bayonet Practice Range –
signed – oil on canvas – 24 x 26in.
(Christie's)   **$770   £440**

VALENTINE PRAX – Nature morte cubiste –
signed and dated 1932 – oil on canvas – 44½ x
38¼in.
(Christie's)   **$8,019   £4,950**

MAURICE BRAZIL PRENDERGAST –
Promenade – signed – watercolour and pencil on
paper – 13¼ x 10¾in.
(Christie's)   **$82,500   £50,547**

PRENDERGAST

MAURICE BRAZIL PRENDERGAST – Still Life With Apples And A Bowl – oil on panel – 8¼ x 13¾in.
(Christie's)   **$55,000**   **£30,728**

GREGORIO PRESTOPINO – Backyard Politics – signed, and signed again and inscribed on the reverse – oil on masonite – 30¼ x 25¾in.
(Christie's)   **$13,200**   **£8,087**

EMILIE PREYER – Grapes, Peaches, Plums And Nuts On A Draped Table – signed – 8¼ x 11in.
(Christie's)   **$21,384**   **£13,200**

ALOIS PRIECHENFRIED – A Rabbi Smoking A Pipe – signed – on panel – 12½ x 10in.
(Christie's)   **$1,633**   **£990**

BERTRAM PRIESTMAN – Crossing The Pyke – signed with initials and dated '09 – oil on canvas – 12¼ x 16in.
(Christie's)   **$1,347**   **£770**

BERTRAM PRIESTMAN – The Ferry – indistinctly signed and dated? – oil on panel – 11 x 15in.
(Christie's)   **$1,386**   **£792**

BERTRAM PRIESTRAM – Ducks On The Pond –
signed and dated '97 – oil on canvas – 15 x 16¼in.
(Christie's) $5,143 £3,080

CARL PROBST – Bygone Days – signed and
dated 1899 – on panel – 18½ x 25in.
(Christie's) $4,537 £2,750

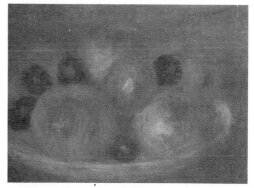

G. THOMPSON PRITCHARD – The Arrival Of
The Sultan – signed – oil on canvas – 75 x 86cm.
(Sotheby's) $3,663 £1,980

DOD PROCTER – Still Life With Apples And
Plums – signed – oil on board – 19 x 27cm.
(Phillips) $4,654 £2,600

CARL PROBST – The Courtship – signed and
dated 1879 – on panel – 21 x 27in.
(Christie's) $12,584 £7,150

DOD PROCTER – A Rocky Coastline – oil on
canvas – 41 x 35.5cm.
(Phillips) $1,476 £900

PROCTER

DOD PROCTER – A Mixed Bunch – signed – oil
on canvas – 51 x 44cm.
(Phillips) **$15,215** **£8,500**

ERNEST PROCTER – The Garden – signed – oil
on canvas – 51 x 61cm.
(Phillips) **$3,580** **£2,000**

ERNEST PROCTER – Summer Holidays – signed
and dated '34 – oil on canvas – 99.9 x 190.5cm.
(Phillips) **$41,000** **£25,000**

ERNEST PROCTER – Brent Knoll, Somerset –
signed and inscribed on the reverse – oil on board
– 22 x 48in.
(Christie's) **$6,429** **£3,850**

MARGARET FISHER PROUT – The Novel –
signed and dated 1937 – oil on board – 78.5 x
88cm.
(Phillips) **$3,135** **£1,900**

PROVENCAL SCHOOL, circa 1450/60 –
Portrait Of A Gentleman – oil on panel – 39.5 x
27.5cm.
(Sotheby's) **$199,815** **£115,500**

ALFRED PROVIS – 'Pet-Rabbits' – signed and dated 1862, and inscribed on old label on the reverse – on panel – 10½ x 15½in.
(Phillips)   **$4,576**   **£2,600**

ALFRED PROVIS – 'Old Abbey Dairy' – signed indistinctly and dated 1861 – on canvas – 11 x 16in.
(Phillips)   **$6,160**   **£3,500**

ALFRED PROVIS – The Reading Lesson – signed – on panel – 10¼ x 13¾in.
(Phillips)   **$3,520**   **£2,000**

CLIFTON ERNEST PUGH – Portrait Of Miriam Karlin – recto – signed and dated '74 – watercolour and bodycolour – 77 x 56cm.; A Portrait Sketch – verso.
(Sotheby's)   **$915**   **£495**

FERNAND DU PUIGAUDEAU – Venise, le Palais du Doge – signed – oil on panel – 12½ x 16¼in.
(Christie's)   **$20,020**   **£11,000**

HOVSEP PUSHMAN – Ten Thousand Yesterdays Are Gathered Here – signed – oil on panel – 17¼ x 23½in.
(Christie's)   **$22,000**   **£12,291**

QUIGNON

FERNAND JUST QUIGNON – Le quai a Pont Aven; Maree Basse – signed – 46 x 71in.
(Christie's) **$5,033** **£2,860**

FRANZ RADZIWILL – Gelbe Hausecke – signed and dated 1934 – watercolour, pen and ink heightened with white on brown paper – 8¾ x 14¼in.
(Christie's) **$7,607** **£4,180**

H. J. QUINTIN – Governor, A Prize Hereford Bull In A Landscape – signed, dated 1848 and inscribed, and inscribed on the reverse – oil on canvas – 61.5 x 75.5cm.
(Sotheby's) **$7,568** **£4,400**

FRANZ RADZIWILL – Im Lande der Deutschen – signed – oil on canvas – 36¼ x 41¼in.
(Christie's) **$54,054** **£29,700**

HENRIETTA RAE – A Bacchante – signed and dated 1885 – oil on canvas – 127 x 63.5cm.
(Sotheby's) **$10,406** **£6,050**

JEAN FRANCOIS RAFFAELLI – Fleurs dans
un Vase – signed – oil on board laid on cradled
panel – 28¼ x 25½in.
(Christie's) $4,204   £2,310

THEODORE JACQUES RALLI – Ah! Jalouse
Entre Les Jalouses! . . . , Victor Hugo – signed –
28½ x 19½in.
(Christie's) $26,730   £16,500

ALEXANDRE RALLI – Le Chevalier – signed and
dated '05 – oil on canvas – 61 x 46.5cm.
(Phillips) $1,680   £1,000

MARY F. RAPHAEL – Britomart And Amoret –
signed and dated '98 – oil on canvas – 185.5 x
119.5cm.
(Sotheby's) $14,190   £8,250

RATCLIFFE

WILLIAM RATCLIFFE – River Town; and
Country Town – watercolour pen and ink – 14 x
18in. and 12 x 14in.
(Christie's) $2,939 £1,760 Two

THOMAS RATHNELL – The Family – signed –
oil on canvas-board – 36 x 48in.
(Christie's) $1,469 £880

MAN RAY – Daffodils – signed – oil on canvas –
24 x 14¼in.
(Christie's) $14,300 £7,989

ABRAHAM RATTNER – Rome, Composition –
signed, and signed again and inscribed on the
reverse – oil on canvas – 39½ x 35¼in.
(Christie's) $12,100 £6,760

LOUISE RAYNER – The Old Town Gate, Rye –
signed, and inscribed on the artist's label attached
to the reverse – watercolour and bodycolour – 9¾
x 14in.
(Christie's) $13,475 £7,700

JOSEPH REBELL – Naples With Capri Beyond –
29¼ x 44½in.
(Christie's)   **$115,830   £71,500**

EDWARD WILLIS REDFIELD – Monhegan
Harbour – signed – oil on canvas – 26¼ x
32¼in.
(Christie's)   **$26,400   £16,175**

ODILON REDON – Le Vase bleu – signed –
watercolour and pencil on paper – 8 x 6in.
(Christie's)   **$34,034   £18,700**

EDWARD WILLIS REDFIELD – A Country Lane
– signed – 32 x 40in.
(Christie's)   **$82,500   £46,092**

ODILON REDON – Decoration – signed – oil
on canvas – 40 x 30¼in.
(Christie's)   **$84,084   £46,200**

REID

ROBERT REID – Autumn – signed and signed again – 32 x 27in.
(Christie's) $60,500   £33,801

ROBERT REID – Ruth – oil on canvas – 20¼ x 16in.
(Christie's) $6,600   £4,043

ROBERT REID – Colorado Springs – signed – oil on canvas – 24 x 34in.
(Christie's) $14,300   £8,761

ROBERT REID – Lady In Pink – signed – oil and charcoal on canvas – 36¼ x 24in.
(Christie's) $4,400   £2,458

ROBERT REID – River Rapids, Springtime – signed – oil on canvas – 26¾ x 30½in.
(Christie's) $93,500   £57,287

FREDERIC SACKRIDER REMINGTON – A
Manchurian Bandit – signed – oil en grisaille on
canvas – 30 x 20¼in.
(Christie's)   **$37,400   £20,895**

PIERRE AUGUSTE RENOIR – La jeune
Paysanne revenant du Marche – signed with
initial – oil on canvas – 8¾ x 6¾in.
(Christie's)   **$29,920   £18,700**

GUIDO RENI – Fortune With A Crown – oil on
canvas – 164 x 131.5 cm.
(Sotheby's)   **$913,440   £528,000**

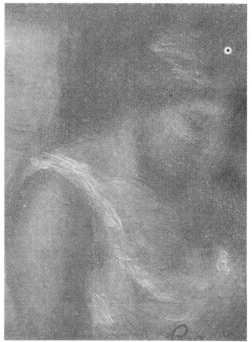

PIERRE-AUGUSTE RENOIR – Buste de jeune
Femme – oil on canvas – 6¾ x 5¼in.
(Christie's)   **$130,130   £71,500**

RENOIR

PIERRE AUGUSTE RENOIR – Portrait d'Henry
Bernstein – signed and dated 1910 – oil on
canvas – 31½ x 25 in.
(Christie's)   **$160,160   £88,000**

PIERRE AUGUSTE RENOIR – La Couseuse –
signed – oil on canvas – 15 x 11 in.
(Christie's)   **$389,620   £242,000**

PIERRE AUGUSTE RENOIR – Coco a l'Eventail
Japonais – signed – oil on canvas – 19¾ x 15¾ in.
(Christie's)   **$760,760   £418,000**

PIERRE AUGUSTE RENOIR – Femme nue
assise se massant le pied – signed – oil on canvas
– 13¾ x 12¾ in.
(Christie's)   **$237,600   £148,500**

PIERRE AUGUSTE RENOIR – Fleurs dans un
Vase bleu et blanc – oil on canvas – 13¾ x
11¾in.
(Christie's) $340,340   £187,000

PIERRE AUGUSTE RENOIR – Buste de Jeune
Fille – signed with initial – oil on canvas – 9¾ x
6¾in.
(Christie's) $149,600   £93,500

PIERRE AUGUSTE RENOIR – Femme en Bleu
en Chapeau assise sur l'Herbe – signed – oil on
canvas – 18½ x 22in.
(Christie's) $566,720   £352,000

ERNEST RENOUX – Auto Portrait – signed and
inscribed – oil on canvas – 56 x 46.5cm.
(Phillips) $470   £280

RENOUX

JULES ERNEST RENOUX – Le Pont Louis-
Philippe en 1927 – signed and inscribed on the
reverse – oil on canvas – 18¼ x 21¾in.
(Christie's) **$1,247** **£770**

AUGUST VON RENTZELL – Plucking The Bird
– signed and dated 1888 – oil on panel – 23 x
17cm.
(Phillips) **$1,260** **£700**

ALAN REYNOLDS – Dying Hyacinth – signed,
inscribed and dated '54, and signed, inscribed and
dated again on the reverse – brown wash,
bodycolour pen and ink – 15 x 11in.
(Christie's) **$1,010** **£605**

SIR JOSHUA REYNOLDS – Portrait Of Sarah
Ottway With Her Daughter – oil on canvas – 142
x 111cm.
(Sotheby's) **$52,976** **£30,800**

PIERRE RIBERA – A Geisha Girl – signed – oil
on board – 44 x 36cm.
(Sotheby's) **$915** **£495**

PIERRE RIBERA – Peking – recto – signed – oil on canvas – 33 x 39cm.; A Ball – verso.
(Sotheby's) **$1,933** **£1,045**

WILLIAM TROST RICHARDS – On The Coast Of Cornwall – signed – oil on canvas – 10¼ x 20in.
(Christie's) **$8,800** **£4,916**

CERI RICHARDS – Blossoms – signed with initials and dated '65 – oil on canvas – 10 x 10in.
(Christie's) **$2,388** **£1,430**

WILLIAM TROST RICHARDS – Day At The Beach – signed – watercolour on paper laid down on board – 8¾ x 14¼in.
(Christie's) **$10,450** **£5,838**

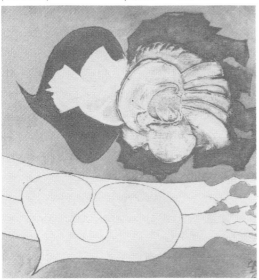

CERI RICHARDS – Abstract Composition – signed with initials and dated '65 – oil on canvas – 25.5 x 25.5cm.
(Phillips) **$2,970** **£1,800**

WILLIAM TROST RICHARDS – At Atlantic City – signed and dated 1877 – oil on canvas – 24¼ x 20¼in.
(Christie's) **$143,000** **£87,616**

RICHARDSON

CHARLES HENRY RICHERT – Landscape –
signed – oil on canvasboard – 13¾ x 17¾in.
(Robt. W. Skinner Inc.) **$475** **£287**

THOMAS MILES RICHARDSON, Jnr. – Figures
On A Road Below Fort Leon, Sicily – signed and
dated 1879, and inscribed on the artist's label –
pencil, pen and brown ink and watercolour
heightened with white – 30¾ x 25¼in.
(Christie's) **$9,625** **£5,500**

CHARLES HENRY RICHERT – Lobster Gear –
signed – watercolour – 10 x 14in.
(Bruce D. Collins) **$231** **£130**

CHARLES HENRY RICHERT – Springtime Brook
– signed – watercolour – 11 x 13in.
(Bruce D. Collins) **$467** **£263**

GERHARD RICHTER – Korsika I – signed and
dated '68 on the reverse – oil on canvas – 34¼ x
35¾in.
(Christie's) **$121,176** **£74,800**

GERHARD RICHTER – Garten – signed and dated 1982 on the reverse – oil on joined canvas – 102½ x 78¾in.
(Christie's) $80,190   £49,500

HERBERT DAVIS RICHTER – Archway, Page Street, With The Construction Of Cleland House Beyond – signed – oil on canvas laid down on panel – 57 x 78in.
(Christie's) $5,482   £3,080

ROBERT RICHTER – After The Bacchanal – signed and dated 1898 – 47½ x 71in.
(Christie's) $9,075   £5,500

RIEDL

G. A. RIEDL – A Swag Of Roses And
Chrysanthemums – signed and dated 1859 – 28¼
x 22½in.
(Christie's)   **$12,474**   **£7,700**

JEAN-PAUL RIOPELLE – Untitled – signed and
dated '60 – oil on canvas – 25½ x 32in.
(Christie's)   **$37,422**   **£23,100**

JEAN-PAUL RIOPELLE – Untitled – signed and
dated '60 – oil on canvas – 21 x 25½in.
(Christie's)   **$35,640**   **£22,000**

JEAN-PAUL RIOPELLE – Vallee de l'oiseau No.
4 – signed and dated '54, and also signed and
inscribed on the reverse – oil on canvas – 76¾ x
37½in.
(Christie's)   **$164,164**   **£90,200**

ALDEN S. LASSELL RIPLEY – Skating On A
Woodland Pond – signed and dated 1935 –
watercolour on paper – 18¾ x 25in.
(Robt. W. Skinner Inc.)   **$2,000**   **£1,117**

PAUL ROBERT – Portrait Of A Lady In A White
Silk Dress And Black Hat – signed and dated 1901
– 28¾ x 23½in.
(Christie's)   **$1,936**   **£1,100**

DAVID ROBERTS – Antwerp Cathedral – signed
and dated 1845 – watercolour over pencil – 35 x
25cm.
(Phillips)   **$6,018**   **£3,400**

DAVID ROBERTS – La Bourse – signed and
dated 1830 – pen and ink and watercolour – 31 x
23cm.
(Phillips)   **$1,770**   **£1,000**

LANCELOT ROBERTS – The Pink Dress –
signed – pastel – 24 x 18in.
(Christie's)   **$7,348**   **£4,400**

441

ROBERTS

WILLIAM ROBERTS – The Bicycle Lesson –
signed – oil on canvas – 24 x 20in.
(Christie's) $16,533   £9,900

WILLIAM ROBERTS – Moving Day – signed and
dated '68 – oil on canvas – 30 x 24in.
(Christie's) $11,748   £6,600

WILLIAM ROBERTS – Mediterranean Folk – signed – oil on canvas – 12¾ x 16½in.
(Christie's) $16,643   £9,350

ANNA MARY ROBERTSON 'Grandma Moses' – Over The River To Grandma's – signed, and dated 1944 and inscribed on the artist's label attached to the reverse – oil on masonite – 14¼ x 28¼in. *(Christie's)* **$46,200 £25,811**

ANNA MARY ROBERTSON 'Grandma Moses' – Come On Old Topsy – signed, and inscribed and dated 1948 on the artist's label attached to the reverse – oil on masonite – 16 x 20in. *(Christie's)* **$28,600 £15,978**

THEODORE ROBINSON – Girl Raking Hay – signed – oil on canvas – 18¾ x 15½in. *(Christie's)* **$374,000 £229,149**

FREDERICK CAYLEY ROBINSON – A Long Story – signed and dated 1907 – oil on card – 8 x 10in. *(Christie's)* **$2,887 £1,650**

THEODORE ROBINSON – Garden At Giverny – signed – oil on canvas – 18¼ x 21¾in. *(Christie's)* **$330,000 £184,371**

ROBSON

FORSTER ROBSON – Nymphs In Woodland –
signed – oil on canvas – 27½ x 41½in.
(Christie's) **$1,347** **£770**

HUGO ROBUS – Dancing Figure – signed –
pencil on cream paper – 12 x 9¾in.
(Christie's) **$3,300** **£2,035**

NORMAN ROCKWELL – Oil Sketch For 'Give Me
A Boy' – signed and inscribed – oil and pencil on
paper – 14½ x 9¼in.
(Christie's) **$3,300** **£1,843**

ERNEST ROCHER – Roses In A Vase With Fruit
In A Porcelain Basket – signed – 23 x 23in.
(Christie's) **$2,722** **£1,650**

NORMAN ROCKWELL – Going To Church –
signed and inscribed – oil on board – 16¼ x
15¼in.
(Christie's) **$6,050** **£3,706**

NORMAN ROCKWELL – The Auto Repair man (Want To Know Why I Use It?) – signed – oil en grisaille on canvas – 11¾ x 17in. *(Christie's)*   **$8,800 £4,916**

NORMAN ROCKWELL – Give Me A Boy – 29 x 22½in.
(Christie's)   **$38,500 £21,509**

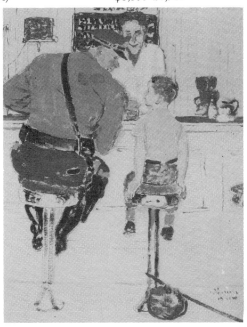

NORMAN ROCKWELL – The Runaway – signed – gouache, crayon and pencil on board – 11½ x 10½in.
(Christie's)   **$10,450 £6,402**

ROCKWELL

NORMAN ROCKWELL – Bread And Jelly –
signed – oil on canvas – 13¾ x 30¼in.
(Christie's) $33,000   £20,219

WILLEM ROELOFS – An Extensive Landscape
With A Sportsman Shooting Duck By A Windmill
– signed – 17½ x 27¾in.
(Christie's) $21,384   £13,200

NORMAN ROCKWELL – Portrait Studio – signed
and inscribed – pencil on board – 12¾ x 11¾in.
(Christie's) $6,600   £4,043

LUDOVIC RODO-PISSARRO – Marble Arch –
signed, inscribed and dated '08 – watercolour and
pencil – 23 x 31cm.
(Phillips) $638   £380

SEVERIN ROESEN – Still Life With Fruit –
signed – oil on canvas in a painted oval – 24 x
20¾in.
(Christie's) $8,800   £5,428

SEVERIN ROESEN – Flowers Of All Seasons – signed and dated 1859 – oil on canvas – 27¼ x 34¼in.
(Christie's)   **$115,500**   **£64,529**

SEVERIN ROESEN, Shop of – Still Life With Flowers – oil on canvas in a painted oval – 24 x 20¾in.
(Christie's)   **$7,150**   **£4,410**

ENRIQUE ROLDAN – An Interior With An Arab Smoking A Pipe – signed – on panel – 19½ x 12in.
(Christie's)   **$7,356**   **£4,180**

GRETCHEN W. ROGERS – Lady In White – signed – pastel on canvas – 30 x 25in.
(Christie's)   **$4,400**   **£2,695**

THOMAS MATHEWS ROOKE – The Vineyard – watercolour heightened with bodycolour – 71 x 51cm.
(Sotheby's)   **$2,310**   **£1,320**

ROSA

HERVE DI ROSA – Sad Vacation – signed and dated '83 – acrylic on unstretched canvas – 73 x 54½in.
(Christie's) $1,801   £990

CHARLES ROSEN – Hanging Branch – oil on canvas – 30¼ x 40¼in.
(Christie's) $16,500   £10,178

RICHARD ROSENBAUM – Royal Post Coaching Scene – signed – watercolour on paper – 21 x 29½in.
(Robt. W. Skinner Inc.) $600   £335

GIULIO ROSATI – The Gift – signed, inscribed and dated 1892 – oil on canvas – 20 x 14in.
(Robt. W. Skinner Inc.) $5,500   £3,072

LEONARD ROSOMAN – No. 7 The Land And The Sea – signed, and inscribed on the reverse – acrylic on canvas – 72 x 72in.
(Christie's) $2,117   £1,210

PERCIVAL LEONARD ROSSEAU – Pointers –
signed – oil on canvas – 10 x 14in.
(Christie's) **$4,950** **£2,765**

PERCIVAL LEONARD ROSSEAU – Irish Setters
– signed and dated 1910 – oil on canvas – 14 x
18in.
(Christie's) **$6,600** **£3,687**

PAUL ROSSERT – Elegant Figures On A Beach –
signed – on panel – 10½ x 15½in.
(Christie's) **$23,595** **£14,300**

ALEXANDER M. ROSSI – The Quarrel – on
canvas – 53 x 76in.
(Phillips) **$4,928** **£2,800**

MOZART ROTTMANN – A Young Jew Reading
– signed – 19¾ x 15¾in.
(Christie's) **$4,646** **£2,640**

GEORGES ROUAULT – Les Deux Amis –
inscribed on the reverse – oil on canvas – 25¾ x
18½in.
(Christie's) **$318,780** **£198,000**

ROUAULT

THOMAS ROWLANDSON – 'The Old Ewe Dressed Lamb Fashion' – signed and indistinctly inscribed – wash over pencil and pen and ink – 22.5 x 17.5cm.
(Phillips)   **$3,186**   **£1,800**

GEORGES ROUAULT – La Femme a la Fleur rouge (Buste) – signed and dated 1925 – oil and mixed media on paper laid on canvas – 26¼ x 19½in.
(Christie's)   **$440,440**   **£242,000**

CHARLES ROWBOTHAM – Positano-Coast Of Amalfi; and Porlezza-Lago Lugano – signed and dated 1901 – watercolour and bodycolour over pencil with scratching out – 21 x 41cm.
(Phillips)   **$2,389**   **£1,350 Pair**

FREDERICK VAN ROYEN – Still Life With Peaches, Grapes And A Glass On A Velvet Cloth – bears a false signature – on canvas laid down on board – 15 x 12½in.
(Phillips)   **$13,650**   **£7,500**

STANLEY ROYLE – The Cottage Garden, Winter – signed and inscribed – oil on canvas – 19½ x 23½in.
(Christie's)   **$7,440**   **£4,180**

JOHN PETER RUSSELL – Belle Ile, Brittany – inscribed, and again on the reverse – oil on canvas – 38.5 x 46cm.
(Sotheby's)   **$27,472**   **£14,850**

SIR WALTER WESTLEY RUSSELL – An Audience – oil on canvas – 20 x 24in.
(Christie's)   **$3,916**   **£2,200**

MARK RUBOVICS – An Elegant Beauty – signed – 12 x 8½in.
(Christie's)   **$1,548**   **£880**

JOHN PETER RUSSELL – Goulphar, Belle Ile, Brittany – signed and dated '03, and inscribed on the reverse – watercolour – 30 x 47cm.
(Sotheby's)   **$13,024**   **£7,040**

RUSSIAN SCHOOL, early 20th century – Portrait Of A Young Girl With Flowers – signed indistinctly – oil on canvas – 24 x 20in.
(Prudential Fine Art Auctioneers)   **$851**   **£460**

RUTHERFORD

HENRY RUTHERFORD – An English Country Market – signed – oil on canvas – 61 x 76cm.
(Phillips) $3,280   £2,000

J. R. RYOTT – William Jackson Of Woodhorn, Northumberland With His Prize Shorthorn Cow – signed, dated 1839 and inscribed – oil on canvas – 66 x 91cm.
(Sotheby's) $7,568   £4,400

THEO VAN RYSSELBERGHE – Paysage du Midi – with monogram – oil on canvas – 33½ x 33¾in.
(Christie's) $24,640   £15,400

THEO VAN RYSELLBERGHE – Bouquet de Fleurs – signed with the monogram and dated '05 – oil on canvas – 16¼ x 12¾in.
(Christie's) $17,820   £11,000

WALTER DENDY SADLER – The Fisherman – signed and dated '81 – oil on canvas – 76.5 x 50.5cm.
(Phillips) $907   £550

SALOME − Liebespaar − signed and dated '83, and inscribed on the reverse − acrylic on canvas − unframed − 75 x 63in.
(Christie's)   **$7,007**   **£3,850**

EMMA SANDYS − The Shell: A Girl Leaning On A Ledge In A River Landscape − signed with monogram and dated 1873 − pencil and coloured chalks heightened with white on stone-coloured paper − 19¼ x 16in.
(Christie's)   **$2,310**   **£1,320**

ANTHONY FREDERICK AUGUSTUS SANDYS − 'Ysoude' − signed, inscribed and dated 1870 − black, red and white chalk − 44 x 33cm.
(Phillips)   **$6,372**   **£3,600**

JOHN SINGER SARGENT − Mrs. George Mosenthal − signed and dated 1906 − oil on canvas − 36 x 28½in.
(Christie's)   **$88,000**   **£53,917**

SARGENT

JOHN SINGER SARGENT – Colourful
Pavements, Sicily – inscribed on the reverse –
watercolour and pencil on paper – 10 x 14in.
(Christie's)   **$11,000**   **£6,145**

JOHN SINGER SARGENT – Portrait Of Lady
Delamere As A Young Girl – signed and dated
1912 – charcoal on paper – 21¾ x 16¾in.
(Christie's)   **$15,400**   **£9,435**

JOHN SINGER SARGENT, Circle of – Portrait Of
An Arab – bears signature – oil on canvas – 22 x
18in.
(Christie's)   **$2,310**   **£1,320**

FRANCIS SARTORIUS – John Beard Holding
Captain Bertie's Sportsman – signed and dated
1769 – oil on canvas – 99 x 124.5cm.
(Sotheby's)   **$68,112**   **£39,600**

JOHN NOST SARTORIUS – H.R.H. The Prince
Of Wales' Racehorse 'Escape' With Trainer And
Jockey Sam Chiffney On Newmarket Heath –
signed and dated 1791 – oil on canvas – 17 x 21in.
(Phillips)   **$55,500**   **£30,000**

LUCIEN GUIRAND DE SCEVOLA – Fleurs dans
un Vase vert – signed – oil on board – 50 x
60.5cm.
(Phillips)   **$924**   **£550**

HENRY SCHAFER – A Continental Town –
signed and dated '78 – 14 x 12in.
(Christie's) **$1,200** **£682**

FRIEDRICH SCHAPER – Hafen in der Ostsee –
signed and dated '94 – oil on canvas laid on board
– 19½ x 23¾in.
(Christie's) **$7,128** **£4,400**

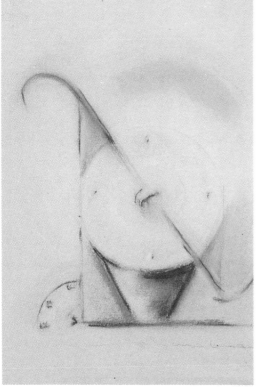

HUGO SCHEIBER – Dancers: The Tango –
signed – gouache with oil on paper – 16½ x
26½in.
(Christie's) **$8,553** **£5,280**

MORTON LIVINGSTON SCHAMBERG –
Composition (1916) – signed – pastel on paper –
8 x 5¼in.
(Christie's) **$17,600** **£9,833**

ANDREAS SCHELFHOUT – A Dog By A Fence
– signed – on panel – 13½ x 11¼in.
(Christie's) **$1,270** **£770**

SCHENDEL

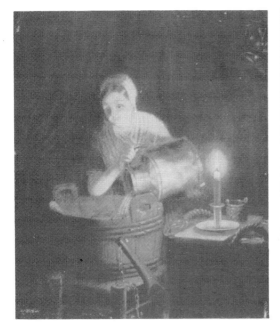

PETRUS VAN SCHENDEL – A Woman Pouring
Water In A Candlelit Interior – signed with
monogram – 21 x 18cm.
(Phillips) $2,520 £1,400

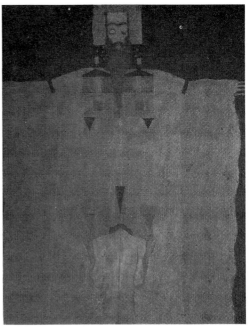

EGON SCHIELE – Vor Gottvater knieender
Jungling – signed with initials – oil, gold and
copper paint on canvas – 31¼ x 23¼in.
(Christie's) $885,500 £550,000

PETRUS VAN SCHENDEL – A Scene From The
Fifth Act Of Romeo And Juliet – signed – oil on
panel – 66.5 x 51cm.
(Phillips) $11,160 £6,200

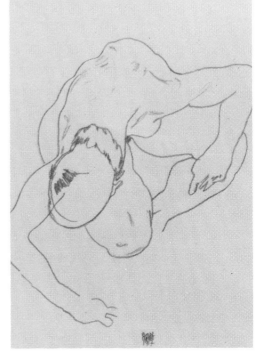

EGON SCHIELE – Kauende Frau – signed and
dated 1917 – soft pencil on paper – 17¼ x 11in.
(Christie's) $29,920 £18,700

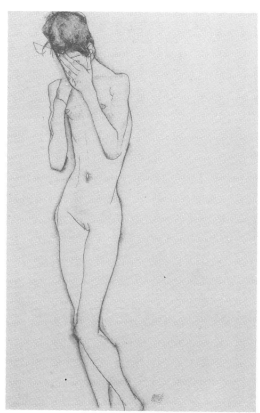

EGON SCHIELE – Stehendes Madchen, Sich Die Hande Vors Gesicht Haltend – signed and dated 1913 – pencil and coloured crayon – 48 x 31 cm.
(Sotheby's) **$136,565** **£71,500**

HAROLD VON SCHMIDT – Trading Post – signed and dated 1937 – oil on canvas laid down on masonite – 23¼ x 53in.
(Christie's) **$15,400** **£9,435**

WALTER ELMER SCHOFIELD – Coast Of Cornwall, England – signed and dated '21 – oil on canvas – 26 x 30in.
(Christie's) **$4,180** **£2,561**

HENRI GUILLAUME SCHLESINGER – La Contemplation – signed and dated 1860 – 32 x 25½in.
(Christie's) **$2,178** **£1,320**

WALTER ELMER SCHOFIELD – Thatched Roofs In Godolphin – dated Nov. 7th, '38 on the reverse – oil on canvas – unframed – 26 x 29¾in.
(Christie's) **$8,250** **£5,054**

SCHOFIELD

HENRY SCHOUTEN – Ducks And Ducklings On A River Bank – signed – 23 x 35in.
(Christie's) **$1,815** **£1,100**

WALTER ELMER SCHOFIELD – Midsummer Night – oil on canvas – 40½ x 48¼in.
(Christie's) **$30,800** **£17,207**

WALTER ELMER SCHOFIELD – Winter Farmyard – oil on canvas – unframed – 20 x 23¾in.
(Christie's) **$8,250** **£5,054**

WILHELM SCHREUER – A Gardener And A Maid In A Courtyard – signed with initials – on panel – 14 x 11½in.
(Christie's) **$726** **£440**

ALFRED SCHONIAN – Poultry In A Farmyard – signed and inscribed – oil on panel – 20 x 25cm.
(Phillips) **$1,476** **£820**

LOUIS DE SCHRYVER – Roses In A Bowl – signed and dated 1881 – 19¼ x 25½in.
(Christie's) **$8,910** **£5,500**

CLAUDE EMILE SCHUFFENECKER – Femme
nue assise sur un Lit – signed and dated 1885,
and signed with initials on the reverse – oil on
canvas – 25½ x 21¼in.
(Christie's)   **$21,120   £13,200**

KURT SCHWITTERS – Portrait Of An Internee
1940-41 (Recto Verso) – signed with initials – oil
on panel.
(Phillips)   **$3,360   £2,000**

ADOLPHE SCHWARZ – Strandhauser an der
Alten Donau; and Hafenwinkel – on board – 10 x
15in.
(Christie's)   **$1,905   £1,155 Pair**

CARL SCHWENINGER – An Alpine Landscape
With Huntsmen By A Torrent – signed – 37½ x
49in.
(Christie's)   **$2,178   £1,320**

KURT SCHWITTERS – Suisse – inscribed by the
artist's son on the reverse – collage – 14.8 x
11.7cm.
(Sotheby's)   **$36,767   £19,250**

SCOTT

SIR PETER SCOTT – Teal On A Pond – signed
and dated 1955 – oil on canvas-board – 24 x 34in.
(Christie's)   **$4,041**   **£2,420**

EDWARD SEAGO – Norfolk Village–Winter –
signed – oil on board – 30.5 x 40.5 cm.
(Phillips)   **$7,518**   **£4,200**

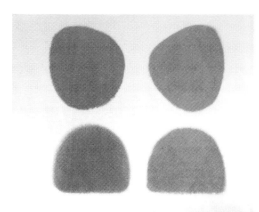

WILLIAM SCOTT – Blue Composition II – signed
with initials – gouache – 20 x 24in.
(Christie's)   **$1,370**   **£770**

EDWARD SEAGO – Cattle In A Lane By The
Dutch House – signed – oil on board – 28 x
30cm.
(Phillips)   **$3,222**   **£1,800**

EDWARD SEAGO – Salthouse – signed – oil on
panel – 11¼ x 14½in.
(Christie's)   **$10,103**   **£6,050**

EDWARD SEAGO – The Watch Tower At Hoorn
– signed and inscribed on the reverse – pen,
brush, ink and watercolour – 11¾ x 18¼in.
(Christie's)   **$1,837**   **£1,100**

EDWARD SEAGO – De Fernando-de-Gloria And
Sagres Off Lisbon – signed – oil on board – 30.5
x 40.5 cm.
(Phillips) $13,425 £7,500

EDWARD SEAGO – The Coast Road In The
Cascais–Portugal – signed – oil on board – 30.5 x
40.5 cm.
(Phillips) $10,382 £5,800

EDWARD SEAGO – Leaning Houses In The
Stroomarkt, Amsterdam – signed and inscribed on
the reverse – pen, ink and watercolour – 10¾ x
14½in.
(Christie's) $2,755 £1,650

COLIN SEALY – Still Life With Jug And Bowl Of
Fruit – pencil and water colour heightened with
white – 14 x 16.5 cm.
(Phillips) $156 £95

EDWARD SEAGO – Sketchbook Of Greece –
comprising fifty-two sketches – pencil – 5¼ x
6¾in.
(Christie's) $7,715 £4,620

ANDRE DUNOUER de SEGONIZAC – Le
Canal – signed – oil on panel – 9¼ x 13in.
(Christie's) $3,603 £1,980

SEIGNAC

GUILLAUME SEIGNAC – Trying On Her New Earrings – signed – oil on canvas – 117 x 79cm.
(Phillips) **$23,400** **£13,000**

ENRIQUE SERRA – A Little Girl In A Wood – signed – on panel – 5½ x 3½in.
(Christie's) **$1,548** **£880**

EISMAN SEMENOWSKY – The Pretty Flower Gatherer – signed and inscribed – 47 x 31cm.
(Phillips) **$6,300** **£3,500**

JAMES SESSIONS – Harbour Reflections – signed and dated '37 – water colour and pencil on paper – 21¾ x 24¾in.
(Christie's) **$2,640** **£1,628**

JAMES SESSIONS – The Bowsprit – signed –
watercolour on board – 15 x 22in.
(Christie's)   **$2,090**   **£1,289**

GEORGES SEURAT – Homme Assis, Lisant, Sur
Une Terrasse (Le Pere De Seurat) – conte crayon –
30.7 x 23.3cm.
(Sotheby's)   **$714,340**   **£374,000**

FRANZ VAN SEVERDONCK – Sheep And
Ducks By A Pond In An Extensive Landscape –
signed and dated 1866 – 9½ x 14¼in.
(Christie's)   **$2,087**   **£1,265**

GINO SEVERINI – La Sette Virtu – signed –
gouache – 68.5 x 93cm.
(Sotheby's)   **$63,030**   **£33,000**

TOM SEYMOUR – Sheep Grazing By A Quiet
River Near A Castle – signed – oil – 11½ x 19½in.
(Anderson & Garland)   **$1,221**   **£660**

BEN SHAHN – Join Or Die – signed – gouache on
board – 30 x 19¾in.
(Christie's)   **$17,600**   **£9,833**

SHAHN

BEN SHAHN – Unemployment – signed – tempera on paper laid down on masonite –
13¾ x 16¾in. *(Christie's)*   **$49,500 £30,536**

JAMES JEBUSA SHANNON – Michaelmas – oil
on canvas – 44½ x 31½in.
(Christie's)   **$24,200   £14,827**

SIR JOHN JAMES JEBUSA SHANNON – Head Of
A Young Girl – signed – oil on canvas – 11 x
9½in.
(Christie's)   **$3,850   £2,200**

FRANK HENRY SHAPLEIGH – Mt. Washington From The Ammonoosuc River – signed – watercolour on paper – 13½ x 9½in.
(Robt. W. Skinner Inc.)   **$850**   **£515**

FRANK HENRY SHAPLEIGH – Mts. Washington and Pleasant From Beecher's Cascades – signed and dated 1874 – oil on canvas – 16 x 10in.
(Bruce D. Collins)   **$1,870**   **£1,056**

DOROTHEA SHARP – A Jug Of Summer Flowers – oil on board – 38 x 46cm. *(Phillips)*
$3,936 £2,400

DOROTHEA SHARP – At The Seaside – signed – oil on canvas – 25 x 30in. *(Christie's)*
$16,533 £9,900

DOROTHEA SHARP – A Vase Of Asters And
Zinnias – signed – oil on board – 43 x 38cm.
(Phillips) **$4,264 £2,600**

DOROTHEA SHARP – By The Sea – oil on
canvas – 30 x 25in.
(Christie's) **$15,614 £9,350**

DOROTHEA SHARP – Ducks On A Pond –
signed – oil on canvas – 14¼ x 18¼in.
(Christie's) $6,853   £3,850

DOROTHEA SHARP – Watering The Garden –
signed – oil on canvas – 25½ x 23½in.
(Christie's) $29,370   £16,500

DOROTHEA SHARP – Mother And Children By
The Sea – signed with initials – oil on canvas –
51 x 61cm.
(Phillips) $16,400   £10,000

DOROTHEA SHARP – At The Seaside – signed
– oil on panel – 11½ x 14½in.
(Christie's) $10,181   £5,720

JOSEPH HENRY SHARP – War Bonnet Song – signed and inscribed – oil on canvas – 25
x 30in. *(Christie's)* $77,000 £43,019

SHARP

JOSEPH HENRY SHARP – Firelight – signed – oil on canvas – 30 x 36¼in. *(Christie's)*
$66,000   £36,874

JAMES SHARPLES – George Washington –
pastel on paper – 9¼ x 7½in.
(Christie's) $22,000   £12,291

DAVID SHEPHERD – An African Bull Elephant
– signed and dated '84, and also signed and again
with initials, inscribed and dated – oil on canvas –
15.5 x 15.5cm.
(Phillips) $2,624   £1,600

GEORGE SHEPHERD – The Captive Wild Man – inscribed – watercolour over pencil – 14.5 x 22cm.
(Sotheby's)   **$770** **£440**

EVERETT SHINN – Winter Night, Paris – signed – oil on board – 9¾ x 11¾in.
(Christie's) **$15,400** **£9,435**

EVERETT SHINN – Nude Study Of A Seated Woman – signed and dated 1940 – charcoal heightened with white on green paper – 25 x 19in.; Still Life With Children's Toys – signed with initials and dated '37 – charcoal on tan paper – 16 x 20in.; Portrait Of A Young Woman Facing Forward – signed – charcoal heightened with white on grey paper – 21½ x 17½in.; and Portrait Of A Young Woman Facing Left – signed and dated 1947 – charcoal heightened with white on grey paper – 25 x 19in.
(Robt. W. Skinner Inc.) **$600** **£363 Four**

EVERETT SHINN – Reading – conte crayon and pencil on paper – 9 x 8in.
(Christie's) **$2,640** **£1,628**

ADOLPH ROBERT SHULZ – Sunset In Florida – signed – oil on canvas – 27 x 34in.
(Christie's) **$2,750** **£1,696**

SICKERT

WALTER RICHARD SICKERT – Neüilly, Dieppe
– signed with initials and inscribed – oil on canvas
– 46 x 56cm.
(Phillips)   **$7,380**   **£4,500**

WALTER RICHARD SICKERT – St. Jacques,
Dieppe – signed and dated 1912 – oil on canvas –
13¼ x 16in.
(Christie's)   **$31,328**   **£17,600**

WALTER RICHARD SICKERT – Chelsea
Hospital – signed – oil on canvas – 14 x 18in.
(Christie's)   **$22,044**   **£13,200**

WALTER RICHARD SICKERT – The Garden,
St. George's Hill House, Bathampton – signed –
oil on canvas – 34¾ x 28½in.
(Christie's)   **$22,962**   **£13,750**

WALTER RICHARD SICKERT – Girl On A Bed,
Mornington Crescent – signed – oil on canvas –
20 x 16in.
(Christie's)   **$47,762**   **£28,600**

WALTER RICHARD SICKERT – Two Ladies In A Garden – signed – oil on canvas – 19 x 29in.
(Christie's)   **$7,440   £4,180**

HENRI LE SIDANER – Le Chambre bleu; Villefranche sur Mer – signed – oil on canvas – 28¾ x 36¼in.
(Christie's)   **$88,000   £55,000**

WALTER RICHARD SICKERT – Rue de la Boucherie, With St. Jacques, Dieppe – signed and indistinctly inscribed – watercolour, bodycolour, pen and brown ink and pencil on blue paper – 9¼ x 12in.
(Christie's)   **$17,451   £10,450**

HENRI LE SIDANER – Bord de Riviere a Gerberoy – signed – oil on panel – 12¾ x 16¼in.
(Christie's)   **$49,280   £30,800**

HENRI LE SIDANER – Les Peniches – signed and dated 1894 – oil on canvas – 12¾ x 16in.
(Christie's)   **$14,256   £8,800**

PAUL SIGNAC – Quai du Louvre – signed and dated 1925 – watercolour and pencil on paper – 11¾ x 17¼in.
(Christie's)   **$24,640   £15,400**

FRANCIS AUGUSTUS SILVA – Coney Island –
signed – oil on canvas – 20 x 36¼in.
(Christie's)   **$17,600**   **£10,783**

MARIE ELENA VIEIRA DA SILVA – Combat –
signed and dated '51 – oil on canvas – 25¾ x
39¼in.
(Christie's)   **$98,010**   **£60,500**

MARIE ELENA VIEIRA DE SILVA – Ville –
signed, dated '56 and inscribed – gouache on
paper – 22¼ x 19¼in.
(Christie's)   **$24,948**   **£15,400**

FRANCIS AUGUSTUS SILVA – Seabright From
Galilee – signed and dated '80, and signed and
dated again and inscribed on the reverse – oil on
canvas – 21 x 42in.
(Christie's)   **$39,600**   **£22,124**

LUCIEN SIMON – Jeune Fille Bretonne – signed
– watercolour on paper – 41¼ x 22¼in.
(Christie's)   **$2,202**   **£1,210**

CHARLES SIMPSON – Out Hunting – signed –
gouache – 22½ x 28½in.
(Christie's) $4,041   £2,420

CHARLES SIMPSON – The Saddling Enclosure –
signed – oil on canvas – 18 x 24in.
(Christie's) $3,490   £2,090

CHARLES SIMPSON – A Pinto (Piebald Horse) –
signed – oil on canvas – 18 x 24in.
(Christie's) $3,674   £2,200

WILLIAM SIMPSON – Large Deodar Tree,
Kunawi, Himalayas – signed, inscribed and dated
1865 – watercolour over pencil – 25 x 35cm.
(Phillips) $2,478   £1,400

CHARLES SIMS – Apples – signed – oil on
canvas laid down on panel – 16¼ x 14¼in.
(Christie's) $4,408   £2,640

CHARLES SIMS – Summertime – signed –
pencil, watercolour and bodycolour – 20¾ x 15in.
(Christie's) $2,755   £1,650

SINCLAIR

JOHN SINCLAIR – The Finish Of The Epsom
Derby, 1822 – oil on canvas – 54 x 84in.
(Phillips)   **$20,350**   **£11,000**

ALFRED SISLEY – Sur les Falaises, la Baie de
Langland; Pays de Galles – signed and dated '97 –
pastel on paper – 11 x 14in.
(Christie's)   **$167,200**   **£104,500**

ALFRED SISLEY – La Ferme du Trou d'Enfer,
Matinee d'Automne – signed and dated '74,
also inscribed – oil on canvas – 17½ x 23¾in.
(Christie's)   **$680,680**   **£374,000**

JOHN SKEAPING – Horse And Jockey – signed
and dated '54 – coloured chalks, pen and black ink
– 15 x 21in.
(Christie's)   **$4,503**   **£2,530**

ALFRED SISLEY – Le Canal du Loing au
Printemps; le Matin – signed and dated '97 –
oil on canvas – 23½ x 28¾in.
(Christie's)   **$460,460**   **£286,000**

JOHN SKEAPING – Before The Off – signed,
inscribed and dated '60 – brush and black ink –
18¼ x 22¼in.
(Christie's)   **$1,468**   **£825**

C. H. SLATER – Still Life With Apples & Plums –
signed – watercolour – 16½ x 12in.
*(Prudential Fine Art
    Auctioneers)*   **$693**   **£420**

MAX SLEVOGT – Garten in Godrammstein mit
Verwachsenem Baum und Weiher – signed and
dated 1910 – oil on canvas – 39 x 32in.
(Christie's)   **$318,780   £198,000**

JOHN FALCONAR SLATER – Poultry In A
Farmyard – signed – oil on board – 17¼ x 23¼in.
(Anderson & Garland)   **$1,850   £1,000**

MAX SLEVOGT – Der Vorgarten der
Steinbartschen Villa in Berlin – signed and dated
1911 – oil on canvas – 33¾ x 41½in.
(Christie's)   **$177,100   £110,000**

MAX SLEVOGT – Dame im weissen Reitkleid zu
Pferde – signed and dated 1910 – oil on canvas
– 71½ x 59in.
(Christie's)   **$35,200   £22,000**

SLINGELAND

JOHN SLOAN – Harmony – signed, dated '06 and inscribed – charcoal on paper laid down on board – 14¾ x 21¾in.
(Christie's)   **$5,500**   **£3,072**

PIETER VAN SLINGELAND – A Hermit Seated Reading – oil on panel – 42.5 x 36cm.
(Sotheby's)   **$38,060**   **£22,000**

GEORGE SLOANE – The Connoiseur – signed and dated 1897 – oil on panel – 8¼ x 10¾in.
(Christie's)   **$5,500**   **£3,072**

JOHN SLOAN – Girl Dressing – bears signature, date 1914 and inscribed – conte crayon on paper – 11¾ x 9½in.
(Christie's)   **$1,870**   **£1,153**

BORLASE SMART – Down-Along St. Ives – signed, and signed and inscribed on the reverse – oil on canvas – 24 x 29in.
(Christie's)   **$3,230**   **£1,815**

JOHN SMART – A Sketch On Draggan Burn – signed, and inscribed on the reverse – oil – 16 x 25 in.
(Messrs. G. A. Key) $982   £540

LEON DE SMET – Bouquet de Fleurs – signed – oil on canvas – 25¾ x 29½ in.
(Christie's) $9,009   £4,950

ELMER BOYD SMITH – Working In The Fields – oil on canvas laid down on masonite – 10¾ x 11¼ in.
(Christie's) $3,520   £1,966

CARLTON ALFRED SMITH – The Stray Cats Treat – signed and dated 1872 – watercolour and bodycolour over pencil – 35 x 24.5 cm.
(Phillips) $3,186   £1,800

FRANCIS HOPKINSON SMITH – A British Harbour Scene – signed and inscribed – gouache and watercolour on paper – 23¼ x 12¾ in.
(Christie's) $4,400   £2,695

SMITH

FRANCIS HOPKINSON SMITH – Beautiful Fountain, Scutari – signed – gouache and pencil on brown paper laid down on board – 12¾ x 24¼in.
(Christie's)   **$4,400**   **£2,695**

FRANCIS HOPKINSON SMITH – Along The French Canal – signed – watercolour, gouache and charcoal on board – 14 x 24in.
(Christie's)   **$7,700**   **£4,750**

GEORGE SMITH – The Valentine – signed and dated 1857 – on panel – 14 x 12in.
(Phillips)   **$2,720**   **£1,700**

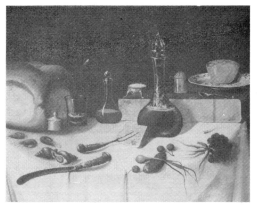

GEORGE SMITH, of Chichester – Still Life With Bread, Cheese And Other Viands With Ale On A Draped Table – oil on canvas – 67 x 82.5cm.
(Sotheby's)   **$12,298**   **£7,150**

HENRY PEMBER SMITH – Mid-day At Venice – signed – oil on canvas – 29¼ x 50¼in.
(Christie's)   **$5,500**   **£3,392**

J. BURRELL SMITH – By The River – watercolour.
(Prudential Fine Art Auctioneers)   **$2,805**   **£1,700**

JAMES BURRELL SMITH – A Figure On A Path In A Mountainous Landscape – signed with monogram – on canvas – 12 x 10in.
(Phillips)   **$1,120**   **£700**

JAMES BURRELL SMITH – A Wooded River
Landscape With A Waterfall – signed and dated
1870 – on canvas – 23½ x 19in.
(Phillips) $4,576 £2,600

JOHN 'WARWICK' SMITH – Cascade On The
Margin Of The Lake Of Lugano – signed –
watercolour over pencil with scratching out – 43
x 31cm.
(Sotheby's) $1,636 £935

JESSIE WILLCOX SMITH – Prayers Before
Breakfast – signed – watercolour, gouache and
charcoal on board – 22¼ x 16¼in.
(Christie's) $22,000 £12,291

SIR MATTHEW SMITH – Portrait Of A Lady,
Three-Quarter Length, In A Yellow Dress – oil on
canvas – 30 x 25in.
(Christie's) $15,614 £9,350

SMITH

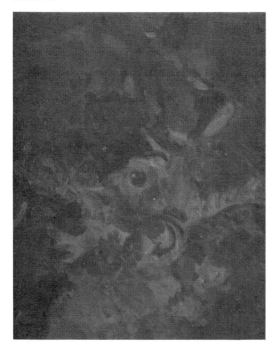

SIR MATTHEW SMITH – Roses In A Vase – oil
on canvas – 18 x 15 in.
(Christie's) $9,185   £5,500

SIR MATTHEW SMITH – Still Life With Fruit,
Leaves And A Clay Figure – signed – charcoal and
pastel – 30 x 22 in.
(Christie's) $3,916   £2,200

SIR MATTHEW SMITH – Still Life With Fruit
And A Jug – signed – watercolour – 9 x 14 in.
(Christie's) $3,490   £2,090

SIR MATTHEW SMITH – Tulips And Fruit –
signed with initials – oil on canvas – 13 x 18 in.
(Christie's) $33,066   £19,800

SIR MATTHEW SMITH – Still Life Of Tulips And
Daisies In A Vase – signed with initials –
watercolour and pencil – 16 x 13¼ in.
(Christie's) $5,874   £3,300

JOHN RICHARD COKE SMYTH — Interior Of
The Church Of The Ursuline Convent, Quebec —
inscribed and dated 1838 — watercolour over
pencil heightened with bodycolour — 9¾ x 8¼in.
(Sotheby's) $10,175 £5,500

ROSAMOND LOMBARD SMITH — Maid In
Boston — signed — oil on canvas — 38 x 25¼in.
(Robt. W. Skinner Inc.) $12,000 £6,703

JOHN RICHARD COKE SMYTH — The Pulpit Of
The Church Of The Ursuline Convent, Quebec —
inscribed — watercolour over pencil heightened
with bodycolour — one 10 x 11¼in.
(Sotheby's) $26,455 £14,300 Two

ISAAC SNOWMAN — An Elderly Jew Reading A
Prayer Book — signed and dated 1928 — oil on
canvas — 56 x 35.5cm.
(Sotheby's) $11,352 £6,600

ARDENGO SOFFICI – Fiori – inscribed and signed – oil on board – 8½ x 14½in.
(Christie's) **$5,346** **£3,300**

RIGOBERTO SOLER – Picking Flowers – signed and dated 1919 – 29 x 35in.
(Christie's) **$29,040** **£17,600**

HENRI SOLLIER – Bateaux en Reparatre – signed – oil on canvas – 46 x 55cm.
(Phillips) **$1,680** **£1,000**

ANDREA SOLDI – Portrait Of The Composer William Defesch (1687-1758) – oil on canvas – 76 x 63.5cm.
(Sotheby's) **$17,974** **£10,450**

HENRI SOLLIER – Dans l'Oliveraie–Cagnes sur Mer – signed – oil on canvas laid down on panel – 38 x 46cm.
(Phillips) **$2,100** **£1,250**

STUART SCOTT SOMERVILLE – Convexion –
signed – pen, brush and indian ink, watercolour
and bodycolour on green paper – 22 x 16cm.
(Phillips) $313   £190

PIERRE SOULAGES – Peinture, 1952 – signed,
inscribed and dated '52 – watercolour on paper –
41 x 30in.
(Christie's) $20,020   £11,000

WILLIAM LOUIS SONNTAG – Fishing – signed
– oil on canvas – 19 x 32¼in.
(Christie's) $41,800   £23,353

WILLIAM LOUIS SONNTAG, Jnr. – Seashore
Play – signed – watercolour and gouache on
paper laid down on board – 14¼ x 21¼in.
(Christie's) $9,900   £5,531

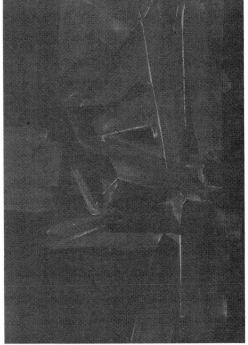

PIERRE SOULAGES – 4 Aout 1961 – signed,
and inscribed on the reverse – oil on canvas – 77
x 51¼in.
(Christie's) $98,010   £60,500

JOHN BULLOCH SOUTER – Netting Crabs –
signed – oil on linen canvas down on board – 51
x 76cm.
(Phillips) $15,580   £9,500

FRANK SOUTHGATE – Fisherman Smoking A
Pipe On The Shores Of An Estuary – signed –
watercolour – 12¾ x 24¾in.
(Christie's) $866   £495

JOSEPH EDWARD SOUTHALL – The Schooner
– signed with monogram and dated 1907 –
watercolour and bodycolour over traces of pencil
– unframed – 38 x 27cm.
(Phillips) $18,040   £11,000

E. F. SOUTHGATE – Duck Shooting – signed and
dated '98 – watercolour – 16 x 20in.
(Messrs. G. A. Key) $218   £120

MOSES SOYER – Dancer – signed – oil on canvas
– 20¼ x 10¼in.
(Christie's) $3,850   £2,358

MOSES SOYER – Seamstresses – signed and dated 1953 – oil on canvas – 36 x 42in.
(Christie's) **$19,800 £11,062**

MOSES SOYER – Seated Dancer – signed –
pastel and charcoal on paper – 25¼ x 17½in.
(Christie's) **$880 £542**

MOSES SOYER – On Leave – signed and dated
'44 – oil on canvas – 16¼ x 12in.
(Christie's) **$5,500 £3,392**

SOYER

RAPHAEL SOYER – Girl In Blue Blouse – signed
– oil on canvas – 18¼ x 14in.
(Christie's)   **$4,620**   **£2,850**

RAPHAEL SOYER – City Children – signed – oil
on canvas – 48¼ x 38in.
(Christie's)   **$66,000**   **£36,874**

RAPHAEL SOYER – Waiting Room – signed –
watercolour and charcoal on paper – 12 x 14½in.
(Christie's)   **$2,200**   **£1,357**

RAPHAEL SOYER – Womanhood – signed – oil
on canvas – 12 x 10in.
(Christie's)   **$2,750**   **£1,684**

RAPHAEL SOYER – Profile – signed – oil on
canvas – 9¾ x 8¼in.
(Christie's)   **$3,850**   **£2,375**

ARMANDO SPADINI – Girl With Cat – signed –
oil on canvas – 43 x 33cm.
(Phillips)   **$6,720**   **£4,000**

AUSTIN OSMAN SPARE – Snake Head – signed
with initials and dated '53 – pencil and coloured
pencils, black chalk and pastel on board – 77 x
51.5cm.
(Phillips)   **$4,290**   **£2,600**

SPANISH SCHOOL – Bullfighting Scenes – signed
and dated 1879-1902 – 18 x 12in.
(Christie's)   **$3,448**   **£2,090 Pair**

RUSKIN SPEAR – Self-Portrait – signed – oil on
board – 23 x 19in.
(Christie's)   **$7,440**   **£4,180**

SPEAR

RUSKIN SPEAR – The Board Meeting – signed, and inscribed on the reverse – oil on board – 16 x 32in.
(Christie's)   **$2,117**   **£1,210**

RUSKIN SPEAR – The Clown – signed – oil on board – 32 x 40½in.
(Christie's)   **$3,132**   **£1,760**

EUGENE SPEICHER – Bouquet In A White Vase – signed – oil on canvas – 20 x 16in.
(Christie's)   **$5,500**   **£3,072**

RUSKIN SPEAR – Footballers – signed – oil on board – 30 x 20in.
(Christie's)   **$2,937**   **£1,650**

CHARLES SPENCELAYH – Luxuries – signed, and inscribed on the reverse – oil on canvas – 46 x 30.5cm.
(Sotheby's)   **$20,812**   **£12,100**

GILBERT SPENCER – In The Garden – signed –
oil on panel – 12¼ x 15½in.
(Christie's) **$962** **£550**

GILBERT SPENCER – Summer Landscape – oil
and pencil on canvas – 18 x 24in.
(Christie's) **$3,122** **£1,870**

GILBERT SPENCER – Thou Shalt Not Commit
Adultery – signed and dated 1927 – pen and black
ink – 22½ x 20½in.
(Christie's) **$4,408** **£2,640**

SIR STANLEY SPENCER – Portrait Of J. L.
Behrend By A Window – oil on canvas – 19½ x
11½in.
(Christie's) **$21,538** **£12,100**

SIR STANLEY SPENCER – The Thames At
Chauntry Court – oil on canvas – 20 x 30in.
(Christie's) **$88,110** **£49,500**

MATTHEW SPENDER – The Bathers – signed
and dated '81 – oil on canvas – 70 x 90cm.
(Phillips) **$1,452** **£880**

THOMAS SPINKS – A Figure Punting In A
Wooded River Landscape – signed and dated 1878
– on canvas – 12 x 18in.
(Phillips) **$2,112** **£1,200**

IGNACE SPIRIDON – A Lesson In Geography –
signed – 20¾ x 16in.
(Christie's) **$11,616** **£6,600**

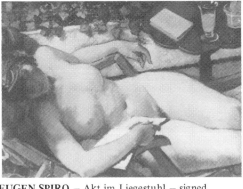

EUGEN SPIRO – Akt im Liegestuhl – signed
and dated '27 – oil on canvas – 30 x 43¾in.
(Christie's) **$11,011** **£6,050**

JAN JACOB SPOHLER – A Wooded River
Landscape With Fishermen Mooring Their Boats –
signed – 11 x 17in.
(Christie's) **$5,362** **£3,520**

JOHANNES FRANCISCUS SPOHLER – A Canal
Scene, Amsterdam – signed and inscribed on a
label on the reverse – oil on panel – 21 x 16cm. –
and companion.
(Phillips) **$3,600** **£2,000 Pair**

ARTHUR SPOONER – Cricket, Tea Interval, Trent Bridge – signed and dated 1938 – oil on canvas – 57 x 36½in. *(Christie's)* $77,341 £43,450

CLARKSON STANFIELD – A Village In The Tyrol – watercolour over pencil – 33 x 44cm. *(Phillips)* $2,212   £1,250

GEORGE CLARKSON STANFIELD – 'Arona, Lake Maggiori' – signed – on canvas – 23½ x 35½in. *(Phillips)* $4,928   £2,800

STANNARD – Summer Flowers In A Blue Vase – watercolour – 27 x 20in. *(Messrs. G. A. Key)* $1,237   £680

STANNARD

ELOISE HARRIET STANNARD – Strawberries On A Cabbage Leaf With A Butterfly – signed and dated 1879 – oil on canvas – 33 x 28 cm.
(Sotheby's) **$14,190** **£8,250**

LILIAN STANNARD – Flower Garden With Fountain In Foreground, And Rose Pergola – signed – watercolour – 13½ x 9½ in.
(Hobbs & Chambers) **$3,600** **£2,000**

SIR HERBERT HUGHES STANTON – Wooded Landscape With A Peasant On A Track – signed and dated 1931 – oil on canvas – 15½ x 19½ in.
(Christie's) **$1,958** **£1,100**

PHILIP WILSON STEER – The Music Room – oil on canvas – unframed – 27 x 32 in.
(Christie's) **$25,718** **£15,400**

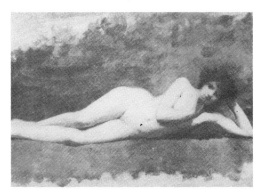

PHILIP WILSON STEER, Attributed to – Reclining Nude – oil on canvas – 33 x 51 cm.
(Phillips) **$1,023** **£620**

EDWARD JEAN STEICHEN – Lake George –
signed and dated, and signed again, dated Oct
12/04 and inscribed on the backing – oil on canvas
laid down on board – 13¾ x 9¾in.
(Christie's) **$26,400** **£16,175**

IRMA STERN – Watutsi Of Uganda – signed on
the reverse – oil on canvas – 60 x 50cm.
(Sotheby's) **$7,733** **£4,180**

CHARLES STENHOUSE – Fishermen On A
Quay – signed – oil on canvas – 19½ x 25½in.
(Christie's) **$3,084** **£1,705**

MARC STERLING – Still Life In Green – signed
– oil on board – 24 x 30cm.
(Phillips) **$672** **£400**

MAURICE STERNE – Peasant Girl, Anticoli –
signed and dated 1922–26 – oil on canvas – 52¾
x 33¾in.
(Christie's) **$13,200** **£8,143**

STEVENS

AGAPIT STEVENS – The Jewel Box – signed and dated 1884 – oil on canvas – 30¼ x 22¼in.
(Robt. W. Skinner Inc.) **$2,500** **£1,515**

NORMAN STEVENS – Classical Landscape – signed, inscribed and dated 1968-69 – oil on canvas – 60 x 84in.
(Christie's) **$1,664** **£935**

WILLIAM LESTER STEVENS – 'Port Clyde' – signed – watercolour and gouache on board – 24 x 30in.
(Robt. W. Skinner Inc.) **$475** **£265**

WILLIAM LESTER STEVENS – Deer Isle, Maine – signed – watercolour – 20 x 29in.
(Bruce D. Collins) **$715** **£403**

JULIUS L. STEWART – The Bather – signed – 28¼ x 19in.
(Christie's) **$6,897** **£4,180**

GEORGE BLACKIE STICKS – A Fishing Village At Sunset – signed and dated 1875 – oil on board – 7½ x 23½in.
(Anderson & Garland) **$1,332** **£720**

MARGARET OLROG STODDART – On The Beach, Hayle, Cornwall – signed and dated 1903, and inscribed on the reverse – watercolour – 24.5 x 34.5cm.
(Sotheby's) **$2,035** **£1,100**

CONSTANTIN STOILOFF – Cossacks Charging – signed – on panel – 12 x 19in.
(Christie's) **$1,936** **£1,100**

JOSEF STOMZNER – An Extensive Hilly Landscape – signed – 21¼ x 26¾in.
(Christie's) **$7,484** **£4,620**

GEORGE ADOLPHUS STOREY – Portrait Of A Lady In White, Full Length Seated, Holding A Book By A Lake – signed and dated 1876 – on canvas – 71¾ x 47¾in.
(Phillips) **$6,720** **£4,200**

ARTHUR CLAUDE STRACHAN – Country Cottages – signed – watercolour heightened with body colour and scratching out – 26 x 18.5cm.
(Sotheby's) **$9,625** **£5,500**

STRANG

WILLIAM STRANG – Portrait Of Rudyard Kipling – signed with initials – charcoal and crayon – 7¾ x 5¼in.
(Christie's)   **$2,117**   **£1,210**

BERNARDO STROZZI, Called il Cappuccino – The Annunciation – oil on canvas – 97 x 130cm.
(Sotheby's)   **$60,896**   **£35,200**

ALFRED WILLIAM STRUTT – A Cavalier's Children, Penshurst Place, Kent – signed – watercolour heightened with bodycolour – 57 x 95cm.
(Sotheby's)   **$13,860**   **£7,920**

GILBERT STUART – Mr. And Mrs. Barney Smith – oil on panel – 38¾ x 29¼in. and 37 x 26¾in.
(Christie's)   **$55,000**   **£33,698 Pair**

GILBERT STUART, After – Portrait Of George
Washinton – oil on canvas – 25¼ x 20½in.
(Sotheby's)   **$936   £506**

WALTER J. STUEMPFIG – Civilization – signed
– oil on canvas – 30¼ x 32¼in.
(Christie's)   **$4,180   £2,578**

WALTER J. STUEMPFIG – The Fisherman's
Family – signed – oil on canvas – 20¼ x 24¼in.
(Christie's)   **$7,700   £4,750**

NICOLAI SUETIN, Circle of – Suprematist
Composition – oil on canvas – 31¼ x 23½in.
(Christie's)   **$14,256   £8,800**

KUMI SUGAI – Animal – signed, and signed and
dated 1954 on the reverse – oil on canvas – 103 x
80cm.
(Sotheby's)   **$84,480   £44,000**

SULLY

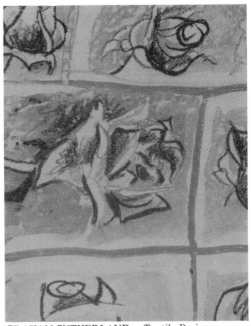

GRAHAM SUTHERLAND – Textile Design:
White Roses On Green – gouache and black chalk
– 15 x 11in.
(Christie's)   **$3,122**   **£1,870**

THOMAS SULLY – Lord Byron – oil on canvas
– 28¾ x 21¼in.
(Christie's)   **$13,200**   **£8,087**

THOMAS SULLY – Flirtation – oil on canvas –
24 x 19¾in.
(Christie's)   **$6,600**   **£4,043**

GRAHAM SUTHERLAND – Chained Beast –
signed and dated 1963 – pen, brush, black ink,
wash and bodycolour – 12½ x 9in.
(Christie's)   **$2,388**   **£1,430**

LEGHE SUTHERS – Farmyard – signed – oil on canvas – 22 x 17¼in.
(Christie's)   **$4,895**   **£2,750**

ALICE MACALLAN SWAN – St. Dorothea – signed with initials and also inscribed on old label on backboard – watercolour and gold paint – 21 x 19.5cm.
(Phillips)   **$796**   **£450**

VICTORIA SWAINE – Nocturne – signed and inscribed on a label, and inscribed and dated – oil on canvas – 66½ x 54in.
(Christie's)   **$4,235**   **£2,420**

MARY SWANZY – The Train Fairwell – signed and dated '49 – oil on board – 14¾ x 10¾in.
(Christie's)   **$1,925**   **£1,100**

SWANZY

MARY SWANZY – Gather Ye Rosebuds While Ye May – oil on canvas – 18 x 21in.
(Christie's)   **$3,306**   **£1,980**

GEORGE GARDNER SYMONS – Winter Landscape Scene – signed – oil on board – 6 x 8½in.
(Robt. W. Skinner Inc.)   **$950**   **£530**

GEORGE GARDNER SYMONS – Early Spring – signed – oil on board – 8¼ x 11in.
(Robt. W. Skinner Inc.)   **$1,100**   **£666**

AUGUSTUS VINCENT TACK – Untitled – oil on canvas laid down on board – 68¼ x 44in.
(Christie's)   **$220,000   £134,794**

ELIZABETH TAGGART – The Ideal Couple – signed, and also signed, inscribed and dated 1976 on the reverse – oil on canvas – 91.5 x 91.5cm.
(Phillips)   **$1,072**   **£650**

ARTHUR FITZWILLIAM TAIT – The Adirondacks, Long Lake – signed and dated '73, and signed and dated again and inscribed on the reverse – oil on canvas – 12 x 18in.
(Christie's) **$14,300 £7,989**

ARTHUR FITZWILLIAM TAIT – Little Pets – signed and dated '99, and signed again, dated and inscribed on the reverse – oil on panel – 9¾ x 14in.
(Christie's) **$11,000 £6,145**

ALGERNON TALMAGE – Cattle In A Field – signed – oil on panel – 14½ x 17½in.
(Christie's) **$2,310 £1,320**

ARNALDO TAMBURINI – In The Cellar – signed and inscribed – 11½ x 9½in.
(Christie's) **$1,548 £880**

TANGUY

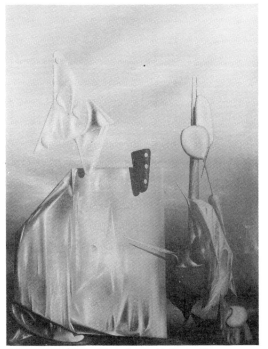

YVES TANGUY – Memoire du Matin – oil on canvas – 50 x 40cm.
(Sotheby's) **$337,920 £176,000**

HENRY OSSAWA TANNER – Moroccan Man – signed, signed again on the reverse – oil on panel – 13 x 9¼in.
(Christie's) **$7,700 £4,717**

YVES TANGUY – Composition – signed and dated '51 – gouache – 49.5 x 32.5cm.
(Sotheby's) **$88,242 £46,200**

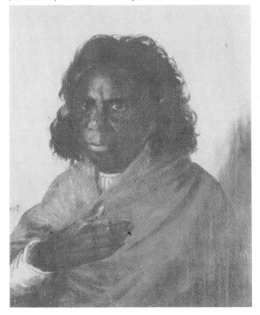

LOUIS TANNERT – An Aboriginal Queen – signed – oil on canvas – 24 x 51cm.
(Sotheby's) **$5,291 £2,860**

ANTONI TAPIES – Trozo de carton sombre Fondo Negro – signed and dated 1959 on the reverse – oil and cardboard collage on canvas board – 22¾ x 42¼in.
(Christie's) $48,048   £26,400

GEORG TAPPERT – Puppen – signed and signed again on the reverse – oil on canvas – 21 x 22in.
(Christie's) $61,600   £38,500

E. TARAZONA – A Scene From The Arabian Nights – signed – 45 x 39¼in.
(Christie's) $1,645   £935

GEORG TAPPERT – Die Loge I – signed – oil on canvas – 21¼ x 33¾in. *(Christie's)*
$320,320 £176,000

TARR

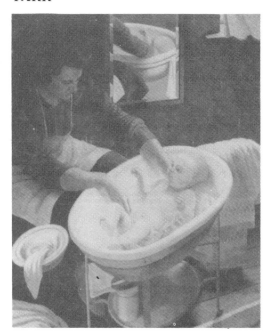

JAMES TARR – Bath Time – oil on panel – 30 x 25in.
(Christie's) $918   £550

ALBERT CHEVALLIER TAYLER – Cattle Watering By A Bridge – signed and dated 1906 – oil on canvas – 15 x 19in.
(Christie's) $7,348   £4,400

FREDERICK TAYLER – Equestrian Portrait Of Kettle Drummer Cuthbert Blaydes Of The 2nd Regiment Of Life Guards – inscribed on the reverse – oil on panel – 65 x 47cm.
(Sotheby's) $2,821   £1,650

JAMES TARR – Donkey And Cart In A Village Street – signed – oil on board – 23½ x 18¾in.
(Christie's) $1,958   £1,100

JOHN FREDERICK TAYLER – An Otter Hunt – signed with initials and dated 1871 – watercolour heightened with bodycolour – 39 x 58.5cm.
(Sotheby's) $3,062   £1,760

LEONARD CAMPBELL TAYLOR – Models From
The Ballet – signed and signed again – oil on
canvas – 37 x 33½in.
(Christie's)   **$11,022**   **£6,600**

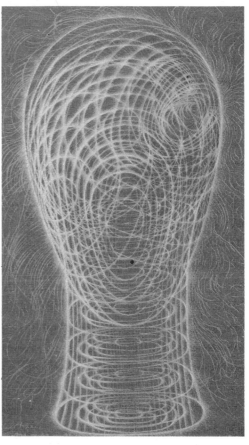

PAVEL TCHELITCHEW – Spiral Interior
Landscape With Hair – signed and dated '52 –
coloured chalks on blue paper – 50 x 32.2cm.
(Sotheby's)   **$10,505**   **£5,500**

LEONARD CAMPBELL TAYLOR – Succulents –
signed – oil on canvas – 26¾ x 23in.
(Christie's)   **$6,980**   **£4,180**

VLADIMIR DE TERLIKOWSKI – Vase de Fleurs
– signed and dated 1935 – oil on canvas – 46.5 x
61.5cm.
(Phillips)   **$537**   **£320**

TERRY

JOSEPH ALFRED TERRY – Reflections –
signed – oil on canvas – 21½ x 17in.
(Christie's)   **$8,566   £4,840**

WILLEM DE FAMARS TESTAS – Vue a
Senouris (province du Fayoum, Egypte) – signed,
and signed and inscribed on the reverse – 20¾ x
31¾in.
(Christie's)   **$4,114   £2,200**

HENRY HERBERT LA THANGUE – A Provencal
Forge – signed – oil on canvas – 76 x 89cm.
(Sotheby's)   **$51,975   £27,500**

HENRY HERBERT LA THANGUE – Fountain
In A Provencal Village – signed – oil on canvas –
27 x 30½in.
(Christie's)   **$45,034   £25,300**

ANTHONY THIEME – Meandering Stream In
Winter Woodlands – signed – oil on canvas – 25¼
x 30¼in.
(Robt. W. Skinner Inc.)   **$1,400   £782**

ROBERT STRICKLAND THOMAS – H.M.
Frigate Leander Getting Under Way – oil on canvas
– 50 x 70cm.
(Sotheby's)   **$11,930   £6,380**

EMMA THOMSEN – Wild Strawberries, Bluebells And Hedge Bindweed On A Bank – signed, and signed on the reverse – on panel – 8 x 10in.
(Christie's) **$24,420** **£13,200**

CARL THOMSEN – A Sunday Afternoon – signed with monogram and dated 1888 – 28 x 23in.
(Christie's) **$71,225** **£38,500**

ALFRED REGINALD THOMSON – Bathers By The Brooklyn Bridge, New York – signed and dated 1925 – oil on canvas – 28¾ x 23½in.
(Christie's) **$5,062** **£2,860**

EMMA THOMSEN – A Still Life With Lilies And Polyanthus – signed with initials and dated 1854 – on panel – 13 x 11in.
(Christie's) **$7,122** **£3,850**

JOHN MURRAY THOMSON – An October Day; and A Sutherland Stable – signed, and signed and inscribed – oil on canvas – 51 x 76cm.
(Sotheby's) **$1,722** **£990 Pair**

507

THOMSON

TOM THOMSON – Spring, Canoe Lake – oil on panel – unframed – 5¼ x 8¾in.
(Christie's) **$8,250** **£5,054**

ARCHIBALD THORBURN – Courtship Display Of Black Grouse – signed and dated 1900 – watercolour – 15 x 22in.
(Prudential Fine Art Auctioneers) **$55,500** **£30,000**

WILHELM THONY – The Drunkard – signed and inscribed – watercolour and pencil on paper – 6½ x 11½in.
(Christie's) **$7,840** **£4,840**

ARCHIBALD THORBURN – A Black Cock On A Rocky Outcrop – signed and dated 1906 – pencil and watercolour heightened with bodycolour on grey paper – 9¾ x 7in.
(Christie's) **$6,930** **£3,960**

WILHELM THONY – Portrait Of A Man – signed – oil on canvas – 18 x 14in.
(Christie's) **$7,128** **£4,400**

ARCHIBALD THORBURN – The Twelfth – signed and dated 1927 – watercolour heightened with white and gum arabic – 17¾ x 22¼in.
(Christie's) **$61,600** **£35,200**

ARCHIBALD THORBURN – Ptarmigan In A Highland Landscape – signed and dated 1899 – watercolour heightened with white on buff-coloured paper – 10¾ x 14¾in.
(Christie's)   **$15,400   £8,800**

WILLIAM THORNLEY – 'Scarborough' Coastal Landscape With Shipping And Figures On Shore – signed – oil on canvas – 11½ x 19½in.
(Barbers Fine Art Auctioneers)   **$1,750   £1,000**

WILLIAM THORNLEY – Figures On The Shore; and Fishing Boats At Anchor Near A Harbour Town At Sunset – signed – on canvas – 10 x 18in.
(Phillips)   **$2,720   £1,700 Pair**

WENZEL THORNOE – The Picnic, Dyrehaven – signed and dated 1883 – 39½ x 87in.
(Christie's)   **$91,575   £49,500**

TIEPOLO

GIOVANNI BATTISTA TIEPOLO – Study For The Head And Right Arm Of Chronos – recto – black chalk on blue paper; Drapery Study – verso – red chalk heightened with white – 318 x 262mm.
(Sotheby's) $109,736 £63,800

LOUIS COMFORT TIFFANY – Mrs. Hinkley Reading – signed with initials – oil on canvas – 26¼ x 18¼in.
(Christie's) $15,400 £9,435

LEOPOLD TILL – A Winter Landscape With Children Skating On A Pond – signed – 18½ x 27¾in. *(Christie's)* **$4,646 £2,640**

CHARLES EFFERIM SMITH TINDALL – A Traveller Camping Under Blue Gums – signed – watercolour – 25.5 x 32cm.
(Sotheby's) $2,645   £1,430

LEOPOLD TILL – Young Revellers In A Town Square – signed – 17¾ x 25¾in.
(Christie's) $4,537   £2,750

LOUIS TIMMERMANS – A Capriccio Venetian Scene – signed – 8¼ x 15¾in.
(Christie's) $2,359   £1,430

DAVID TINDLE – View From A Window – signed and dated '59 – oil on board – unframed – 48 x 72in.
(Christie's) $2,755   £1,650

JAMES JACQUES JOSEPH TISSOT – The Queen Of Sheba – signed – oil on panel – 15½ x 21½in.
(Sotheby's) $12,540   £6,600

TJELLWIJ

TJELLWIJ – Portrait Of A Bearded Gentleman
Wearing A Dark Coat – signed and dated 1835 –
oil on canvas – 72 x 58cm. – and companion.
(Phillips) **$1,800** **£1,000 Pair**

BEN TOBIAS – Sainte-Adresse – signed and
inscribed – oil on canvas – 46 x 56cm.
(Phillips) **$1,764** **£1,050**

RALPH TODD – Fetching Water – signed – oil on
canvas – 56 x 38cm.
(Sotheby's) **$4,989** **£2,640**

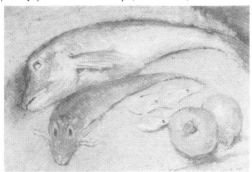

ARTHUR RALPH MIDDLETON TODD – Still
Life Of Fish, Prawns And Onions – signed – oil on
board – 13¾ x 17½in.
(Christie's) **$385** **£220**

GIOVANNI BATTISTA TODESCHINI – Flowers
In A Japanese Bowl – signed – 22¾ x 17in.
(Christie's) **$2,068** **£1,100**

JAN TOOROP – Young Girl In Spring – signed – soft pencil on paper – 8¾ x 12in.
(Christie's)   **$12,342   £6,600**

MAX TODT – The Musician – signed – on panel – 9½ x 7in.
(Christie's)   **$3,097   £1,760**

JAN TOOROP – Thirsty For Justice – signed and dated 1900 – coloured crayons and watercolour on paper – 27½ x 25¾in.
(Christie's)   **$7,040   £4,400**

JAN TOOROP – Mother And Child – signed, dated and inscribed – pastel and pencil on paper – 10½ x 6½in.
(Christie's)   **$10,285   £5,500**

TOOROP

JAN TOOROP – Life's Guardian – signed –
crayon – 41 x 85in.
(Sotheby's)   **$25,080**   **£13,200**

FRANK W. W. TOPHAM – Continental Scene,
Figures Outside Farm Buildings – oil on canvas –
23 x 30in.
*(Barbers Fine Art
Auctioneers)*   **$1,312**   **£750**

FRANK WILLIAM W. TOPHAM – A Young Girl
Standing At A Fountain, Assissi – signed – on
panel – 8½ x 7in.
(Phillips)   **$640**   **£400**

TRYGVE TORKILDSEN – La Place de la
Concorde – signed and indistinctly dated – oil
on canvas – 13¼ x 16¼in.
(Christie's)   **$600**   **£330**

E. TORRINI – Clerical Assistance – signed –
watercolour – 15 x 22in.
(Bruce D. Collins)   **$412**   **£232**

HENRI DE TOULOUSE-LAUTREC – Le Depart
– signed with the monogram – pen and ink and
pencil on paper – 6 x 9¾in.
(Christie's)   **$73,920**   **£46,200**

PIETRO TORRINI – Back From Market – signed
– 14 x 10½in.
(Christie's)   **$2,541**   **£1,540**

HENRI DE TOULOUSE-LAUTREC – Tete De
Femme De Profil; Etude De Mary Hamilton –
pencil on paper – 6¾ x 8in.
(Christie's)   **$7,199**   **£3,850**

MICHELE TOSINI, Called Michele di Ridolfo del
Ghirlandaio – The Virgin And Child With The
Infant Saint John The Baptist – oil on panel – 95
x 76cm.
(Sotheby's)   **$64,702**   **£37,400**

HENRI DE TOULOUSE-LAUTREC – La
Clownesse assise (Mlle. Cha-u-ka-O) – soft pencil
on thin paper laid down on board – 18½ x 14¼in.
(Christie's)   **$64,064**   **£35,200**

TOUSSAINT

FERNAND TOUSSAINT – The Commissioned
Portrait – signed – oil on canvas – 149 x 129cm.
(Sotheby's) **$107,822 £63,800**

FERNAND TOUSSAINT – Reading Time –
signed – oil on canvas – 28½ x 21in.
(Sotheby's) **$20,900 £11,000**

CHARLES TOWNE – A Gentleman With His Bay Hunter And A Spaniel In A River
Landscape – signed – oil on canvas – 70 x 86cm.
(Sotheby's) **$45,254 £24,200**

FRANCIS TOWNE – A Hilly Landscape With
Travellers – signed and dated 1790 – pen and ink
and watercolour – 38 x 54cm.
(Phillips)   **$17,700**   **£10,000**

HENRY SPERNON TOZER – 'By The Hearth' –
signed with monogram and dated '93 – on canvas
– 9 x 12in.
(Phillips)   **$1,320**   **£750**

LEE TOWNSEND – The Cock Fight – signed –
oil on canvas – 50¼ x 40in.
(Robt. W. Skinner Inc.)   **$400**   **£223**

JULES TRAYER – A Good Book – signed – 21 x
16in.
(Christie's)   **$4,537**   **£2,750**

HENRY SPERNON TOZER – The Lepidopterist
– signed and dated '05 – 9 x 13in.
(Phillips)   **$2,720**   **£1,700**

ADOLPH TREIDLER – Nude – signed – watercolour – 12 x 21in.
(Bruce D. Collins)   **$467**   **£263**

TREVELYAN

JULIAN TREVELYAN – Close Hauled – signed and dated '62 – oil on canvas – 16 x 20in.
(Christie's) **$1,347** **£770**

WILLIAM HENRY HAMILTON TROOD – The Best Of Friends – signed and dated 1890 – canvas laid down on board – 15 x 12in.
(Christie's) **$2,904** **£1,650**

JOHANN ZOETELIEF TROMP – At The Seaside – signed – 30½ x 38in.
(Christie's) **$35,640** **£22,000**

DWIGHT WILLIAM TRYON – Night – signed and dated 1916, and signed, dated and inscribed on the reverse – oil on panel – 10¼ x 14in.
(Christie's) **$13,200** **£8,143**

WILLIAM HENRY HAMILTON TROOD – Dejeuner – signed and dated 1899 – 31½ x 47¼in.
(Christie's) **$32,076** **£19,800**

DWIGHT WILLIAM TRYON – Summertime – signed – oil on canvas – 9 x 12¼in.
(Christie's) **$3,300** **£1,843**

JAMES TUCKER – Utility And The Graces – signed, tempera on board – 20 x 24in.
(Sotheby's) $1,925 £1,100

HENRY SCOTT TUKE – Comrades – signed and dated 1924 – oil on canvas – 81 x 122cm.
(Sotheby's) $41,580 £22,000

TUKE

HENRY SCOTT TUKE – Johnny Jacket –
inscribed on the reverse – oil on panel – 7¾ x
10¾in.
(Christie's)   **$14,602   £8,250**

HENRY SCOTT TUKE – Samuel Under A Tree,
Jamaica – signed, inscribed and dated – oil on
board – 13¾ x 18½in.
(Christie's)   **$8,761   £4,950**

JOHN TUNNARD – Take Off – signed and
inscribed on the reverse – oil on gesso-prepared
board – 20 x 24in.
(Christie's)   **$7,009   £3,960**

JOHN TUNNARD – Untitled (Fishes) – signed
and dated '63 – charcoal, brush and ink and wash
with white heightening – 36.5 x 54.5cm.
(Phillips)   **$1,790   £1,000**

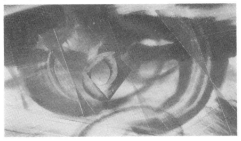

JOHN TUNNARD – Maelstrom – signed, inscribed
and dated '67 – watercolour, ink and gouache –
37 x 55cm.
(Phillips)   **$2,327   £1,300**

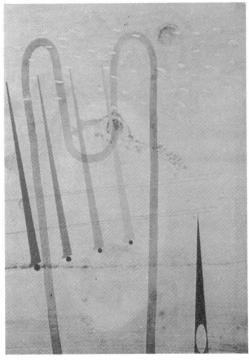

JOHN TUNNARD – Composition – signed and
dated 1939 – watercolour, brush, black ink and
pencil – 22 x 15in.
(Christie's)   **$3,699   £2,090**

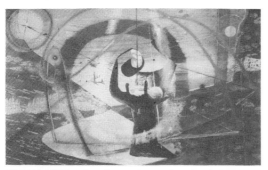

JOHN TUNNARD – Penumbra – signed and dated
'57 – gouache – 14½ x 21¼in.
(Christie's) $3,916 £2,200

CHARLES FREDERICK TUNNICLIFFE –
Summer Ford – signed – watercolour – 17½ x
26in.
(Christie's) $2,741 £1,540

JOHN TUNNARD – Composition – oil on board
– 12¾ x 16½in.
(Christie's) $7,832 £4,400

GEORGE TURNER – Figures On A Bridge Before
A Cottage In A Wooded River Landscape – signed
– on canvas – 14½ x 19in.
(Phillips) $2,464 £1,400

CHARLES FREDERICK TUNNICLIFFE –
Chaffinches – signed with monogram –
watercolour and bodycolour – 9¾ x 7½in.
(Christie's) $1,566 £880

JOSEPH MALLORD WILLIAM TURNER –
Windsor Castle From The Great Park – signed –
watercolour over pencil – 8¾ x 12¼in.
(Sotheby's) $90,992 £48,400

TURNER

WILLIAM EDDOWES TURNER – Charley, A Dapple Grey Hunter In A Stable – signed, dated '67 and inscribed – oil on canvas – 50 x 61.5 cm.
(Sotheby's) **$1,222** **£715**

LAURITS TUXEN – The Coronation Of Czar Nicolas II – 55½ x 71 in.
(Christie's) **$18,315** **£9,900**

JOHN HENRY TWACHTMAN – Dredging In The East River – signed – oil on canvas – 11¾ x 17¾ in.
(Christie's) **$41,800** **£25,610**

JOHN HENRY TWACHTMAN – Gloucester – oil on canvas – 18 x 14 in.
(Christie's) **$49,500** **£30,328**

JOHN HENRY TWACHTMAN – Cascades – signed – oil on canvas – 30 x 24¾ in.
(Christie's) **$93,500** **£57,287**

CY TWOMBLY – Untitled – signed and dated '67 on the reverse – gouache and crayon on paper – 19¼ x 26¾in.
(Christie's) $53,460 £33,000

JAMES GALE TYLER – Battleships At War – signed – oil on canvas – 30 x 42in.
(Christie's) $12,100 £7,413

JAMES GALE TYLER – Naval Battle – signed – oil on canvas – 30 x 42in.
(Christie's) $11,000 £6,739

CARROLL S. TYSON – 'Gravel Pit, Long Pond, Mount Desert Island, Maine' – signed and dated 1944, and inscribed and signed – oil on canvas – 30 x 36in.
(Robt. W. Skinner Inc.) $500 £303

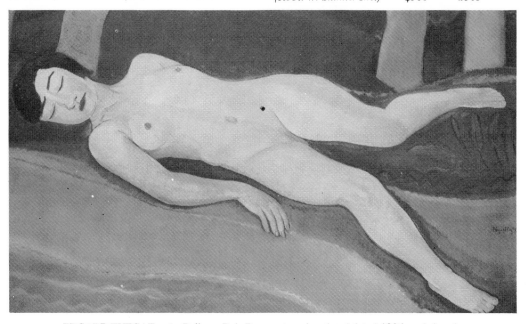

EDGARD TYTGAT – La Belle au Bois Dormant – signed and dated 1924, and signed, dated and inscribed on the reverse – oil on canvas – 32¼ x 40in. *(Christie's)*
$64,064 £35,200

UFER

WALTER UFER – Adobe Village – signed on the reverse – oil on canvas – 20¼ x 26¼in.
(Christie's) **$11,000** **£6,785**

FRANZ RICHARD UNTERBERGER – Amalfi– Golfe de Salerne – signed, and signed and inscribed on the reverse – 31½ x 27in.
(Christie's) **$32,670** **£19,800**

LEON UNDERWOOD – Portrait Of A Woman – signed with initials and dated 1910 – pencil, brown and indian ink, watercolour and bodycolour – 54.5 x 42.5cm.; verso – Study Of A Woman.
(Phillips) **$1,072** **£650**

FRANZ RICHARD UNTERBERGER – An Alpine Lake Landscape With A Goatherd By A Chalet – signed – 28 x 43½in.
(Christie's) **$6,776** **£3,850**

FRANZ RICHARD UNTERBERGER – A View Of The Grand Canal Towards Santa Maria Della Salute – signed – oil on canvas – 83 x 72cm.
(Phillips) **$39,600** **£22,000**

JOHN WILLIAM UPHAM – A West View Of The Ruins Of Walton-in-Gordano Church And Castle, Somerset; and A Traveller Entering The Gatehouse Of Torre Abbey, Devon – one signed and dated 1803, one inscribed on reverse – watercolour over pencil, one with scratching out – 28 x 37cm.
(Sotheby's)　　　　**$808**　　**£462 Pair**

LESSER URY – Dorf (Domburg) mit Kirche – signed and dated 1912 – oil on canvas – 20 x 28in.
(Christie's)　　**$15,840**　　**£9,900**

LESSER URY – Seelandschaft – signed – oil on canvasboard – 8¾ x 12¼in.
(Christie's)　　**$9,009**　　**£4,950**

LESSER URY – Landschaft mit Baumen – signed – pastel on paper – 14¾ x 19¾in.
(Christie's)　　**$22,022**　　**£12,100**

LESSER URY – Seelandschaft – signed – pastel on paper – 26 x 18¼in.
(Christie's)　　**$22,022**　　**£12,100**

MAURICE UTRILLO – Sacre Coeur De Montmartre, Square Saint Pierre – signed and dated 1934 – oil on card laid down on canvas – 9½ x 12¼in.
(Christie's)　　**$94,435**　　**£50,500**

UTRILLO

MAURICE UTRILLO – Paysage a Saint-Pierre-de-Bost, en Creuse – signed and dated 1926 – oil on canvas – 28¾ x 39½in. *(Christie's)* $177,100 £110,000

MAURICE UTRILLO – Vue du Sacre Coeur – signed and dated 1923 – gouache on paper – 11¼ x 15¾in. *(Christie's)* $45,760 £28,600

MAURICE UTRILLO – La Maison de Mimi Pinson – signed and inscribed – charcoal on paper – 17¾ x 18¾in. *(Christie's)* $18,018 £9,900

MAURICE UTRILLO – Place Ravignan – signed – oil on panel – 16¼ x 19¾in. *(Christie's)* $120,120 £66,000

MAURICE UTRILLO – Rue a Hyeres – signed – oil on canvas – 23¾ x 32in. *(Christie's)* $283,360 £176,000

UTRILLO

MAURICE UTRILLO – Montmartre – signed and inscribed – watercolour and gouache on paper – 12¼ x 9¼in.
(Christie's)   **$65,824**   **£35,200**

MAURICE UTRILLO – Le Moulin De La Galette – signed, and signed on the reverse – gouache – 27 x 20.5cm.
(Sotheby's)   **$50,424**   **£26,400**

MAURICE UTRILLO – Une Rue a Montmartre – signed and inscribed – oil on canvas – 15 x 18in.
(Christie's)   **$102,080**   **£63,800**

MAURICE UTRILLO – La Grande Rue a Poissy – signed and inscribed – oil on canvas – 18¼ x 21½in.
(Christie's)   **$150,150**   **£82,500**

MAURICE UTRILLO – Scene de Rue – signed – watercolour and charcoal on paper – 14½ x 19in.
(Christie's)   **$66,880**   **£41,800**

MAURICE UTRILLO – La Basilique D'Ars – signed and dated 1929 – oil on canvas – ·25¾ x 31¾in.
(Christie's)   **$163,680   £88,000**

MAURICE UTRILLO – Les Cafes de Village – signed – oil on board – 19½ x 28¾in.
(Christie's)   **$340,340   £187,000**

UTRILLO

MAURICE UTRILLO – Eglise en Andorre – signed and dated 1935 – oil on canvas – 21¼ x 28¾in. *(Christie's)* $160,160 £88,000

MAURICE UTRILLO – Le Moulin de la Galette – signed – oil on canvas – 18¾ x 23¼in. *(Christie's)* $260,260 £143,000

MAURICE UTRILLO – La Belle Gabrielle et la Rue Saint-Vincent – signed and inscribed – oil on board – 18 x 21½in. *(Christie's)* $177,100 £110,000

JULES EMMANUEL VALADON – A Young Boy Crouched Before A Stove – signed – oil on panel – 27 x 21cm. *(Phillips)* $990 £550

GIOVANNI DOMENICO VALENTINO – A
Kitchen Interior – on canvas – 37¾ x 52¼in.
(Phillips) **$9,100** **£5,000**

FELIX VALLOTTON – Sortie Du Bain – signed
and dated – oil on canvas – 37¾ x 39 ¼in.
(Christie's) **$49,368** **£26,400**

GEORGES VALMIER – Composition cubiste –
signed – watercolour, pen and ink on paper – 6¾
x 4in.
(Christie's) **$17,600** **£11,000**

GEORGES VALMIER – Composition cubiste –
signed – collage – watercolour, pen and ink on
paper – 5¼ x 5¾in.
(Christie's) **$17,600** **£11,000**

LOUIS VALTAT – La Seine et le Pont de Bir
Hakeim – signed – oil on canvas laid on panel –
8¼ x 11in.
(Christie's) **$9,801** **£6,050**

LOUIS VALTAT – Paysage de Choisel – signed –
oil on canvas – 21¾ x 28¾in.
(Christie's)   **$52,052   £28,600**

JOHN VARLEY – The Old Redhouse Battersea –
signed and dated 1831 – watercolour over traces
of pencil – 14 x 20cm.
(Phillips)   **$1,858   £1,050**

LOUIS VALTAT – Bouquet de Fleurs dans un
vase – oil on panel – 10¼ x 8in.
(Christie's)   **$12,012   £6,600**

JOHN VARLEY – The Bridge At Beddgelert,
Merionethshire – signed and dated 1815, and
signed again on the verso – watercolour with
scratching out – 30 x 46.5cm.
(Sotheby's)   **$3,657   £2,090**

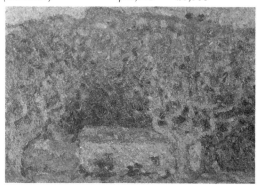

LOUIS VALTAT – Maisons Sous Les Oliviers –
signed – oil on canvas – 17¾ x 21¾in.
(Christie's)   **$26,741   £14,300**

JOHN VARLEY, Jnr. – The Mosque Of Sultan
Selim, Cairo; and The Horsemarket, Cairo – signed,
and inscribed on original labels attached to
backboard – oil on board – 26.5 x 20cm.
(Sotheby's)   **$1,322   £715 Pair**

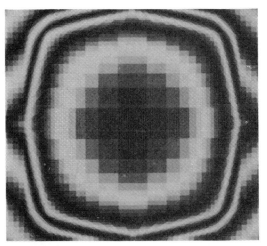

VICTOR VASARELY − Rell-Z − signed, inscribed and dated 1973 on the reverse − acrylic on canvas − 39½ x 39½in.
(Christie's) $12,012   £6,600

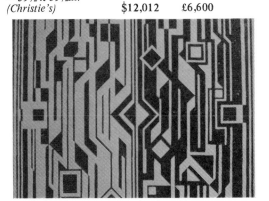

VICTOR VASARELY − Gizeh II − signed, and signed and dated 1955-62 − oil on canvas − 120.5 x 120.5cm.
(Sotheby's) $42,592   £24,200

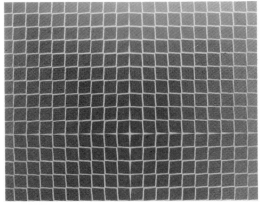

VICTOR VASARELY − Quasar 2 − signed, inscribed and dated 1965 on the reverse − acrylic on canvas − 69 x 69in.
(Christie's) $26,730   £16,500

VICTOR VASARELY − Xingou − signed and dated '49-51, and inscribed by the artist on a label attached to the reverse − oil on panel − 120 x 100cm.
(Sotheby's) $57,024   £29,700

KEITH VAUGHAN − Pallas Athene − watercolour and bodycolour − 9½ x 11¼in.
(Christie's) $2,887   £1,650

533

VAUGHAN

ELIHU VEDDER – Absorbed – signed and dated 1883, and signed, dated again and inscribed on the reverse – oil on canvas laid down on board – 11¾ x 15¾in.
(Christie's) $7,700   £4,750

KEITH VAUGHAN – Miner Adjusting A Cutter – signed and dated '52 – watercolour, bodycolour, brush, pen, black and grey wash and pencil, heightened with white chalk – 14½ x 10¾in.
(Christie's) $4,307   £2,420

ELIHU VEDDER – The Questioner Of The Sphinx – signed and dated 1863 – oil en grisaille on paper laid down on canvas – 6¾ x 5½in.
(Christie's) $19,800   £12,214

ELIHU VEDDER – Leaning Trees Near Viareggio – signed – oil on canvas laid down on masonite – 17¼ x 10½in.
(Christie's) $2,420   £1,492

ELIHU VEDDER – Orte – signed and inscribed – oil on canvas laid down on masonite – 10½ x 14in.
(Christie's) $3,300 £2,035

ELIHU VEDDER – Vesuvius – signed with initial – oil on paper laid down on canvas – 5¾ x 10¼in.
(Christie's) $3,080 £1,900

ELIHU VEDDER – Near Perugia, 1867 – signed with initial and dated '67 – oil on paper laid down on canvas – 11¼ x 8¼in.
(Christie's) $3,080 £1,900

ELIHU VEDDER – Bordighera – signed – oil on panel – 12½ x 8in.
(Christie's) $7,150 £4,410

ELIHU VEDDER – Near Perugia – signed with initial and dated '91, and signed and dated again on the reverse – oil on board – 7¾ x 12½in.
(Christie's) $7,700 £4,750

VEDDER

ELIHU VEDDER – Roadside Figure And Umbrella – signed – pastel on tan paper laid down on canvas – 15 x 24½in.
(Christie's) $1,540   £950

ELIHU VEDDER and ALFRED PARSONS – Luna, Christmas, 1882 – signed with initial – watercolour and pastel and black and blue ink on artist's board – 12¼ x 11in.
(Christie's) $6,050   £3,732

BRAM VAN VELDE – Composition – signed on the reverse – gouache on cardboard – 73 x 55cm.
(Sotheby's) $23,232   £13,200

WILLEM VAN DE VELDE, the Younger – Dutch Men Of War With A Galleon And Other Shipping In Choppy Seas – signed with initials – oil on canvas – 56.5 x 71cm.
(Sotheby's) $285,450   £165,000

WILHELM VELTEN – A Coach Halted Outside A Farmhouse – signed – on panel – 6¼ x 9½in.
(Christie's) $3,267   £1,980

EUGENE JOSEPH VERBOECKHOVEN – Deer In A Wooded Landscape – signed and dated '51 – on panel – 9½ x 11¾in.
(Christie's) $11,192   £6,050

JULES VICTOR VERDIER – A Reclining Nude – 28 x 36in. *(Christie's)*
$6,352 £3,850

SIMON VERELST – Portrait Of A Lady, Three Quarter Length, Seated – oil on canvas – 124.5 x 99cm.
(Sotheby's)   **$24,596   £14,300**

SIMON PIETER VERELST – A Vase Of Flowers – signed – on canvas – 25¾ x 20½in.
(Phillips)   **$309,400   £170,000**

VERHAECHT

TOBIAS VERHAECHT – Nimrod Supervising The Building Of The Tower Of Babel – oil on panel – 137 x 165cm.
(Sotheby's)　　　**$144,628**　**£83,600**

JAN HENDRIK VERHEYEN – A Dutch Town Scene – signed and dated 1824 – on panel – 20½ x 25½in.
(Christie's)　　　**$40,986**　**£25,300**

FRITS VERMEHREN – A Difficult Task – signed with initials and dated 1894 – 15¼ x 12in.
(Christie's)　　　**$8,547**　**£4,620**

JAN HENDRIK VERHEYEN – Figures In A Garden Before A Dutch Town – signed and dated 1813 – oil on panel – 29 x 32cm.
(Phillips)　　　**$1,530**　**£850**

JOHANN FREDERICK NIKOLAI VERMEHREN – Poppies And Daisies In A Vase – signed – 20¼ x 17¾in.
(Christie's)　　　**$1,548**　**£880**

ANDREAS FRANCISCUS VERMEULEN – A
Market Stall At Night – signed and dated 1863 –
on panel – 24¼ x 19¾in.
(Christie's)　　　**$2,541**　　**£1,540**

EMILE VERNON – The Billet doux – signed –
36½ x 28½in.
(Christie's)　　　**$8,019**　　**£4,950**

VERNIER – Entree du port de Boulogne –
signed, inscribed and dated '90 – 25 x 39in.
(Christie's)　　　**$2,359**　　**£1,430**

J. VERNIER – A Quayside – signed and dated
'91? – 21 x 25in.
(Christie's)　　　**$2,359**　　**£1,430**

LIBERALE DA VERONA – The Madonna And
Sleeping Christ Child – tempera on panel – 77 x
50.5cm.
(Sotheby's)　　　**$27,593**　　**£15,950**

VERONESE

PAOLO VERONESE, and Studio – The Martyrdom Of Saint Catherine – oil on canvas – 86.5 x 106cm.
(Sotheby's) $83,732   £48,400

FRANCOIS VERWILT – A Horseman With Servants And Hounds In A Landscape – signed – on panel – 16½ x 21¾in.
(Phillips) $10,920   £6,000

ANTHONIE VERSTRAELEN – Figures On The Ice Near A Gateway To A Town – signed twice in monogram – oil on panel – 33 x 54cm.
(Sotheby's) $28,545   £16,500

ALFRED H. VICKERS – A Lakeside Ruin, Vale Of Clwyd – signed, and also inscribed on the reverse – on canvas – 8 x 16in.; also a companion.
(Phillips) $2,720   £1,700 Pair

GEORGE VERTUE – The Royal Progress Of Queen Elizabeth – signed – watercolour – 16 x 22in.
(Sotheby's) $38,258   £20,350

ROBERT VICKREY – Nassau Church – signed – tempera on masonite – 21¼ x 30in.
(Christie's) $9,350 £5,223

VICTORIAN SCHOOL – Highland Landscapes –
oil – various small sizes.
(Messrs. G. A. Key) $21   £12

VICTOR VIGNON – L'Entree du Village d'
Evecquemont – signed – oil on board – 10½ x
16¼in.
(Christie's) $8,910   £5,500

MACARIO VITALIS – Bouquet de Fleurs –
signed and dated '38 – oil on canvas – 25½ x
21¼in.
(Christie's) $1,603   £990

VIVREL

ANDRE VIVREL – Les Coquelcots – signed – oil on canvas – 81 x 100cm. *(Phillips)*
$2,688 £1,600

MAURICE DE VLAMINCK – Le Carrefour Du
Village – signed – watercolour and pen and brush
and indian ink – 45 x 54cm.
(Sotheby's)   **$31,725   £16,610**

MAURICE DE VLAMINCK – Nature morte aux
Livres – signed – oil on canvas – 17¼ x 21¼in.
(Christie's)   **$49,280   £30,800**

MAURICE DE VLAMINCK – Voilier sur une
Fleuve – signed – oil on canvas – 23¾ x 32in.
(Christie's)   **$168,245   £104,500**

MAURICE DE VLAMINCK – Nature Morte Aux
Fleurs – signed – oil on canvas – 17¾ x 14¼in.
(Christie's)   **$90,508   £48,400**

MAURICE DE VLAMINCK – Scene de Village;
Coucher de Soleil – signed – oil on canvas –
23¾ x 28¾in.
(Christie's)   **$105,600   £66,000**

MAURICE DE VLAMINCK – Village sur une
Colline – signed – watercolour, pen, brush and
indian ink on paper – 18½ x 24½in.
(Christie's)   **$22,000   £13,750**

MAURICE DE VLAMINCK – Les Toits du
Village – signed and dated 1914 – oil on canvas
– 32¼ x 25¾in.
(Christie's)   **$105,600   £66,000**

VLAMINCK

MAURICE DE VLAMINCK – Paysage Orageux –
signed – oil on canvas – 18¼ x 21¾in.
(Christie's)   **$68,068**   **£37,400**

MAURICE DE VLAMINCK – Paysage Aux
Maisons – signed – gouache and watercolour – 34
x 43.3cm.
(Sotheby's)   **$18,909**   **£9,900**

MAURICE DE VLAMINCK – Paysage Orageux –
signed – oil on canvas – 25¾ x 28¾in.
(Christie's)   **$91,520**   **£57,200**

MAURICE DE VLAMINCK – Le Moulin – signed
– gouache, brush and black ink on paper – 17¼ x
20¾in.
(Christie's)   **$20,020**   **£11,000**

MAURICE DE VLAMINCK – Le Village – signed
– oil on canvas – 25¾ x 32in.
(Christie's)   **$110,110**   **£60,500**

MAURICE DE VLAMINCK – Le Chemin du
Village – signed – oil on canvas – 15 x 18¼in.
(Christie's)   **$66,880**   **£41,800**

MAURICE DE VLAMINCK – Nature morte aux
Fleurs – signed – oil on canvas – 23¼ x 18¾in.
(Christie's) $96,800 £60,500

MAURICE DE VLAMINCK – Nature morte aux
Fleurs – signed – oil on canvas – 23¾ x 21¼in.
(Christie's) $91,520 £57,200

MAURICE DE VLAMINCK – Bouquet de Fleurs – signed – oil on canvas – 23¾ x 28½in.
(Christie's) $120,120 £66,000

VLAMINCK

MAURICE DE VLAMINCK – Bouquet de Fleurs dans un Vase blanc – signed – oil on canvas – 21¾ x 15in.
(Christie's)   **$120,120**   **£66,000**

MAURICE DE VLAMINCK – Les Toits de Paris – signed – oil on canvas – 23¾ x 28¾in.
(Christie's)   **$110,110**   **£60,500**

MAURICE DE VLAMINCK – Pecheur au Bord de la Riviere – signed – oil on canvas – 15 x 18½in.
(Christie's)   **$52,800**   **£33,000**

MAURICE DE VLAMINCK – Paysage; Route De Village – signed – oil on canvas – 24 x 31¾in.
(Christie's)   **$133,705**   **£71,500**

MAURICE DE VLAMINCK – La Route – signed – oil on canvas – 23¾ x 28¾in.
(Christie's)   **$113,135**   **£60,500**

JOHANNES GYSBERT VOGEL – An Eastern Beauty – signed – 39 x 28½in.
(Christie's)   **$2,323**   **£1,320**

LUCIEN VOGT – Reflections – signed – oil on canvas – 46 x 61cm.
(Phillips)　　　**$1,176**　　　**£700**

ROBERT WILLIAM VONNOH – New England Hills – signed and dated 1901 – oil on canvas laid down on board – 19¼ x 23¼in.
(Christie's)　　　**$8,800**　　　**£4,916**

ALEXIS VOLLON – Les Bords de la Seine – signed and dated 1924 – 13 x 16¼in.
(Christie's)　　　**$1,742**　　　**£990**

ROBERT WILLIAM VONNOH – Gathering Geese – signed – oil on canvas – 18¼ x 21½in.
(Christie's)　　　**$14,300**　　　**£7,989**

VINCENT DE VOS – Les Animaux Amis – signed and dated '56 – oil on canvas – 49 x 67cm. *(Phillips)*
$9,000 £5,000

VUILLARD

EDOUARD VUILLARD – Jeune Femme au Bouquet de Fleurs – pastel and charcoal on paper – 14¼ x 8½in.
(Christie's)   **$10,560   £6,600**

EDOUARD VUILLARD – La Jardiniere – oil on board – 9¼ x 6¾in.
(Christie's)   **$56,056   £30,800**

EDOUARD VUILLARD – Nature morte; Fleurs sur un Table devant un Fauteuil – signed with initials – oil on board – 15 x 18¼in.
(Christie's)   **$130,130   £71,500**

EDOUARD VUILLARD – Madame Vuillard au Bureau – oil on canvas – 16¼ x 13in.
(Christie's)   **$260,260   £143,000**

EDOUARD VUILLARD – Madame Vuillard au Petit-Dejeuner – oil on paper laid down on canvas – 28¾ x 36¼in.
(Christie's) $540,540   £297,000

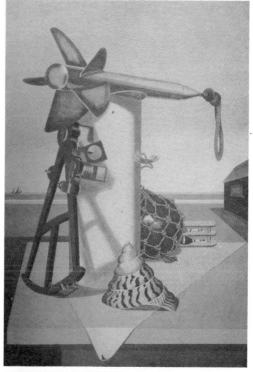

A. DE VYLDER – Flirtation – indistinctly signed – on panel – 20 x 17in.
(Christie's)   **$1,815**   **£1,100**

EDWARD WADSWORTH – North Sea – tempera on panel – 34 x 24in.
(Christie's)   **$137,060**   **£77,000**

ALEXANDER VON WAGNER – A Good Smoke – signed – oil on panel – 18 x 14cm. – and Her Sunday Best. *(Phillips)*
$3,600 £2,000 Pair

WAGNER

LOUIS WAIN – Barrister Cat; and Green Eyed Cat – signed – watercolour heightened with bodycolour – 12 x 9in.
(Sotheby's)   **$1,309**   **£770 Two**

FERDINAND WAGNER – The Huntress – signed and dated '85 – 68 x 37in.
(Christie's)   **$12,705**   **£7,700**

ALFONS WALDE – Einsamer Berghof (Tirol) – signed, inscribed and dated on the artist's label on the reverse – oil on board – 13 x 20¾in.
(Christie's)   **$26,400**   **£16,500**

EHRNFRIED WAHLQUIST – A Wooded River Landscape With A Man In A Boat And Children At A Jetty – signed and dated 1868 – 22 x 32¾in.
(Christie's)   **$6,105**   **£3,300**

ALFONS WALDE – Tiroler Bauernhof am Kaisergebinge – signed, inscribed and dated on the artist's label on the reverse – oil on board – 13 x 20¾in.
(Christie's)   **$35,200**   **£22,000**

DAME ETHEL WALKER – Portrait Of A Girl Seated, Wearing A Red Wrap – signed – oil on canvas – 31 x 23in.
(Christie's)   **$7,788   £4,400**

DAME ETHEL WALKER – The Watchers By The Sea – oil on canvas – 72 x 48in.
(Sotheby's)   **$4,862   £2,860**

DAME ETHEL WALKER – Elsa Lanchester As Prue, In 'Love For Love', By Congreve – oil on canvas – 24 x 20in.
(Christie's)   **$10,903   £6,160**

DAME ETHEL WALKER – Portrait Of A Lady In A White Dress And Black Shawl, Seated On A Red Sofa – oil on canvas – 50 x 40in.
(Christie's)   **$1,886   £1,078**

WALKER

DAME ETHEL WALKER – Watering The Garden
– oil on canvas – 30 x 25 in.
(Christie's) $8,266   £4,950

SAMUEL EDMUND WALKER – The Trysting
Place – signed and dated 1904 – on canvas – 14 x
11 in.
(Phillips) $1,920   £1,200

WILLIAM AIKEN WALKER – Daily Chores –
signed with initials conjoined – oil on board –
6¼ x 12¼ in.
(Christie's) $9,900   £6,065

DAME ETHEL WALKER – Still Life Of Flowers
In A Jug – signed – oil on canvas – 36 x 25 in.
(Christie's) $13,777   £8,250

WILLIAM AIKEN WALKER – Wash Day –
signed with initials conjoined – oil on board – 9¼
x 12¼ in.
(Christie's) $9,350   £5,768

WILLIAM AIKEN WALKER – Washing Clothes – signed with conjoined initials – oil on
board – 6¼ x 12¼in. *(Christie's)* $7,700 £4,301

WILLIAM AIKEN WALKER – A Cotton Picker With A Basket; and A Negro With An
Umbrella And A Bag – signed – oil on board – 20 x 10cm. *(Sotheby's)*
$4,070 £2,200 Two

WALKER

WILLIAM AIKEN WALKER – The Cotton Field
– signed with initials conjoined – oil on board –
8¾ x 12¼in.
(Christie's)   **$6,600**   **£4,071**

WILLIAM AIKEN WALKER – Picked Cotton –
signed with initials conjoined – oil on board –
unframed – 9¼ x 12¼in.
(Christie's)   **$5,500**   **£3,392**

ALFRED WALLIS – A Yacht – gouache on paper
laid down on panel – 10¾ x 12¾in.
(Christie's)   **$2,571**   **£1,540**

WILLIAM AIKEN WALKER – A Walk In The
Cotton Fields – signed with initials conjoined –
oil on board – 12¼ x 6¼in.
(Christie's)   **$3,850**   **£2,375**

ALFRED WALLIS – Ships And Harbour – signed
– blue crayon – 11¾ x 15¾in.
(Christie's)   **$1,837**   **£1,100**

ELLEN WARD – Off The Coast Of Maine –
signed and dated – oil on canvas – 8 x 13in.
(Bruce D. Collins) **$247** **£139**

ALFRED WALLIS – A Three-Masted Brig –
recto; A View Of St. Ives – verso – signed both
sides – coloured crayons – 11 x 15in.
(Christie's) **$2,204** **£1,320**

JAMES WARD – The Woodman's Companions –
signed – oil on panel – 18.5 x 32.5cm.
(Sotheby's) **$4,138** **£2,420**

JAMES WARD – The Wagonner's Horse – oil on panel – 42.5 x 52.5cm. *(Christie's)*
$6,171 **£3,300**

WARD

JOHN WARD – The Piazza del Popolo, Rome –
signed twice, inscribed and dated 1961 and 1962
– pen, brown ink and water colour – 32 x 47.5cm.
(Phillips)   **$1,353**   **£820**

JOHN WARD – The Artist Painting A Still Life Of
Flowers – signed and dated 1946 – watercolour
and pencil – 12¼ x 18in.
(Christie's)   **$1,771**   **£1,012**

ARTHUR WARDLE – Portraits Of Two Lakeland
Terriers – signed – oil on canvas – 13 x 20in.
(Phillips)   **$4,160**   **£2,600**

ANDY WARHOL – Cupid With Pussy Cats –
signed – pen and ink and water colour on paper –
35.5 x 51cm.
(Sotheby's)   **$9,680**   **£5,500**

ANDY WARHOL – Do You See My Little Pussy?
– signed with the initials – felt tip pen and
watercolour on paper – 35 x 27.5cm.
(Sotheby's)   **$6,969**   **£3,960**

ANDY WARHOL – Flowers – signed with initials
and dated '64 – silkscreen on canvas – 5 x 5in.
(Christie's)   **$8,408**   **£4,620**

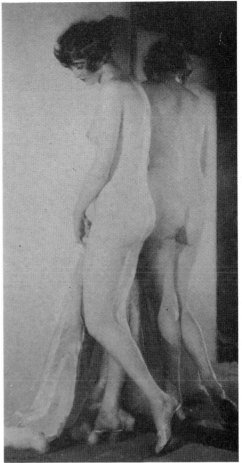

EVERETT LONGLEY WARNER – Late Thaw –
signed – pastel on board – 9½ x 6½in.
(Robt. W. Skinner Inc.) **$600** **£363**

CHARLES WATELET – A Nude In Front Of A
Mirror – signed and dated 1929 – 53½ x 31in.
(Christie's) **$28,512** **£17,600**

JOSEPH WARNIA-ZARZECHI – Entertaining The Pasha – signed and dated 1896 – oil on canvas –
61 x 98½in. *(Sotheby's)* **$192,280** **£101,200**

WATELIN

LOUIS WATELIN – Champ de Fleurs et Bois –
oil on hardboard – 39 x 32.5cm.
(Phillips) $638   £380

JOHN WILLIAM WATERHOUSE – Fair
Rosamund – signed and dated 1916, and signed
and inscribed on an old label on the reverse – 38 x
28½in.
(Christie's) $101,750   £55,000

JOHN WILLIAM WATERHOUSE – The Favourites Of The Emperor Henorius – 37 x 64½in.
(Christie's) $9,680   £5,500

HOMER RANSFORD WATSON – Stairway,
Isle Of Orleans – signed with initials and
inscribed on the reverse – oil on board –
unframed – 6½ x 9¼in.
(Christie's) $770 £471

LESLIE JOSEPH WATSON – Fishing By The
Lighthouse – signed – oil on canvas – 20 x 24in.
(Christie's) $1,469 £880

SIR JOHN WATSON-GORDON, Circle of –
Portrait Of Members Of The MacDonald Family –
oil on canvas – 168 x 209cm.
(Sotheby's) $3,762 £2,200

SPENCER WATSON – Portrait Of Mrs. Dorothy
Mulloch – signed – oil on canvas – 91.5 x 71cm.
(Sotheby's) $5,984 £3,520

GEORGE FREDERICK WATTS – A Portrait
Head Of Henry Phillips – charcoal – 71 x 61cm.
(Phillips) $637 £360

WAUGH

FREDERICK JUDD WAUGH – Restless Sea –
signed – oil on canvas – 43¾ x 60¾in.
(Christie's) $16,500   £9,218

JAMES WEBB – Breezy Day, Portsmouth –
signed and dated 1869, and signed and inscribed on
the reverse – 36 x 54½in.
(Christie's) $28,512   £17,600

JAMES WEBB – 'Istanbul' – signed – on canvas –
24 x 35½in.
(Phillips) $7,744   £4,400

WILLIAM EDWARD WEBB – Shipping In A Stiff
Breeze Off A Port – signed and dated '85 – 12 x
24in.
(Christie's) $1,839   £1,045

WILLIAM JAMES WEBB – Gathering Roses In
The Holy Land – signed with monogram and
dated 1868 – oil on canvas – 79 x 64cm.
(Sotheby's) $4,919   £2,860

AUDREY WEBER – A Busy London Street –
signed, tempera on board – 30 x 21in.
(Sotheby's) $4,114   £2,420

MAX WEBER – The Gesture – signed and inscribed on an old label attached to the stretcher – oil on canvas – 18 x 22in. *(Christie's)* $20,900 £12,805

MAX WEBER – Three Women – signed and dated '10 – watercolour and gouache on paper laid down on board – 13¾ x 10¾in.
(Christie's) $33,000 £18,437

MAX WEBER – Solo – signed and dated 1918 – oil on canvas – 24 x 18in.
(Christie's) $26,400 £16,175

WEBER

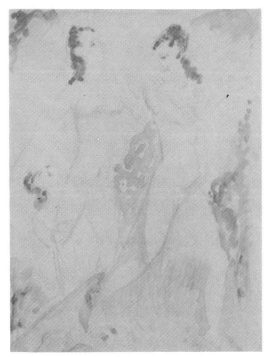

MAX WEBER – Three Girls – signed and dated 1912, and signed again, dated and inscribed on the reverse – watercolour and pencil on board – 10 x 8in.
(Christie's)   **$1,540**   **£950**

WILLIAM WEEKES – Her Lord And Master– signed and dated 1879, and signed and inscribed on the reverse – 44¼ x 34in.
(Christie's)   **$8,131**   **£4,620**

WALTER ERNEST WEBSTER – Puppets – signed, and also signed and inscribed on a label on the reverse – oil on canvas – 68 x 56cm.
(Phillips)   **$5,370**   **£3,000**

EDWIN LORD WEEKS – Figures On A Roadside In Nice – signed and inscribed – on canvas – 10½ x 8½in.
(Phillips)   **$2,400**   **£1,500**

BERTHA WEGMANN – In The Woods – signed
and dated 1880 – 15 x 12in.
(Christie's) $15,147 £9,350

GUSTAVE ADOLPH WEIGAND – Blue Mountain
Lake – signed – oil on canvas – 24 x 20in.
(Bruce D. Collins) $935 £528

CAREL WEIGHT – Strange Encounter, A View
From The Artist's Studio – signed – oil on
board – 10 x 14in.
(Sotheby's) $2,244 £1,320

CAREL WEIGHT – The Paper Mill – signed – oil
on board – 16¼ x 19¼in.
(Christie's) $4,041 £2,420

CAREL WEIGHT – Walkers On A Path – signed –
oil on board – 19½ x 23in.
(Christie's) $4,672 £2,640

WEIGHT

CAREL WEIGHT – Edwin La Dell's Cottage –
oil on canvas – 18 x 24in.
(Sotheby's) **$5,236 £3,080**

CAREL WEIGHT – From The Window, Winter
1984 – signed – oil on canvas board – 40.5 x
30.5cm.
(Phillips) **$1,312 £800**

JULIAN ALDEN WEIR – Blossom Time – signed
– oil on canvas – 20¼ x 24¼in.
(Christie's) **$41,800 £23,353**

CAREL WEIGHT – Dream About A Flower –
signed on the reverse – oil on canvas – 30¾ x
20in.
(Christie's) **$6,245 £3,740**

JULIAN ALDEN WEIR – Nassau, Bahamas –
signed and dated – oil on canvas – 32¼ x
36¼in.
(Christie's) **$440,000 £269,588**

JULIAN ALDEN WEIR – The Old Laurel Bush –
oil on canvas.
(Christie's)   **$16,500   £10,109**

JOHANNES WEISS – Portrait Of An Artist
Smoking A Pipe – signed and dated 1835 – 25 x
20in.
(Christie's)   **$5,346   £3,300**

JULIAN ALDEN WEIR – A Homage To Whistler
– signed – oil on canvas – 17¼ x 11¼in.
(Christie's)   **$49,500   £27,655**

DENYS G. WELLS – The Portfolio – signed and
dated '57 – oil on canvas – 21¼ x 17¼in.
(Christie's)   **$3,524   £1,980**

WENBAN

SION LONGLEY WENBAN – River Landscape – signed and dated 1889 – oil on canvas – 6¼ x 13in.
(Sotheby's) **$1,526** **£825**

RICHARD WESTALL – 'A Storm In Harvest' – oil on canvas – 22¼ x 28¼in.
(Phillips) **$11,100** **£6,000**

WILLIAM WENDT – View From The Hill – signed – oil on canvas – 19¾ x 30in.
(Christie's) **$12,100** **£7,413**

STOW WENGENROTH – Red Berries – signed – watercolour – 6½ x 10in.
(Bruce D. Collins) **$385** **£217**

CONSTANT WESTCHILOFF – The 'Liselliot' – signed – oil on canvas – 25 x 34in.
(Robt. W. Skinner Inc.) **$1,500** **£837**

JULIUS WENTSCHER – The Sea Shore – signed and dated 1904 – 46½ x 82¾in.
(Christie's) **$11,192** **£6,050**

CORNELIS WESTERBEEK – A Shepherd With His Flock In An Extensive Landscape – signed – oil on canvas – 32 x 51cm.
(Phillips) **$1,350** **£750**

GEORGE FAULKNER WETHERBEE – Spring Passes – signed – oil on canvas – 31 x 50in.
(Christie's) $6,980   £4,180

HARRY VAN DER WEYDEN – Menton – signed, inscribed and dated 1939 – oil on canvas laid down on board – 36 x 57cm.
(Phillips) $2,506   £1,400

RICHARD WEATHERBY – Trewerne–After The Storm – signed and inscribed on the reverse – oil on canvas – 25 x 30in.
(Christie's) $2,204   £1,320

FRANCIS WHEATLEY – Dairy Maids Outside A Cottage – signed and dated 1789 – oil on canvas – 46 x 56cm.
(Sotheby's) $11,313   £6,050

HARRY VAN DER WEYDEN – The Derelict – signed and dated 1923 – oil on canvas – 50¾ x 65¼in.
(Sotheby's) $4,884   £2,640

ALFRED WHEELER – Study Of Two King Charles Spaniels – signed – on board – 5¼ x 6¾in.; also Two Studies Of Terriers – signed with initials – on board.
(Phillips) $2,240   £1,400 Three

ROWLAND WHEELWRIGHT – Girl On A Beach – signed – oil on canvas – 20¼ x 24¼in.
(Christie's) $5,511 £3,300

ROWLAND WHEELWRIGHT – Farm Girl Riding A White Horse Leading A Bay Horse Through A Gate – signed – oil on canvas – 71 x 92cm.
(W. H. Lane & Son) **$4,125** **£2,500**

JAMES ABBOTT MacNEIL WHISTLER – On The Beach, Hastings – signed – pastel on brown paper – 13½ x 9½in.
(Christie's) **$66,000** **£36,874**

ETHELBERT WHITE – Still Life Of Fruit On A Table – signed – oil on canvas – 21 x 25½in.
(Christie's)   **$1,468**   **£825**

JAMES ABBOTT McNEILL WHISTLER – A Street, Ajaccio, 1900 – pencil on cream wove paper – 13.5 x 8cm.
(Sotheby's)   **$9,355**   **£4,950**

THOMAS WHITCOMBE, Circle of – After The Battle – oil on canvas – 44 x 59cm.
(Sotheby's)   **$2,069**   **£1,210**

ETHELBERT WHITE – Betty At The Washtub – signed – oil on panel – 17½ x 13½in.
(Christie's)   **$1,309**   **£748**

WHITE

ETHELBERT WHITE – The Sluice, Amberley Wildbrooks – oil on board – 10½ x 14in.; and six paintings.
(Christie's)   **$1,732**   **£990 Seven**

ETHELBERT WHITE – A Summer's Afternoon On The River – signed – watercolour – 10¼ x 13¼in.
(Christie's)   **$1,058**   **£605**

GEORGE WHITE – Charles II – signed and dated 1702 – pencil on vellum – 14 x 10.5cm.
(Phillips)   **$1,858**   **£1,050**

ETHELBERT WHITE – On The River – signed – oil on board – 16 x 20in. *(Sotheby's)*
     $4,301   **£2,530**

GEORGE HARLOW WHITE – The Log House In The Forest – signed and dated 1875 – water-colour over pencil – 5¼ x 8½in.
(Sotheby's) $569 £308

FREDERIC WHITING – The Green Boat – signed – oil on canvas board – 34 x 44cm.
(Phillips) $5,740 £3,500

JOHN WHITE – The Gossips – signed – oil on canvas – 26 x 21½in.
(Christie's) $1,251 £715

WILLIAM JOHN WHITTEMORE – Queen Anne's Lace – signed and dated 1886 – oil on canvas – 9 x 12in.
(Christie's) $6,050 £3,732

FREDERICK WILLIAM NEWTON WHITEHEAD – Cattle Grazing In A Wooded River Landscape – signed and inscribed – on canvas – 11¾ x 19½in.; also a companion.
(Phillips) $2,112 £1,200 Pair

JOHN WHORF – Winter Night – signed and dated '40 – watercolour and pencil on paper – 15 x 21¾in.
(Christie's) $2,420 £1,492

WHORF

JOHN WHORF – Three Women In A Park –
signed – oil on board – 17 x 13in.
(Christie's)   **$2,860   £1,764**

DUNCAN McGREGOR WHYTE – Boating On A
Lake – oil on canvas – 16¼ x 13in.
(Christie's)   **$5,390   £3,080**

ERNEST HERBERT WHYDALE – The Circus –
signed twice and dated 1924 – black chalk,
watercolour and bodycolour – 35.5 x 51.5cm.
(Phillips)   **$2,640   £1,600**

CHARLES WHYMPER – 'Chibi'; and 'Fuji',
Japanese Favourites Of The Earl Of Sandwich –
signed and dated 1903 – oil on canvas – 14 x
19in.
*(Prudential Fine Art
    Auctioneers)*   **$5,022   £3,100 Pair**

WILLIAM WIDGERY – Beckey Falls; and Coombe
Ball Mill, near Brislestowe, North Devon – signed –
18 x 12in.
(Christie's)   **$1,161   £660**

GUSTAVE ADOLPH WIEGAND – Autumn
Reflections – signed – oil on canvas – 24 x 20in.
(Bruce D. Collins)　　**$1,045**　　**£590**

CHARLES MAYES WIGG – Study Of A Beached
Sailing Vessel In A Storm – monogrammed –
watercolour – 11 x 15in.
(Messrs. G. A. Key)　　**$491**　　**£270**

GUY CARLETON WIGGINS – Broad Street
Winter – signed – oil on board – 12 x 16in.
(Christie's)　　**$14,300**　　**£7,989**

GUY CARLETON WIGGINS – Winter Landscape
– signed – oil on canvas – 25¼ x 30in.
(Christie's)　　**$15,400**　　**£8,603**

GUY CARLETON WIGGINS – The Stock
Exchange – signed – oil on canvasboard – 12 x
16in.
(Christie's)　　**$8,250**　　**£4,609**

GUY CARLETON WIGGINS – Fishing Boats At
Rockport – signed, and signed again, dated 1916
and inscribed on the reverse – oil on canvas laid
down on board – 16 x 12in.
(Christie's)　　**$5,280**　　**£3,257**

WIJNGAERDT

ANTHONIE JACOBUS WIJNGAERDT – A Heathland With Figures – signed – on panel – 8 x 12in.
(Christie's) **$4,356** **£2,640**

IRVING RAMSEY WILES – Poppies And Crystal – signed – oil on board – 13½ x 19½in.
(Robt. W. Skinner Inc.) **$1,700** **£1,030**

LEMUEL WILES – A Well Read Book – oil on canvas – 11¾ x 18¼in.
(Christie's) **$14,300** **£8,821**

FRANK WILL – Notre Dame – signed and inscribed watercolour and pencil on paper – 17¾ x 23¾in.
(Christie's) **$3,326** **£1,760**

FRANK WILL – Le Treport – signed and inscribed - watercolour, charcoal and pencil – 17¾ x 21¾in.
(Christie') **$2,286** **£1,210**

FRANK WILL – Montmartre – signed – watercolour and pencil on paper – 21¼ x 17½in.
(Christie's) **$3,326** **£1,760**

ARCHIBALD WILLARD – Rough Ride – oil on canvas – 22¼ x 30¼in.
(Christie's)   **$2,860**   **£1,764**

ARTHUR WILLETT – Hunting Scenes With Huntsmen And Hounds In Village; And In Open Country – signed – watercolour – 5 x 19½in.
(Hobbs & Chambers)   **$1,656**   **£920 Pair**

KYFFIN WILLIAMS – Welsh Blacks – oil on canvas – 48 x 48in.
(Christie's)   **$1,443**   **£825**

KYFFIN WILLIAMS – Nant Paris – oil on canvas – 36 x 36in.
(Christie's)   **$1,443**   **£825**

TERRICK WILLIAMS – Harbour, Low Tide – signed – oil on canvas – 10¾ x 16in.
(Christie's)   **$5,451**   **£3,080**

TERRICK WILLIAMS – Passing Clouds, Concarneau – signed – oil on canvas – 10¼ x 16in.
(Phillips)   **$9,152**   **£5,200**

WILLINGALE

C. WILLINGALE – Portrait Of John Willingale, 'Saviour Of Epping Forest' – signed and dated 1832 – watercolour – 14½ x 21½in.
(Prudential Fine Art Auctioneers) $567   £350

DAVID FORRESTER WILSON – The Tea Party: The Scobie Sisters – signed – oil on canvas – 102 x 102cm.
(Phillips) $19,680   £12,000

CHARLES EDWARD WILSON – The Beautiful Rose – signed – watercolour – 53 x 35cm.
(Phillips) $9,735   £5,500

WILLIAM E. WINNER – Near The Beach, Gloucester – signed, and signed again, dated '77 and inscribed on the reverse – oil on canvas – 26¼ x 20¾in.
(Christie's) $7,150   £4,410

PETER DE WINT – The Entrance To St. John's College, Cambridge – watercolour over pencil – 10½ x 14¾in.
(Sotheby's) $14,889   £7,920

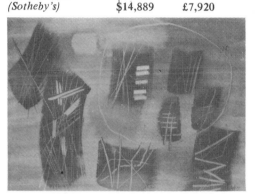

FRITZ WINTER – Untitled – signed and dated '54 – watercolour, gouache and oil on cardboard – 28¾ x 38¾in.
(Christie's) $4,989   £3,080

WILLEM WISSING, Studio of – A Portrait Of Brigadier General Richard Morris – oil on canvas – 50 x 40in.
(Phillips) $7,770   £4,200

WILLIAM FREDERICK WITHERINGTON – Gathering Watercress On The Banks Of The River Mole, Surrey – signed and dated 1855 – oil on canvas – 68.5 x 89cm.
(Sotheby's) $26,741   £14,300

WILLIAM FREDERICK WITHERINGTON – The Homestead – signed and dated 1855 – oil on canvas – 68.5 x 89cm.
(Sotheby's) $30,855   £16,500

KARL WITKOWSKI – Fixing His Grip – signed – oil on canvas – 28 x 20in.
(Christie's) $6,050   £3,380

WOLFE

EDWARD WOLFE – Girl On A Chair – oil on canvas – 30½ x 20½in.
(Christie's)   **$17,912   £10,120**

EDWARD WOLFE – Girl In A Green Jumper, Brenda Bourne – signed – pastel – 22¼ x 16¾in.
(Christie's)   **$2,213   £1,265**

EDWARD WOLFE – A Malay Girl – pastel – 23¾ x 18¼in.
(Christie's)   **$3,465   £1,980**

EDWARD WOLFE – Still Life Of Lilies In A Pot – oil on canvas – 31¾ x 22¼in.
(Christie's)   **$5,005   £2,860**

ALFRED WOLMARK – The Power Station – oil on canvasboard – 15¾ x 11¾in.
(Christie's)　　　　$6,461　　**£3,630**

ALFRED WOLMARK – Two Ballet Dancers – signed and dated '37 – oil on panel – 30¾ x 16in.
(Christie's)　　　　$5,874　　**£3,300**

ALFRED WOLMARK – The Card-Players – signed – oil on canvas – 15¾ x 21in.
(Christie's)　　　　$3,622　　**£2,035**

ALFRED WOLMARK – Still Life Of Flowers And Fruit – signed with a monogram – oil on canvas – 20 x 15½in.
(Christie's)　　　　$5,005　　**£2,860**

WOLMARK

ALFRED WOLMARK – Breton Man – signed with initial – oil on canvasboard – 18½ x 15¾in.
(Christie's) $10,786 £6,060

ALFRED AARON WOLMARK – The Fishmarket, Concarneau – signed – oil on canvas board – 46 x 37.5cm.
(Phillips) $9,845 £5,500

ALFRED WOLMARK – Cissy Esdaile – signed – oil on canvas – 47¼ x 25in.
(Sotheby's) $8,131 £4,620

ALFRED AARON WOLMARK – Christ And The Woman Taken In Adultery – signed indistinctly – oil on canvas – 76 x 51cm.
(Phillips) $1,611 £900

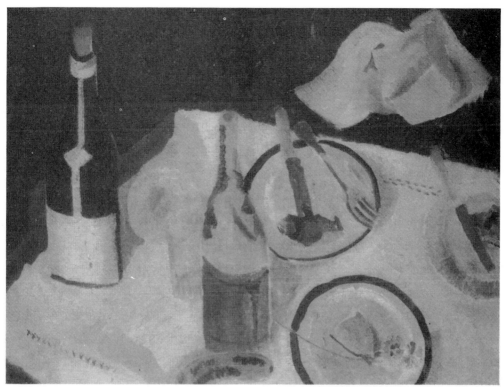

CHRISTOPHER WOOD – Still Life On A Table –
oil on canvas – 24 x 29in.
(Sotheby's) **$40,656 £23,100**

CHRISTOPHER WOOD – Seagulls On The Rocks,
Cornwall – water colour and bodycolour over
pencil – 35.5 x 24.5cm.
(Phillips) **$3,217 £1,950**

CHRISTOPHER WOOD – Dahlias In A Jug – oil
on canvasboard – 40 x 30cm.
(Sotheby's) **$14,553 £7,700**

WOOD

J. WOOD – Clipper Off Lighthouse – signed –
oil on canvas – 21 x 31in.
(Bruce D. Collins)　　**$687**　　**£388**

W. R. C. WOOD – Pasture Gate – signed and
dated 1907 – oil on canvas – 18 x 22in.
(Bruce D. Collins)　　**$1,980**　　**£1,118**

THOMAS WATERMAN WOOD – His First Vote,
1868 – signed and dated 1868 – oil on canvas –
20 x 10½in.
(Christie's)　　**$65,000**　　**£36,315**

DAVID WOODLOCK – A Little Girl In A Flower
Garden – signed and dated '97 – watercolour over
traces of pencil – 35 x 24.5cm.
(Phillips)　　**$2,566**　　**£1,450**

DAVID WOODLOCK – Watering The Flowers –
signed – watercolour – 50 x 34.5cm.
(Phillips) **$1,593** **£900**

GEORGE WRIGHT – Winter – signed – oil on
canvas – 35.5 x 51cm.
(Sotheby's) **$17,028** **£9,900**

GEORGE HAND WRIGHT – Back To Earth –
signed in pencil – etching – 9 x 12in.
(Bruce D. Collins) **$165** **£93**

ETHEL WRIGHT – A Woman In An Interior –
signed – oil on canvas – 57 x 36½ in.
(Sotheby's) **$12,584** **£7,150**

GILBERT SCOTT WRIGHT – Tally Ho! – signed
– 20 x 28in.
(Christie's) **$19,332** **£10,450**

WRIGHT

GILBERT SCOTT WRIGHT — The Meet — signed —
18 x 24in.
(Christie's)   **$4,646**   **£2,640**

JOHN MICHAEL WRIGHT — Portrait Of Anne,
Countess Of Carlisle, Half Length, Seated Wearing
A Blue Dress, A Letter In Her Left Hand —
inscribed on the letter — oil on canvas — 61 x
74cm.
(Sotheby's)   **$11,313**   **£6,050**

MARGARET WRIGHT — Summer On The
Garelock — oil on panel — 15½ x 19¾in.
(Christie's)   **$4,812**   **£2,750**

ROBERT W. WRIGHT — Feeding Time — signed and dated '95 — on panel — 5 x 4in.; also a
companion — unsigned. *(Phillips)*   **$3,907 £2,220 Pair**

ALEXANDER HELWIG WYANT – Woods And Brook – signed – oil on canvas – 12 x 16in.
(Christie's)   **$3,080**   **£1,900**

ANDREW WYETH – The French Connection (1980) – signed – watercolour, tempera and drybrush on paper – 27 x 20in.
(Robt. W. Skinner Inc.)   **$85,000**   **£47,486**

HORTENSE DE VIVEFAY WYATT – Portrait Of Charles I – signed, inscribed and dated 1853 – oil on canvas – 92 x 69cm.
(Sotheby's)   **$1,504**   **£880**

ANDREW WYETH – Fish Nets, Nova Scotia – signed – watercolour and drybrush on paper – 14¾ x 19¾in.
(Christie's)   **$41,800**   **£23,353**

WYETH

NEWELL CONVERS WYETH – Seeking The New Home – signed – oil on canvas – 34 x 47in. *(Christie's)* $66,000   £36,874

W. L. WYLLIE – The Battle Of Jutland – signed – engraving – 13½ x 28in. *(Greenslade & Co.)*   **$222**   **£120**

WILLIAM LIONEL WYLLIE – Yachts Racing In The Solent – signed – watercolour – 7 x 13in. *(Worsfolds)*   **$991**   **£590**

RICHARD WYNDHAM – Autumn Landscape – oil on canvas – 25 x 30in. *(Christie's)*   **$9,735**   **£5,500**

JACK BUTLER YEATS – The Violence Of The Dawn – signed and inscribed – oil on canvas – 61 x 91.5cm.
(Sotheby's)   **$45,738   £24,200**

FRED YATES – Lloyd's Bank, Penzance – signed, and inscribed on the reverse – oil on board – 46 x 30cm.
(Phillips)   **$462   £260**

GIDEON YATES – South East View Of Old London Bridge – signed and dated 1831 – pen and grey ink and watercolour – 11¾ x 21¼in.
(Christie's)   **$2,138   £1,320**

JACK BUTLER YEATS – The Old Picnic Ground – signed, and inscribed on a label on the reverse – oil on canvas – 35.5 x 53.5cm.
(Sotheby's)   **$31,186   £16,500**

GIDEON YATES – West View Of New London Bridge From The Southwark Bridge – signed and dated 1832, and signed, inscribed and dated 1833 on a label – pen and grey ink and watercolour – 12½ x 22in.
(Christie's)   **$7,128   £4,400**

JACK BUTLER YEATS – South Pacific – signed, and inscribed on the reverse – oil on canvas – 61 x 91.5cm.
(Sotheby's)   **$37,422   £19,800**

YEATS

JACK BUTLER YEATS – Fair Day – signed – oil on panel – 8¾ x 13½in. *(Christie's)*
$30,010 £21,000

JACK BUTLER YEATS – The Tinker – signed –
watercolour – 14½ x 10¼in.
(Christie's)   **$18,601   £10,450**

JACK BUTLER YEATS – Under The Lamp Post
– signed – oil on board – 35.5 x 23cm.
(Sotheby's)   **$6,776   £3,850**

JACK BUTLER YEATS – Homing Cattle Dealers
Approaching Dun Laoghaire – signed – oil on
board – 9 x 14¼in.
(Christie's)   **$37,202**   **£20,900**

JACK BUTLER YEATS – Reading – signed and
dated 1903 – pencil – 19 x 25.5cm.
(Sotheby's)   **$2,618**   **£1,540**

JACK BUTLER YEATS – The Derelict Ship –
signed – oil on canvas – 46 x 61cm.
(Sotheby's)   **$23,232**   **£13,200**

JACK BUTLER YEATS – Something Happening
In The Street – signed – oil on panel – 11¼ x
16¼in.
(Christie's)   **$35,244**   **£19,800**

JACK BUTLER YEATS – A Moment Of Time –
signed and inscribed – oil on canvas – 14 x 18¼in.
(Christie's)   **$35,244**   **£19,800**

JACK BUTLER YEATS – And So My Brother
Hail And Farewell For Evermore – inscribed – oil
on canvas – 13¾ x 20½in.
(Christie's)   **$50,908**   **£28,600**

YEATS

JACK BUTLER YEATS – Loathe To Depart –
signed – oil on canvas – 18 x 25in.
(Sotheby's)   **$65,824**   **£37,400**

JACK BUTLER YEATS – The New Song –
signed – oil on board – 9 x 14in.
(Sotheby's)   **$19,360**   **£11,000**

FRANS YKENS, Circle of – A Still Life Of Roses
In A Glass Vase Standing On A Ledge – on panel –
18½ x 11¾in.
(Phillips)   **$18,800**   **£10,000**

FRANS YKENS – Flowers In A Glass Vase With
Fruit In A Wan-Li Kraak Porselein Bowl, Melons
And Dead Birds On A Table – signed – 86.7 x
123.2cm.
(Christie's)   **$131,313**   **£72,150**

PIETER YKENS – The Birth Of The Virgin –
signed – oil on copper – 75 x 112.5cm.
(Sotheby's)   **$6,089**   **£3,520**

ATELIER D'ADRIAEN YSENBRANDT – The
Lamentation – 54.5 x 38.8cm.
(Christie's) **$20,202 £11,100**

CHRISTIAN ZACHO – A Wooded River Landscape With Ducks – signed and dated 1907 – 30 x
24¾in.
(Christie's) **$3,459 £1,870**

ANTHONY YOUNGS – The New Boat – signed and dated '54 and inscribed on a label on the
reverse – oil on board – 53 x 91.5cm. *(Sotheby's)* **$1,193 £682**

ZACHO

CHRISTIAN ZACHO – A Wooded Landscape
With A Drover, And Cattle Watering At A River –
signed and dated 1894 – 61½ x 86in.
(Christie's) **$20,350 £11,000**

CHRISTIAN ZACHO – A Wooded River Landscape With Figures In A Boat – signed and dated
1893 – 62¾ x 80¾in.
(Christie's) **$17,297 £9,350**

OSSIP ZADKINE – Western – signed – gouache
on paper – 24 x 18in.
(Christie's) **$11,011 £6,050**

OSSIP ZADKINE – Deux Nus – signed, dated
1919 and inscribed – pencil – 24 x 15.5cm.
(Phillips) **$1,680 £1,000**

ZAG – The Bowls Players – signed – watercolour
on paper laid down on card – 8¾ x 5¼in.; and ten
other watercolours by S. de Albertis, E. Pagliano,
P. Bonolo and C. Balestrini and others.
(Christie's) **$4,136 £2,200 Eleven**

GIUSEPPE ZAIS, Follower of – A pair of pastoral
scenes – oil on canvas – 20½ x 27in.
(Sotheby's)   **$50,424   £26,400 Pair**

EUGENIO ZAMPHIGI – A Favourite Melody –
signed – pencil and watercolour – 21 x 14¼in.
(Christie's)   **$1,322   £715**

W. ZAJICEK – Gutzenstadle, Vienna – signed and inscribed – watercolour heightened with
white – 3¾ x 5½in. *(Christie's)*   **$1,628   £880**

ZAMPHIGI

EUGENIO ZAMPIGHI – Her Favourite Tune –
signed – 23½ x 18in.
(Christie's)   **$9,256**   **£4,950**

EUGENIO ZAMPIGHI – Her Favourite Tune –
signed – 24 x 18in.
(Christie's)   **$6,352**   **£3,850**

EUGENIO ZAMPIGHI – Parlour Gossip – signed – oil on canvas – 56 x 76cm. *(Phillips)*
$8,424 £5,200

EUGENIO ZAMPIGHI – He Loves Me, He Loves
Me Not – signed – 9½ x 13in.
(Christie's)   **$5,445**   **£3,300**

ANTONIO ZANCHI, Circle of – Hagar and
Ishmael – 58 x 79in.
(Christie's)   **$26,950**   **£15,400**

HANS ZATZKA – The rendez-vous – signed –
26¾ x 18½in.
(Christie's)   **$3,872**   **£2,200**

ZAO WOU-KI – Nuit Transfigure – signed and
dated '59 – oil on canvas – 73 x 100cm.
(Christie's)   **$56,760**   **£33,000**

A. ZERNADI – Guido Reni drawing Beatrice
Cence in prison the night before her execution –
53½ x 68in.
(Christie's)   **$3,702**   **£1,980**

ZEWY

CARL ZEWY – A Tyrolean Flower Girl – signed
– on panel – 11 x 8½in.
(Christie's) **$3,097** **£1,760**

EUSTACE PAUL ZIEGLER – Mount McKinley
Pack Train – oil on canvas – 18¼ x 24¼in.
(Christie's) **$7,700** **£4,750**

GEORG FREDERIK ZIESEL – Still Lives Of
Flowers In Glass Vases – signed – oil on
glass – 39.5 x 31.5cm.
(Sotheby's) **$33,616** **£17,600 Pair**

BERND ZIMMER – Untitled – signed and dated
'82 – gouache on cardboard mounted on linen –
63 x 51¼in.
(Christie's) $2,494   £1,540

AURELIO ZINGONI – The Chimneysweep –
signed and dated 1881 – oil on canvas – 81 x
66cm.
(Phillips) $8,100   £4,500

BERND ZIMMER – Uberhangender Baum, Schnee – signed, inscribed and dated '85 on the
reverse – oil and dispersion on canvas – 70¾ x 90½in. *(Christie's)* $10,692   £6,600

ZINKEISEN

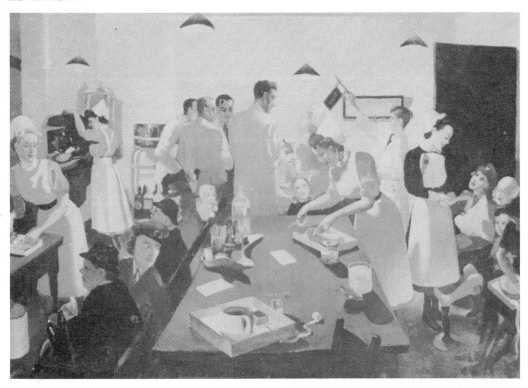

ANNA ZINKEISEN – The Casualty Department –
signed – oil on canvas – 30 x 42in.
(Sotheby's)   **$5,236**   **£3,080**

DORIS ZINKEISEN – Still Life With Fruit And
Wine – signed – oil on canvas – 18 x 16in.
(Christie's)   **$1,049**   **£580**

DORIS ZINKEISEN – Cafe In The Champs
Elysees – signed – oil on canvas – 24 x 20in.
(Sotheby's)   **$14,520**   **£8,250**

DORIS ZINKEISEN — Benacre Commander-Champion Suffolk Punch — signed — oil on canvas — 28 x 36in. *(Sotheby's)* **$3,465** **£1,980**

DORIS ZINKEISEN — The Donkey Cart — signed — oil on canvas — 41 x 51cm. *(Phillips)* **$792 £480**

ZINKEISEN

DORIS ZINKEISEN – Hyde Park – signed – oil on canvas – 13¼ x 21¼in.
(Christie's)   **$1,801   £1,012**

DORIS ZINKEISEN – Mevagissey Harbour – signed – oil on canvas – 16 x 20in.
(Christie's)   **$2,896   £1,600**

DORIS ZINKEISEN – Les Folies Bergeres – signed – oil on canvas – 24 x 29in.
(Christie's)   **$3,328   £1,870**

DORIS ZINKEISEN – At The Races – signed – oil on canvas – 28 x 36in.
(Sotheby's)   **$3,553   £2,090**

DORIS ZINKEISEN – Ascot – signed – oil on canvas – 19¾ x 30in.
(Christie's)   **$6,737   £3,850**

DORIS ZINKEISEN – Cafe Scene – signed – oil on canvas – 20 x 24in.
(Christie's)   **$7,240   £4,000**

DORIS ZINKEISEN – A Sudden Halt – oil on canvas – 63.5 x 76cm. *(Phillips)*
$1,485 £900

JOHN ZOFFANY – Portrait of George Colman, Snr – oil on canvas – 29½ x 24½in.
(Sotheby's) $41,140   £22,000

EMILE ZOIR – Portrait Of A Lady, Seated, Full Length – signed – 70 x 48in.
(Christie's) $7,122   £3,850

WILLIAM ZORACH – The Red Barn – signed –
watercolour on paper – 15 x 21 in.
(Robt. W. Skinner Inc.)   **$1,200**   **£670**

WILLIAM ZORACH – Robinhood Cove – signed
and dated 1926 – watercolour – 15 x 21½in.
(Bruce D. Collins)   **$6,820**   **£3,853**

WILLIAM ZORACH – Maine Houses – signed and
dated 1918 – watercolour on paper laid down on
board – 18¼ x 15¼in.
(Christie's)   **$4,180**   **£2,335**

ANDERS ZORN – A Portrait Of Sir Ernest Cassel – signed and dated '86 – watercolour – 15
x 21¾in. *(Sotheby's)*   **$209,000**   **£110,000**

ANDERS ZORN – A Portrait Of Miss Anna Cassel, Later Mrs. A. E. Jenkins – signed and dated – watercolour and gouache – 38¾ x 26in.
(Sotheby's) **$376,200 £198,000**

ANDERS LEONARD ZORN – Betty Nansen (A. 190) – signed and dated 1905 – etching on laid paper – 9¾ x 6¾in.
(Christie's) **$854 £462**

ANDERS LEONARD ZORN – Morakulla (Dalecarlian Girl) – signed and dated 1904 – 12 x 10in.
(Christie's) **$77,330 £41,800**

ANDERS LEONARD ZORN – Signe – signed and dated 1912 – 35¾ x 24in.
(Christie's) **$529,100 £286,000**

ZORN

ANDERS LEONARD ZORN – Prince Paul
Troubetzkoy I (Asplund 218, Hjert & Hjert 139) –
signed and dated 1908 – etching on van Gelder
Zonen – 11¾ x 7¾in.
(Christie's)   **$1,831**   **£990**

ANDERS LEONARD ZORN – Paul Verlaine I
(A. 93; H. & H. 65) – signed and dated 1895 –
etching on fine laid paper – 9½ x 6¼in.
(Christie's)   **$1,729**   **£935**

ANDERS LEONARD ZORN – Pa Stranden (On The Beach) – signed and dated 1910 – 21¾
x 29¼in. *(Christie's)*   **$172,975**   **£93,500**

ANDERS LEONARD ZORN – In Mourning –
signed and dated '81 – pencil and watercolour
heightened with gum arabic – 19¼ x 13¼in.
(Christie's)   **$97,680   £52,800**

ANDERS LEONARD ZORN – A Spanish Girl
Playing A Mandolin – signed and dated '84 –
watercolour – 20½ x 13in.
(Christie's)   **$183,150   £99,000**

ANDERS LEONARD ZORN – Pa sangkanten (On
The Bed) – signed and dated 1910 – 35¾ x 24¼in.
(Christie's)   **$407,000   £220,000**

FRITZ ZUBER-BUHLER – Puppy Love –
signed – coloured chalk heightened with white –
16½ x 13in.
(Christie's)   **$1,628   £880**

JACOPO ZUCCHI, Circle Of – The Four Elements – on copper – 19¾ x 15½in.
(Phillips) $22,560 £12,000